A

Tr

ACCES

THE
GEORGIAN BUILDINGS
OF BRISTOL

THE
GEORGIAN BUILDINGS
OF BRISTOL

by

WALTER ISON
F.S.A.

KINGSMEAD PRESS

First published in mcmlii
by Faber and Faber Limited
Reprinted 1978
Kingsmead Press
Rosewell House
Kingsmead Square
Bath

© *Walter Ison*

SBN 901571 88 1

To
CECIL FARTHING
F.S.A.

Printed in Great Britain by
REDWOOD BURN LIMITED
Trowbridge & Esher

Introduction to the 1978 Reprint.

When this book was published, in 1952, Bristol was a war-scarred city, and the central area east of the High Street presented a desolate wasteland surrounding the ruined churches of St. Mary-le-Port and St. Peter. Now, a large part of the historic core of Bristol has been replanned and rebuilt in a style all too typical of our post-war 'city centres'. A few Georgian buildings, such as The Friars, survive in this unsympathetic environment, an island of anonymous buildings virtually isolated from the rest of Bristol by a wide ring road. One happy outcome of this redevelopment has been its effect on nearby Portland Square, where the pre-war degradation of many handsome houses has given way to their restoration as prestige offices. Perhaps it is not too late for King Square and Brunswick Square to benefit in the same way, although the south side of Brunswick Square lies under threat of demolition and the west side has been completed without regard to the original intended design. Some squares and crescents in Clifton and Hotwells also show evidence of a steady improvement in their conservation, notably in Dowry Square and Windsor Terrace.

Several of Bristol's major Georgian buildings have been cleaned and restored, most notably Coopers' Hall in King Street, which now serves as a handsome foyer for the Theatre Royal. St. Nicholas' Church has also been well restored, although without its splendid Rococo ceiling, to serve as a church museum. The Gothick bath-house at Arno's Court, Brislington, has gone but its charming colonnaded front has been effectively rebuilt as an architectural feature at Portmeirion, North Wales.

Finally, it is worth mentioning that in his very generous review of this book, Mr. Howard Colvin questioned my attribution of Redland Chapel to William Halfpenny. Since then I have had the good fortune to find confirmatory evidence in a supplementary volume of the King's Maps and Topographical Drawings (British Museum), where two views of Redland Chapel are signed by Halfpenny as inventor (architect) and delineator.

Walter Ison.

PREFACE

BRISTOL'S wealth of eighteenth- and early nineteenth-century buildings, in extent and variety, is not surpassed by that of any English city save London, while Bath alone has a more consistently splendid array of street architecture of this period. Yet, while Bath has received something like due attention from architectural historians, only one full-length study of Bristol's Georgian architecture has, until now, been published, and that one might well be considered too restrictedly selective to present a balanced picture. Selection has, of necessity, been resorted to in compiling the present book, but it is hoped that the range of buildings here described and illustrated is wide enough to give a fair representation of the subject. It is for this reason that several buildings no longer existing have been included in the survey. On the other hand there are omissions that must, at first, seem serious. For example, no more than a passing mention has been made of Vanbrugh's King's Weston House, but this building has already been fully described and illustrated in *Country Life's* 'English Homes', Period IV, Vol. II, and an adequate description could only have been included here at the expense of some work that might otherwise have remained unrecorded. For the same reason it was decided to omit any account of Goldney House and garden, as these were so well illustrated and described in the issues of *Country Life* for 6th and 17th August, 1948.

The material for this book has been largely derived from research among contemporary newspapers, and from the study of leases and building accounts. The archives of the Bristol Corporation have proved a most fruitful source of information, and here I must pay my first debt of gratitude by thanking the City Archivist, Miss Elizabeth Ralph, F.S.A., and her staff, past and present, for the help so unstintingly given me. My thanks for much kindness of a like nature are due also to the officials of the Central Library; to Mr. James Ross, M.A., F.L.A., until lately librarian; to Mr. H. W. Maxwell, director, and the staff of the City Art Gallery; and to Dr. F. S. Wallis, D.Sc., Ph.D., director of the City Museum.

I am indebted to Mr. George Sutton and Mr. Frank Uttley, of the Society of Friends, to the Rev. E. J. D. Hellier, the Rev. J. Coram-Davies, B.A., and the Rev. F. Vyvyan-Jones, for their kindness in allowing me to peruse records in their care; to Messrs. Osborne, Ward, Vassal & Co., for giving me access to the accounts relating to the building of Redland Chapel; and to all members of Bristol University who have helped me in various ways. Lastly, I would assure all those, not mentioned by name, who have given me advice and information, that they have my heartfelt thanks.

Christ Church steeple

CONTENTS

PREFACE   *page* 7

A GENERAL SURVEY OF THE GEORGIAN
    DEVELOPMENT   21

THE ARCHITECTS AND BUILDING
    CRAFTSMEN   30
    Allen, James   30
    Arthur, Nathaniel   31
    Bridges, James   31
    Busby, Charles Augustus   32
    Cockerell, Charles Robert   32
    Edney, William   33
    Foster, James and Thomas   34
    Glascodine, Samuel and Joseph   34
    Greenway, Francis Howard   35
    Hague, Daniel   36
    Halfpenny, William   37
    Henwood, Luke   38
    Patys, The   39
    Seward, Henry Hake   44
    Smirke, Robert   44
    Stocking, Thomas   44
    Strahan, John   45
    Stratford, Ferdinando   46
    Thomas, Joseph   47
    Tully, George and William   47
    Wallis, John   49
    Woods of Bath, The   49

CHURCHES AND CHAPELS   52
    St. Mary Redcliffe, Strahan's Gallery and Organ-Case   52
    Redland Chapel   54
    Wesley's New Room, Broadmead   61
    The Friends' Meeting House, The Friars   62
    St. Nicholas' Church   65
    St. Michael's Church   70
    Christ Church   72
    St. Paul's Church   76
    The Unitarian Chapel, Lewin's Mead   81

[9]

CONTENTS

St. Thomas's Church   *page* 84
Holy Trinity Church, Hotwells   88

PUBLIC BUILDINGS   90

The Old Council House   90
Barber-Surgeon's Hall   91
The City Library   93
Merchant-Taylors' Hall   94
The Exchange   95
Coopers' Hall   05
The Markets   106
The Old Post Office   108
The Assembly Room, Prince Street   108
Bristol Bridge   114
The Theatre Royal   123
Merchants' Hall   127
The Clifton Hotel and Assembly Rooms   130
The Commercial Rooms   134
The Council House   135

DOMESTIC BUILDINGS   140

Queen Square   140
St. James's Square   149
Orchard Street   152
Nos. 10, 11 and 12 Guinea Street   156
Dowry Square and Chapel Row   157
Prince Street   161
Redland Court   164
No. 59 Queen Charlotte Street, Queen Square   170
No. 40 Prince Street   171
King Square   173
Clifton Hill House   177
Arno's Court   181
The Royal Fort   190
Albemarle Row   198
Dowry Parade   201
Boyce's Buildings, Clifton   202
Brunswick Square   204
Redcliffe Parade   209
College Street   210
Park Street   211
The Colonnade, Hotwells   213
Berkeley Square and Crescent   214
Great George Street   217
Portland Square   220
The Mall, Clifton   223
Prince's Buildings   224
St. Vincent's Parade   225
Windsor Terrace   226
Royal York Crescent   228
Cornwallis Crescent   231

CONTENTS

Saville Place, Clifton   *page* 233
Belle-vue, Clifton   234
The Paragon, Clifton   235
Clifton Vale, Caledonia Place and New Mall, Clifton   237

BIBLIOGRAPHY   239

INDEX   241

William Hilliard's monument,
by Thomas Paty,
in St. Mark's Church, College Green

ILLUSTRATIONS

THE PLATES
at the end of this book

PLANS

1. A Plan of Bristol by Jacobus Millerd, published in 1673
2. A Plan of Bristol by John Rocque, published in 1745
3. A Plan of Bristol by Benjamin Donne, published in 1826

THE CHURCHES AND CHAPELS

4. Redland Chapel. The exterior from the south-west
5. Redland Chapel
   a. The interior, looking east
   b. The interior, looking west
6. Redland Chapel
   a. Detail of the altar-piece
   b. Detail of the dado-capping
7. *a.* Wesley's New Room. The interior
   b. The Friends' Meeting House, The Friars. The interior
8. *a.* St. Nicholas' Church. The steeple
   b. Christ Church. The steeple
   c. St. Paul's Church. The steeple
9. *a.* St. Nicholas' Church. The exterior from the north-west
   b. St. Michael's Church. The exterior from the south-west
10. St. Nicholas' Church. The interior, looking east
11. Christ Church
    a. The interior, looking east
    b. The interior, looking south-west
12. *a.* St. Michael's Church. The interior, looking east
    b. St. Paul's Church. The interior, looking east
13. *a.* The Unitarian Chapel, Lewin's Mead. The principal front
    b. St. Thomas's Church. The east front

[13]

c. Holy Trinity Church, Hotwells. The south front, central feature

THE PUBLIC BUILDINGS

14. *a.* The old City Library. The exterior. (Drawing by E. Cashin, 1823)
   b. William Halfpenny's first 'Draught for an Exchange'
15. Designs for the Exchange, made during 1738-9, by William Halfpenny
16. The Exchange. The principal front in Corn Street
17. *a.* The old Post Office and part of the Exchange
   b. Coopers' Hall. The exterior
18. *a.* Bristol Bridge. (Drawing by H. O'Neill, 1823)
   b. Merchants' Hall. The exterior. (Drawing by H. O'Neill, 1823)
19. *a.* The Theatre Royal. A general view of the auditorium from the stage
   b. The Clifton Hotel and Assembly Rooms. The front facing The Mall
20. The Commercial Rooms
   a. The front in Corn Street
   b. The lantern-light of the great room
21. The Council House
   a. The exterior
   b. The former Council-chamber

THE DOMESTIC BUILDINGS

22. Queen Square
   a. The north-east angle, looking into Queen Charlotte Street. (Drawing by S. Jackson, 1824)
   b. A general view of the south-east angle. (Drawing by T. Rowbotham, 1827)
23. Queen Square
   a. The south row. Front of No. 38
   b. The south row. Front of No. 29
24. St. James's Square
   a. Houses on the west side
   b. Houses in the south-east angle
25. Orchard Street
   a. The south block on the east side
   b. The north block on the west side

26. Nos. 10-12 Guinea Street
27. *a.* Chapel Row, Dowry Square
    b. Dowry Square. Houses on the north and east sides
28. Nos. 66, 68 and 70 Prince Street
29. *a.* No. 12 St. James's Barton
    b. No. 59 Queen Charlotte Street
30. Redland Court
    a. The south front
    b. The south front: Detail of pedimented centre
31. Redland Court
    a. The south front. (Engraved drawing by J. and H. S. Storer, 1825)
    b. The north front
32. Prince Street. The west side, with No. 40 and the Assembly Room. (Drawing by E. Cashin, 1825)
33. *a.* Dowry Square. Houses on the west side
    b. King Square. The south-west side
34. Clifton Hill House
    a. The design for the elevation, from Ware's 'Complete Body of Architecture'
    b. The garden front, facing east
35. Arno's Court
    a. A general view of the exterior
    b. The entrance front
36. Arno's Court
    a. The Bath-house. The exterior
    b. The Gateway
37. Arno's Court. The Castle
    a. A general view of the exterior from the south (Drawing by T. Rowbotham, 1827)
    b. The courtyard, looking west
38. The Royal Fort
    a. The architect's model
    b. do. with the upper stories removed
39. The Royal Fort. The west front
40. The Royal Fort
    a. The south front
    b. The north front
41. Albemarle Row

42. *a.* Dowry Parade
    b. Prospect House, Clifton Green
43. Brunswick Square
    a. The south side
    b. The east side
44. *a.* Redcliffe Parade
    b. The Colonnade and Rock House, Hotwells
45. Berkeley Square
    a. The west side
    b. The north side
46. *a.* Berkeley Crescent
    b. Saville Place
47. Great George Street
    a. The front of No. 3
    b. The front of No. 7 (The Georgian House)
48. *a.* Portland Square. The west side
    b. The Mall, Clifton. The south side
49. *a.* Portland Square. The central feature of the south side
    b. Windsor Terrace. Nos. 5 and 6
50. Royal York Crescent
    a. A general view from the west end. (Engraving by Willis, *c.* 1850)
    b. A general view from the east end
51. Cornwallis Crescent
    a. The concave front, facing the garden
    b. The convex front, facing the roadway
52. The Paragon
    a. The convex front, facing the garden
    b. The concave front, facing the roadway
53. *a.* Clifton Vale
    b. Caledonia Place

EXTERIOR DETAILS

54. Entrance doorways
    a. No. 10 St. James's Square
    b. No. 16 St. James's Square
    c. No. 28 Orchard Street
    d. No. 7 Dowry Square
55. Entrance doorways
    a. No. 16 Queen Square (now removed)

b. Arno's Court: The mansion

c. No. 2 Albemarle Row

d. No. 7 Albemarle Row

56. *a*. The Royal Fort. The entrance doorway

    b. Portland Square. A typical doorway

    c. The Paragon. A typical porch

    d. Prince's Buildings. The porch of No. 9

INTERIOR DETAILS

57. *a*. Redland Court. The entrance hall

    b. The Royal Fort. The entrance hall

58. *a*. Redland Court. The main corridor

    b. Clifton Hill House. The entrance hall

59. The Royal Fort

    a. The main corridor

    b. The staircase hall

60. *a*. Redland Court. Ceiling of the main staircase well

    b. Clifton Hill House. Ceiling of the staircase hall.

    c. The Royal Fort. The staircase hall, wall decoration

    d. The Royal Fort. Ceiling of the staircase hall

61. Arno's Court

    a. The dining-room ceiling

    b. Ceiling of the staircase hall

62. *a*. Redland Court. The south-east reception-room

    b. Clifton Hill House. The north-east reception-room

63. *a*. Arno's Court. Interior of the Bath-house

    b. The Royal Fort. The large drawing-room

64. *a*. Bishop's House, Clifton Green. The hall and staircase

    b. Redland Court. The main staircase

    c. Clifton Hill House. The staircase

    d. No. 7 Great George Street. Detail of the staircase balustrade

LINE DRAWINGS
in the text

1. Plans—(*a*) Redland Chapel   *page* 50

       (*b*) Wesley's New Room, Broadmead

       (*c*) Friends' Meeting House, The Friars

       (*d*) Unitarian Chapel, Lewin's Mead

2. Plans—(*a*) St. Nicholas' Church. (*b*) Christ Church.   51

       (*c*) St. Paul's Church

ILLUSTRATIONS

3. St. Mary Redcliffe. Strahan's design for the gallery
   and organ case   *page* 53
4. Redland Chapel. West elevation   56
5. Friends' Meeting House, The Friars, East elevation   64
6. The old Council House. Corn Street elevation (Reconstruction based on various early 19th-century
   drawings)   91
7. Barber-Surgeons' Hall. Exchange Avenue elevation   92
8. The Exchange. Ground-story plan   99
9. The Exchange. North elevation towards Corn Street   101
10. The Exchange. South elevation towards the Market   102
11. The Exchange. Cross section   104
12. The Market. High Street elevation   107
13. The Assembly Room. Prince Street elevation   111
14. The Assembly Room. Interior   113
15. Bristol Bridge. Elevation   123
16. The Clifton Hotel and Assembly Rooms. Elevation
    towards The Mall   132
17. Queen Square. William Halfpenny's 'North Prospect'   145
18. No. 29 Queen Square. Elevation   148
19. St. James's Square. Elevation of two houses forming
    the central feature of the east side   151
20. Redland Court. Ground-story plan   165
21. No. 40 Prince Street. Elevation   173
22. Clifton Hill House. Ground-story plan   179
23. Arno's Court. Ground-story plan   183
24. The Royal Fort. Ground-story plan   192
25. The Royal Fort. Dining-room doorway   197
26. No. 5 Albemarle Row, Hotwells. Elevation   200
27. No. 5 Albemarle Row. Ground-story plan   201
28. Boyce's Buildings, Clifton. Elevation   203
29. Brunswick Square. Elevation of the south side   206
30. No. 7 Great George Street. Elevation   218
31. No. 7 Great George Street. Ground-story plan   219

DECORATIONS

No. 5 Guinea Street. Detail of ceiling plasterwork   *title page*
Christ Church steeple   8
William Hilliard's monument, by Thomas Paty, in St.
   Mark's Church, College Green.   11

[18]

ACKNOWLEDGEMENTS

THE author and publishers of this book are deeply grateful to the Committee and Director of the City Art Gallery, Bristol, for permission to use the following illustrations, mostly from drawings in the Braikenridge Collection: Plates 14a, 18a, b, 22a, b, 37a, 64d. Grateful thanks are also tendered to the Committee and Director of the City Museum, Bristol, for permission to reproduce the plans forming Plates 2 and 3 (Desmond Tripp, photographer).

The plates listed immediately below have been made from photographs in the collections of the National Buildings Record, by arrangement with the Director and Deputy Director, whose help and co-operation are most gladly acknowledged by the author. Mr. V. Turl was responsible for the following photographs: Plates 4, 5a, b, 6a, b, 11a, b, 12a, 20a, 21a, 23a, 29b, 47a, b, 54c, Mr. R. F. Wills was the photographer of Plates 12b, 20b, 21b, 26, 30a, b, 31b, 33b, 34b, 35a, b, 36a, b, 37b, 39, 40a, b, 41, 42b, 44a, 45b, 46a, b, 48b, 49b, 50b, 51b, 52a, b, 53a, b, 55b, 56a, c, d, 57a, b, 58a, b, 59a, b, 60a, b, c, d, 61a, b, 62a, b, 63a. b, 64a, b, c.

The following illustrations were specially taken for this book by Mr. G. L. Dafnis, and are the author's copyright: Plates 8a, b, c, 9a, 13a, b, c, 17a, b, 19b, 25a, b, 27a, b, 28, 29a, 33a, 42a, 43a, b, 44b, 48a, 49b, 51a. Plates 10, 16, 23b, 45a, are reproduced from photographs by Mr. A. F. Kersting, and Plates 24b, 54a, b, d, 55a, c, d, 56b, from photographs by Mr. C. D. Ruding Bryan. Plate 7b, from a photograph by Veale & Co., is reproduced by kind permission of Messrs. Oatley & Brentnall, F. & A.R.I.B.A. Plate 19a, from a photograph by Mr. Herbert Felton, is reproduced by kind permission of the Arts Council of Great Britain. Plate 24a is from a copyright photograph by Mr. F. H. Crossley, F.S.A.

The vignette decorations were drawn by Leonora Ison, while all other drawings in the text are by the author.

A GENERAL SURVEY OF
THE GEORGIAN DEVELOPMENT

At the beginning of the eighteenth century Bristol was the third richest city and the second largest port in England, with a population exceeding 25,000. Physically, however, it was still a medieval city, scarcely different in extent and appearance from that represented by James Millerd's *Exact Delineation*, published in 1673. Indeed, the later and amended issues of this most informative survey clearly show the insignificance, relative to the size of the place, of the additions made between 1670 and 1700—merely a few streets and courts by the Avon and along the main roads out of the city. Bristol, then, was still very like London before 1666, for here no salutary fire had caused a brick-and-stone phœnix to rise from the ashes of timber-framed houses, with jutted stories and gabled fronts, ranged in narrow streets and tortuous lanes. Nevertheless, London's calamity had been an object lesson for other cities to profit by, and henceforth all new building was to be conducted with a greater regard for safety from fire risks.

The troubled times of the seventeenth century had not been propitious for building, but by 1700 stability had returned and the tide of prosperity was steadily rising. Now the grandiose plans of the Corporation for developing the Marsh area, found ample support from wealthy merchants and such speculating builders as the house-carpenters John Price and Peter Wilkins. It was, presumably, towards London that the Corporation's surveyors turned for inspiration when they planned the spacious layout of Queen Square and Prince Street, and they must have based their conditions for 'the uniform building of houses' on the London regulations of 1667.

The success of Queen Square may have inspired the privately-promoted building, in 1707–16, of a square in the north-lying parish of St. James. Although the central area of St. James's Square is small, its houses were comparable in size and style to those in Queen Square. In both developments the fronts were built of red brick, with stone quoins marking the party-walls, and stringcourses defining the three stories in which the sash-windows were evenly spaced. These fronts were uniformly finished with a continuous eaves-cornice of wood, boldly pro-jecting and containing the boxed gutter at the foot of the steeply-pitched roof of pantiles.

So popular was the residential square that this layout was now to be adopted wherever the circumstances permitted. Even Orchard Street, begun in 1717 with a clear width of 30 feet, was increased in width to 50 feet in its northern half so that this portion might rank as a 'square'. The spacious Dowry Square, near the Hot-well and outside the City Liberties, was laid out around 1720 by George Tully (pages 47–9), a house-carpenter and speculative builder, who later became one of the leading architect-surveyors in Bristol. While the house-fronts in Orchard Street, and the first-built ones in Dowry Square, have many features in common with those of the two earlier squares, an important change was made by omitting the wooden eaves-cornice and continuing the wall face to form a parapet, finished with a stone coping well above the gutter level. This measure was taken to minimize still further the risk of fire spreading from house to house, and doubtless was based on the London Act of 1707. The necessity for building control about this time is shown by the Common Council's appointment, in March 1718, of a committee whose duty was to take action against trespass by building owners, for it had apparently become a common practice, when houses were being rebuilt, to encroach on the public thoroughfare 'which if not prevented in time will render them impassable'.

As a general rule it may be observed that the houses built during the period 1700–25 have, at their best, a quality of naïve charm, and their ornamental details exhibit some spirited craftsmanship, but from the standpoint of architectural finesse they are often uncouth. The vernacular Renaissance style then in general use had not been properly assimilated by the Bristol craftsmen, by the masons even less than by the carpenters. Even when Classical detail was correctly rendered it was liable to misapplication, as in the absurd use made of superimposed orders and pediments to adorn the fronts of some houses in Queen Square. The wooden doorcases, which are rarely found, are usually superior in all details to the stone examples, and the most perfect work of the period is to be found in the fine church furniture, for some of which London craftsmen are known to have been responsible.

There are, of course, some exceptions to this generalization. The old Council House, built in 1701–4, had a florid but reasonably well-designed front in the vernacular Renaissance style of the time, while the stone front of Bishop's House on Clifton Green, a work dated 1711, is excellent in composition and correct in detail. The erection of Vanbrugh's great house at King's Weston, begun soon after 1710, was not without some effect on Bristol building styles, and Vanbrugh's Baroque mannerisms appear, along with more orthodox Palladian influences, in the work of John Strahan and William Halfpenny.

John Strahan (pages 45–6) advertised his presence in Bristol during 1725, and soon found patrons among the wealthy merchant class. It was almost certainly he who designed the twin houses, Nos. 68 and 70 Prince Street, built about 1726 for John Hobbs. A few other buildings of similar style and date are probably by the same hand, but Redland Court, built after 1732 for John Cossins, was Strahan's most important work in Bristol, for it must now appear that he was not the architect of Redland Chapel, built 1740–3. This much-admired building was probably designed by William Halfpenny (pages 37–8), who appears to have worked in Bristol at various times between 1728 and 1756, occasionally in the employment of the Corporation, to whom he submitted several abortive designs for the Exchange. The Coopers' Hall, begun in 1744, is certainly his work, and two houses in Prince Street, as well as the Assembly Room there, could reasonably be assigned to him.

Building of the long-projected Exchange was begun early in 1741 and completed in 1743, to the design of John Wood the elder, of Bath. This noble building, the first in Bristol to exhibit the Palladian revival in its full purity of form and splendour of detail, could not have failed to interest and inspire the builders in the city, but even more effectively influential was Isaac Ware's design for Clifton Hill House, erected between 1746–50. These influences, and an intelligent study of the pattern-books then appearing with increasing frequency, were potent in forming the building style of Thomas Paty (pages 40–3), who had worked as a carver at the Exchange, and as the mason for Clifton Hill House. It is only necessary here to single out Albemarle Row (1762) and the south side of Brunswick Square (1766) as two variants of a terrace-house composition with a central feature that might be regarded as a brick-and-stone version of Ware's design for Clifton Hill House. Paty's style was to set the standard for Bristol house-building during the last half of the eighteenth century, for many houses not actually designed by him were infused with his details. His pattern-book classical masonry appears in the houses of King Square, mostly built around 1760, and Brunswick Square, both of which were laid out by George Tully. Dowry Chapel, the Friends' Meeting House in The Friars, and probably Wesley's Chapel in Broadmead, all buildings of pronounced similarity, were erected to Tully's plans around 1746–8 and have stonework details by Paty, or in his manner.

A long-deferred and much-debated public work of great importance was begun early in 1761—the rebuilding of Bristol Bridge, and the widening and general improvement of the ways leading thereto. The lengthy and involved story of this undertaking is fully told elsewhere (pages 114–23), and it will suffice to say here that in 1763, before construction of the new bridge had begun, the architect James Bridges (pages 31–2) was impelled by the thwarting intrigues of others to leave Bristol, whither he had come in 1755, probably from America. Even in this short period of practice in the city Bridges had carried out a considerable body of work. He was employed to rebuild the parish churches of St Werburgh (1758–61) and St Nicholas (begun 1762), but his finest building was the Royal Fort (1761). It must also be fairly obvious that he designed Arno's Court, built about 1760, with its Gothic bath-house and castellated stable-court. Here, and at the Fort, the stuccowork was executed by Thomas Stocking (pages 44–5), and the carving by Thomas Paty, who was later engaged as architect to complete St Nicholas' Church and Bristol Bridge.

Thomas Paty, later assisted by his sons John and William (page 43), was now moving towards a pre-eminent position in the city's building activities, being responsible for rebuilding the parish churches of St Michael (1775–7) and Christ Church (1786–90). To Paty fell the major share of work involved in carrying out a further series of street improvements, centring on the formation of Union and Bridge streets, and provided for by an Act obtained in 1765. Streets and terraces of houses now arose with typical Paty fronts, mostly conforming to the following specification, which is applicable to so much in Bristol but actually related to the sale of building plots in Bath Street, begun in 1787: 'The Front of each House (shall) be cased with the best Stock Brick, ornamented with Pillasters, Fascia Course, Scill Course, Arches over the Windows, Scills, Cornice, and Coping, as per Elevation, all of Free-stone, well cleansed and finished with a Hard Stone Plinth to the Heighth of the Ground Floor.' The house-fronts in Clare Street, formed in 1771 to Paty's designs, were very similar, but the stately four-storied buildings fronting on to Bridge Street were entirely faced with ashlar. The beautiful Bath freestone was now being used more frequently and extensively, and it was to predominate over all other facing materials in the great schemes undertaken during the late 1780s.

Around 1785 the building tradesmen of Bristol, like those of Bath, became infected with a mania for speculative house-building. The first symptoms, such as the erection of Sion Row in Clifton, were by no means abnormal, but the rapid increase of the fever is shown by the number of undertakings mentioned in a letter that *Sarah Farley* published on 24th May 1788. The writer of this, after offering some gratuitous advice to the various architects and builders, lists the works then proposed or actually in progress. Some were of a semi-public nature, such as the rebuilding of Christ Church and the Unitarian Chapel in Lewin's Mead, the building of St Paul's Church and the new Infirmary. But the majority of the undertakings were speculative. Houses were now rising near Brandon Hill (Berkeley Square), in Great George Street, Park Street and around College Street, while the ground had been prepared for others on the site of the Red Lodge gardens. Then there were the extensive operations on Kingsdown—Kingsdown Parade, Alfred, Paul, and Oxford streets—and the new square and streets in the recently-created parish of St Paul. On 30th April 1791 *Sarah Farley* stated that

'So great is the spirit of building in this city and its environs, exclusive of public buildings, that we hear ground is actually taken for more than three thousand houses; which will require some hundreds more journeymen artificers than are already employed'.

The most spectacular projects belong to this 1790–1 phase—such as Portland Square in the eastern suburb, and Windsor Terrace, Royal York Crescent and Cornwallis Crescent in Clifton. The inspiring force behind some of the largest undertakings was James Lockier, a builder, timber-merchant, and upholder. The architects principally involved were William Paty, whose father and brother had died in 1789, and Daniel Hague (page 36). In the background were the attorneys who arranged the land deals and finances, and who waited to profit by the failure of others.

There is evidence to prove that one Bath architect, John Eveleigh, was employed to survey sites and prepare plans for three building schemes in Clifton, but nothing exists to prove his connection with any executed buildings except, perhaps, Windsor Terrace, the original design for which has a startling resemblance to Eveleigh's Camden Crescent in Bath. In all events, the stylistic influence of Bath was now very strong, and it must be obvious that the terraces, squares and crescents begun in Bristol and Clifton during the late 1780s were intended to rival those of the neighbouring city. How far the Bristol builders were from achieving this object can be seen by comparing, say, Portland or Berkeley Square and Cornwallis Crescent with their Bath counterparts, St James's Square and Lansdown Crescent.

A great scheme promoted by a syndicate headed by T. G. Vaughan, the banker, might in realization have surpassed even the splendours of Bath. In April 1791 this company purchased Tyndall's Park, ground partly freehold and partly held on short lease from the Dean and Chapter of Bristol. An Act of Parliament was obtained, in 1792, to permit this leasehold land to be granted for 1,000 years to the syndicate, so that they could begin 'a regular and grand plan of building, including a Crescent, Square, Circus, several streets, &c'. James Wyatt, then at the height of his fame, prepared the designs, and on 29th August 1792 a sale was held of thirty-eight lots of ground 'for building houses in the grand Crescent'. About the same time a scheme was proposed for building a terrace of sixty houses near Ashley Down.

Before the end of 1792 distinct signs of instability were appearing in this vast fabric of speculation. Resources were running out and loans were no longer forthcoming. During December, James Lockier opened a tontine subscription to raise funds for completing Royal York Crescent, and in the following February a similar scheme was promoted by Samuel Worrall in connection with King's Parade in Whiteladies Road, but both measures proved abortive. Disaster was now inevitable, for on 1st February 1793 war broke out between France and England, and a general financial panic ensued. The firm of Lockier, MacAulay and Co. were declared bankrupt towards the end of March, and the failure of many lesser firms rapidly followed. Building work came to a general standstill, there were numerous forced sales of unfixed materials, and more than 500 houses were left in various stages of construction, to remain without protection until the early 1800s. The promotors of the Tyndall's Park scheme showed considerable courage in the face of this general collapse, by advertising, during August 1793, for 'MASONS and CARPENTERS, upon Contract, for the prosecution of this Plan of Building'. Their brave show of optimism went unrewarded by success, however, and Wyatt's great crescent rose no higher than its foundations. Even these were to disappear when Repton remade the park for Colonel Tyndall, to whom the property reverted in 1798.

There were some thirty-four roofless houses in Royal York Crescent, dominating an equal number in Cornwallis Crescent, while Richmond Place, Belle Vue, York Place, Saville Place and part of The Mall presented the same dismal picture. Berkeley Square, Charlotte and Great George streets were in no better state, while Portland Square was said to 'nod in concert with one or two streets near it'. In his *First Impressions*, published in 1807, the antiquary James Malcolm wrote—'I do not recollect a more melancholy spectacle, independent of human sufferings, than a walk on a dull day through the silent and falling houses in the Western environs of this city; almost all of which are so nearly finished as to represent the deserted streets occasioned by a siege, or the ravages of a plague. Nor can one fail of reflecting

[27]

on the ruin many families must have suffered, to occasion such a picture of desolation.'

Many of the houses built during this period of speculation conform to a good standard, particularly those in the schemes with which the Patys were associated. The houses in Berkeley Square, for instance, are well constructed, with fronts of ashlar and, in many cases, back elevations of fine brickwork dressed with stone. Internally, they have stone staircases with balustrades of enriched ironwork, Good plasterwork and chimney-pieces of Adamesque design adorn the principal rooms, which often have doors and fittings of mahogany. On the other hand, neglect and wartime damage have made obvious the scamped construction and poor finish of some terrace-houses in Clifton, where the rubble-stone fronts were faced with cement and adorned with meagre stone trimmings, the chief ornament being a doorcase of stock pattern. Then, too, the drainage problem was often shirked. The houses of Kingsdown Parade originally had cesspools which overflowed during storms and discharged their unsavoury contents into the streets of lower level, while other houses were built with cesspools beneath them.

The building trades were slow to recover from the debacle of 1793, but signs of revival were apparent by 1805. The shells of several houses in the Clifton crescents and terraces now found purchasers, usually speculating builders such as the Greenways (pages 35–6), who completed them for resale. Windsor Terrace was finished on a greatly reduced scale soon after 1807, by John Drew, who then began to build a new loftily-sited crescent, The Paragon, although many houses still remained unfinished in the two great crescents. In fact, the last gaps in Royal York Crescent were not closed until around 1820, while the completion of Cornwallis Crescent was even longer delayed and, owing to the establishment of a right-of-way, never fully achieved.

In Bristol, as in Bath, the early nineteenth century saw the end of the conservatism that, in past years, had generally operated against the employment of architects from outside the city, and this period is especially noteworthy for several public buildings that were designed by London practitioners, generally exponents of the fashionable Greek revival. The Commercial Rooms, erected 1810–11, were the work of C. A. Busby (page

32), the successful entrant in a limited competition. One of Soane's pupils, H. H. Seward (page 44), designed the new Hotwell House (1816) and the County Gaol (1820), both buildings that have been demolished. Then there are two fine early works by C. R. Cockerell (pages 32–3)—The Philosophical and Literary Institute of 1820–3, and Holy Trinity Church, Hotwell Road, of 1829–30. Robert Smirke (page 44) is well represented by a typical church, St George's Brandon Hill, completed in 1823, and by the equally typical Council House of 1824–7.

The Fosters (page 34) were probably outstanding among the local architects of this time. James Foster, a pupil and assistant of William Paty, designed the Upper and Lower Arcades, charming essays in the Grecian manner that were erected in 1824–5, and he rebuilt Clifton Parish Church in 1819–22. Clifton Vale, Caledonia Place and the New Mall, designed about 1834 by the firm of Foster and Okeley, were strikingly original and yet maintained the best traditions of Georgian terrace-house design. Among succeeding architects Charles Dyer—designer of the Victoria Rooms—was an outstanding classicist, whereas R. S. Pope and C. Underwood began well enough—the former with St Mary's-on-the-Quay and the Royal Western Hotel, now Brunel House, both built around 1838, and the latter with some fine Grecian terraces and villas in Clifton—but soon they elected to follow the path of indiscriminate eclecticism that was, perhaps, the inevitable reaction from the Georgian taste for uniformity.

[29]

THE ARCHITECTS
AND BUILDING CRAFTSMEN

ALLEN, James

James Allen, statuary and architect, was described in *The New Bristol Guide* for 1804 as 'an ingenious, scientific, and the principal architect of Bristol'. This, to say the least, is very misleading, for at no time did Allen occupy a position at all comparable with that held in their times by George Tully, James Bridges, or the Patys and their successors, the Fosters. The son of John Allen, a joiner, James Allen was described as a carver when admitted a free burgess on 18th September 1780. In 1788 he was one of the three surveyors appointed to administer the Act of 1788, regulating building within the City Liberties. Allen's house and yard were then in Thomas Street, and his surveyorship probably extended over Redcliffe, St Thomas's, and Temple parishes. In 1787 he had the bitter experience of seeing his design for St Paul's Church, Portland Square, set aside in favour of one by Daniel Hague, but Allen was more fortunate in 1789 when his plans for rebuilding St Thomas's Church were approved. Sharing the common lot of so many then engaged in building, he became bankrupt in 1793 and during August of that year his house and yard were sold. The Bristol Directory for 1795 shows that he was then living at Eugene Street, off Temple Street, and describes him as an 'architect and drawing master'. During 1796 he was engaged on works of repair to St Mary Redcliffe, and it was perhaps for convenience that he then shared No. 3 Cathay, Redcliffe, with his brother John, a music master. By 1800 he had moved to Berkeley Place, where he continued to practice as an architect and drawing master. Five years later he appears as a mason, living on Stoney Hill, and in 1811 he was called in to advise on repairs to Mangotsfield Parish Church. The present writer has found nothing bearing on Allen's subsequent activities.

ARTHUR, *Nathaniel*

It is probable that much of the mid-eighteenth century wrought ironwork in Bristol was made by Nathaniel Arthur, a black-smith, who was made a free burgess on 1st July 1727, by order of the Common Council and on payment of a £10 fine. The gates at Redland Court and Redland Chapel are certainly his, and from these it is possible to identify him as the author of a fine gate originally standing before No. 29 Queen Square, and the area railings to some houses in Albemarle Row.

BRIDGES, *James*

James Bridges appears to have come from the American colonies about 1756, to practice as an architect and builder in Bristol, where he had premises at first on St Michael's Hill, and then on The Back. He is best remembered as the designer of Bristol Bridge, and as the involved history of its building is told elsewhere (pages 114–23), it must suffice to say here that the Trustees first consulted Bridges in 1757, accepted his proposals in 1758, and appointed him their surveyor in 1760. Then followed a long period of frustration for Bridges, brought about by the vacillations of the Trustees and the sustained opposition of John Wallis, who wished to see another design carried out by Ferdinando Stratford, of Gloucester. At length, mortified by intrigues and fretted by disappointments, Bridges resigned his surveyorship and in October he left Bristol for the West Indies. This drastic move seemed to break the spell exercised by Wallis over the Trustees, for on 21st November following they decided to proceed with Bridges' design, under Thomas Paty's direction.

Two of Bristol's parish churches were rebuilt to Bridges' designs—St Werburgh's in Corn Street, and St Nicholas' by Bristol Bridge. Except for its tower, the medieval church of St Werburgh was taken down towards the close of 1758, and Bridges' new building was finished in 1761. This church, which was demolished in 1877, appears to have been a most efficient essay in the late-Gothic style of Bristol, both externally and internally, whereas the Gothic exterior of St Nicholas' enclosed a partly Rococo interior. There is no evidence, however, to show whether this mixture of styles was due to Bridges, who began the rebuilding in 1762, or to Thomas Paty, by whom the church was finished when Bridges had left Bristol.

In March 1758 Bridges was employed by John Cossins, of Redland Court, to design a pair of houses that were to provide a source of revenue for Redland Chapel. Redland Hill House is probably the surviving twin of the pair designed by Bridges, who then submitted plans, estimates, and a model for the new mansion that Thomas Tyndall was to build in the Royal Fort. This splendid house was finished in 1761 and in its decoration Bridges had the collaboration of Thomas Paty, for the stone and wood carving, and Thomas Stocking, for the plasterwork. The same team was almost certainly responsible for the contemporary mansion of Arno's Court, with its Gothic bath-house and the fantastic 'Black Castle' stable-court.

Another of Bridges' buildings was of a transitory nature. This was a 'Temple for Fireworks Display' erected in Queen Square for the festivities held on 22nd September 1761, to celebrate the coronation of George the Third. This Temple 'consisted of a grand Pile of Architecture, composed of three different Orders (designed by Mr BRIDGES, an expert Architect). It was 73 Feet high, rais'd on a rustic Boffement in the form of an Athenian Temple, terminated by two Pavilions, extending 46 Feet in Front, and consisting of three transparent Pieces'.

BUSBY, *Charles Augustus*

Mr Antony Dale's study of *Fashionable Brighton* contains a full account of the life and works of Charles Augustus Busby (1788–1834), who is represented in Bristol by one building, the Commercial Coffee Rooms in Corn Street, erected in 1810–11. In 1816, however, Busby submitted two alternative plans for the gaol it was then proposed to build on the Castle hill. These are preserved in Plan-Book E, and while one is quite orthodox and consequently uninteresting, the other shows a most ingenious arrangement with a courtyard shaped like a kidney, formed by two intersecting parabolas around which are placed the cells and airing yards, one side for males and one for females, so disposed that every prisoner could be kept under the surveillance of the keepers in their towers. These projected into each court and were linked with the central administration block.

COCKERELL, *Charles Robert*

Charles Robert Cockerell was the architect of three buildings in

Bristol, each exceeding the last in merit and interest. The Freemasons' Hall, at the corner of Park Street and Museum Avenue, was the first, being erected as the Philosophical and Literary Institution in 1820–3. The two straight fronts, of unequal length but balanced in design, are rather uninspired, but the 'tholos' portico at the corner is most effective, and beautifully detailed. The reconstructed interior was completely gutted during the late war. This building was followed, in 1829–30, by Holy Trinity Church, Hotwells, which is described in this study. In the Bank of England, Broad Street, dating from about 1844, we have a work of Cockerell's maturity. The splendid front has a Doric pseudo-portico of three bays, recessed between low pavilions. The attic story is arcaded and surmounted by a triangular pediment.

EDNEY, William

William Edney, the greatest of Bristol's blacksmiths, was admitted a free burgess on 18th December 1706, by order of the Common Council and on payment of a £2 fine. A splendid craftsman and designer in the style of Tijou, he executed in 1710 the magnificent gates that originally separated the nave and chancel of St Mary Redcliffe, and it is recorded that he received £110 for this work. The large pair of gates, now set in an arch at the west end of the nave, are hung on tall and narrow pilaster-standards and surmounted by an elaborate overthrow. Each gate is divided by a lock-rail of open scrollwork into two panels, the lower one almost square and braced by diagonal bars, while the upper one is formed of scrollwork and pendant bars. The panels display the usual array of Tijouesque ornaments—acanthus-leaves and bosses, hart's-tongue ferns, and satyr masks, while the stepped overthrow is decorated with flaming urns and contains a Baroque cartouche with the City Arms, surmounted by a helmet and a crest that forms its finial. This is Edney's one documented work in Bristol, but if style, craftsmanship, and the presence of his initials in a monogram, are to be taken as evidence, he must have been responsible for the screens and gates made for the Temple Church in 1726. These had many features in common with the chancel gates of St Nicholas', which belonged to the last years of Queen Anne's reign, and were probably Edney's work. The gates of St

[33]

Nicholas' and the Temple were destroyed during the late war, but the superb sword-rest at the former was recovered from the ruins and has been placed, after careful restoration, in the Lord Mayor's Chapel (St. Mark's, College Green).

FOSTER, *James and Thomas*

An advertisement in *Felix Farley* on 26th February 1800, in which James Foster announced that 'he is carrying on the business of architect at 24 Orchard Street', shows that he began to practise on his own account very soon after the death of William Paty, whose apprentice and assistant he had been. By virtue of this apprenticeship Foster was admitted a free burgess on 10th February 1806, and in that year he was joined in practice by his son and namesake, described as a statuary. The Bristol Directory for 1820 shows that James Foster and Son were then at No. 10 Culver Street, while No. 24 Orchard Street was tenanted by Thomas Foster, architect, who had become a free burgess on 18th June 1818, by his marriage with a freeman's daughter. The exact relationship between James and Thomas Foster is not clear, but they were in practice together by 1826, when their address was at No. 13 Orchard Street. In 1828 the firm was styled Foster and Okeley, James and Thomas Foster having been joined in practice by William Ignatius Okeley, who was apprenticed to Thomas Foster and became a free burgess on 21st September 1830.

Foster and Son were responsible for the Upper and Lower Arcades, built in 1825 and finely designed in the Grecian style, and for the irresilient Gothic rebuilding of Clifton Parish Church, while the firm of Foster and Okeley designed the splendid terrace-houses of Clifton Vale, Caledonia Place and the New Mall.

GLASCODINE, *Samuel and Joseph*

Samuel Glascodine, a house-carpenter, was admitted a free burgess on 12th January 1737, by vote of the Common Council and on payment of a fine of £8. In 1741 he obtained the contract for the carpenter's work at the new Exchange, and in 1746 he was similarly engaged at Clifton Hill House. The Corporation gave him considerable employment as an architect and surveyor, and for them he designed and built the Exchange

Markets and the former Post Office, next to the Exchange. The fine mansion in Stokes Croft that he built for his own occupation still stands as part of the former Baptists' College. Samuel Glascodine must have died shortly before 1761, when the business passed to his son Joseph, who was described as a millwright and carpenter when admitted a free burgess on 11th November 1772. Joseph Glascodine lived at Stokes Croft until 1805, when he sold the property to the Baptists and moved to No. 84 Redcliffe Street, to reside in the district for which he had been appointed City Surveyor. By 1809 he had resigned the millwright's and carpenter's business to his son, but continued to practise as City Surveyor. His name appears for the last time in the Bristol Directory for 1819, when his address was No. 6 Alfred Place.

GREENWAY, Francis Howard

Messrs Olive Greenway, John Tripp Greenway, and Francis Howard Greenway—their exact relationship is not clear—came from Mangotsfield to Bristol about 1805, to practise as 'stonemasons, architects, builders, &c' with premises at No. 7 Limekiln Lane. Francis Greenway appears to have been the architect member of the co-partnership, and in 1806 he undertook to design, and his firm to build, the Hotel and Assembly Rooms at the head of The Mall, Clifton. At the same time the firm speculated by purchasing unfinished houses in Clifton, which they completed and then sold. On 2nd May 1809 the co-partners were declared bankrupt, and a sale of their assets followed. These included a 'valuable stock of marble in blocks, handsome modern chimney-pieces, Painswick stone slabs, Pennant and other paving stones, figures in plaster of Paris, after the antique, some finished to represent bronze, and two ornamental Gothic chimney-tunnels intended for Portumnia Castle'.

Shortly before this failure Francis Greenway had made a contract with one Colonel Doolan, whereby he undertook to finish No. 34 Cornwallis Crescent for the sum of 1,300 guineas. Some time after the bankruptcy, Greenway declared that Doolan had also agreed to pay an additional £250 for the unfinished shell of the house, but when asked to produce the contract he said it had been mislaid. The document then reappeared in mysterious circumstances, and when examined it was found to bear an endorsement, apparently witnessed by Isaac

Cooke, the attorney, confirming Greenway's statement regarding the extra payment. Doolan, however, denied all knowledge of this endorsement, which Cooke declared to be a forgery, and for this Greenway was arrested. Charged at the Bristol Assizes on 23rd March 1812, he pleaded guilty and received sentence of death, but this was later commuted to one of life transportation, due, perhaps, to the special circumstances of his crime. It was clear that he had no thought of personal gain, but wished rather to assist his creditors, and it is quite possible that there had been some verbal agreement about the extra payment. He was transported to Australia in 1813, there to become the father of that continent's architecture. Olive and John Tripp Greenway appear to have recovered from their financial troubles, and continued to practise at Limekiln Lane until about 1820.

HAGUE, *Daniel*

Daniel Hague, mason, was admitted a free burgess on 16th August 1762, having served as an apprentice to Thomas Manley, a well-known Bristol mason who was concerned in building Brunswick Square. Hague has been execrated as the architect of St Paul's Church, built in 1789–94, but he also designed its setting in Portland Square, which has been described as the best of Bristol's late eighteenth-century building schemes. It is, of course, possible that in this last work he was assisted by Paty and Sons, who were his associates in building the Infirmary. If not an inspired architect, Hague must have been a very capable mason and surveyor, for he was frequently called in to give advice to building committees. He seems to have prospered from the extensive building operations that went on during the late eighteenth century, for besides his own activity as a mason, he had interests in brick-making, stone-quarrying and lime-burning, and he appears to have weathered the financial storms of 1793. The Bristol Directory for 1775 gives his address as No. 20 Montague Street, but by 1790 he had removed to premises in Wilder Street, just north of Brunswick Square. Here he continued to live after his retirement about 1805, when the business was taken over by his son. Hague senior appears to have died about 1816, in which year his son changed the trade of mason for that of linen-draper.

[36]

HALFPENNY, William

William Halfpenny—whose slender claim to fame depends less on his few buildings than on the influence his numerous pattern-books exerted on contemporary builders—worked in several capacities in Bristol during the second quarter of the eighteenth century. Little is known of his early life beyond the fact that his first recorded building is Holy Trinity Church, Leeds, erected 1721–7. This suggests that he was born about the turn of the century and that he was a native of Yorkshire, where his name is not uncommon. He was probably apprenticed to a house-carpenter, and, like many building tradesmen of the time, he adopted the style of architect whenever it suited his purpose. Certain statements in Batty Langley's writings have brought about the general belief that Halfpenny's true name was Michael Hoare. Against this may be set the facts that all his Bristol papers and drawings are signed 'William Halfpenny', and while some twenty books were published under that name, only one appears to have been written by 'Michael Hoare'—a *Builders' Pocket Companion* dated 1728. The only book of Halfpenny's that has any direct bearing on Bristol is *Perspective made Easy*, which contains engraved views of the Drawbridge, the Hotwell and St Vincent's Rocks, the north prospect of Queen Square, and his first design for an Exchange. The book was not dated but the British Museum copy, unfortunately destroyed, was inscribed 1731, which is the publication date given in a scathing notice of Halfpenny's book in Thomas Malton's *Treatise on Perspective*. If this date is correct, then we may assume that Halfpenny was in Bristol about 1728, perhaps in the employ of Strahan, with whom some tenuous links can be established. It is significant that Strahan died about 1740, the time when Halfpenny first appears to be working on his own account in Bristol.

During 1739–40 Halfpenny once again directed his efforts towards obtaining the important commission of designing the proposed new exchange, submitting at different dates four alternative schemes which were all eventually rejected by the building committee. This did not deter him from tendering a price for the carpenter's work to the Exchange, but here again he was disappointed, for Wood and the committee gave the contract to Samuel Glascodine. Halfpenny was also employed to a small extent by the Corporation in surveying and valuing their properties, although the bulk of such work went to John Jacob de Wilstar, whose drawings have the engaging naïvety of some early cartography. The Plan-Books contain signed drawings made by Halfpenny during 1742, including a drainage layout and plan of the conduit at Jacob's Wells, and a plan of the ground bounded by Baldwin and King streets, with various properties shown in different colours and the drawing embellished with a magnetic compass, draughtsman's dividers, and a scale. The Audit Books record sundry small payments to Halfpenny for these services, such as one of 7s. 6d. for his survey of the old Coopers' Hall on the Exchange site.

On 22nd May 1742, Halfpenny signed an agreement with John Cossins, of Redland Court, whereby he undertook to supervise the work of finishing Redland Chapel, for which, it now seems certain, he had made the design. About the same time he submitted a scheme for adding wings to the existing Infirmary, his drawing being engraved by Toms and published during 1742, although the design was rejected later in favour of one by George Tully. The Coopers' Hall in King Street, hitherto Halfpenny's best known work in Bristol, was begun during 1743.

The following buildings in Bristol might also have been designed by Halfpenny, on evidence of date and style. The Assembly Room in Prince Street, built 1754–5, and now demolished except for the mutilated remains of the ground-story. No. 40 Prince Street, built 1740–1, and destroyed during an air raid. Clifton Court, Clifton Green, built for Martha Dandervall, about 1742–3.

The presence in Bristol of William Halfpenny's brother and collaborator John, is shown by an advertisement appearing in *The Bristol Oracle* for 27th July 1745, announcing proposals for engraving and publishing a perspective view of St Mary Redcliffe, drawn by John Halfpenny. An advertisement in *Felix Farley*, for some issues during July 1754, announcing the publication of *Perspective made Easy*, suggests the appearance of a new edition and the possibility of Halfpenny's being in Bristol about that time.

HENWOOD, Luke

Luke Henwood, of No. 34 College Street, appears to have

practised as an architect and surveyor from about 1790 until 1830, but the present writer has found only two items concerning him. In 1812 Henwood was acting as architect for rebuilding All Saints' Street and the alms-houses of that parish, and during 1827–8 he was appointed one of the City Surveyors.

PATYS, The

The name of Paty figures so prominently in Bristol's eighteenth-century building history that its bearers deserve a detailed study beyond the scope of the present work. It is a matter for regret that evidence regarding some of them, and their relationship one to the other is either inconclusive or altogether lacking. It is, of course, probable that widespread research would reveal more than is contained in the following.

James Patty

A carver named James Patty, son of James Patty, late of Bristol, was admitted a free burgess on 9th March 1708, by virtue of his being the apprentice of Thomas Kilby, a mason. A second James Patty, whose entry appeared in the Bristol Directories from 1775 to 1795, was presumably the son of the former. Practising as a carver and gilder, he lived at No. 32 Broadmead, and was appointed a waywarden of St James's Parish in 1786.

James Paty (1)

The first recorded work of any note by a Paty was the carving of the Quarter-Jack figures for Christ Church clock. These were executed in 1728, presumably by James Paty, a carver and freestone-mason who was admitted a free burgess on 15th April 1721. The fact that he was called upon to pay a fine of £15 suggests that this Paty was not a native of Bristol, nor did he serve his apprenticeship there. He was considerably employed by the Corporation, and during 1739–41 he acted as principal mason and carver at the Library then building in King Street. The Chamberlain's Audit-Books contain details of his charges for carving the ornaments there. In the absence of contrary evidence, and having regard to James Paty's talents, it seems reasonable to assume that he designed the front of the Library, and that of the very similar house, No. 32, formerly standing in College Green. His will, proved 25th February 1747, shows that he lived in Merchant Street, and that he bequeathed his entire estate to his wife.

James Paty (2)

James Paty, a carver, of 21 Horse Street, whose name appears only in the Directory for 1775, was presumably a son of the first James Paty and brother to Thomas Paty, for the baptismal registers of St Augustine's, in which parish they both lived, show that James and Thomas Paty each named a daughter in honour of the other's wife. By marrying the daughter of Peter Tomkins, a mariner and freeman, James Paty was admitted a free burgess on 12th July 1755. He participated in building schemes in which Thomas Paty was interested, such as Park Street, and he was probably the James Paty who designed the Theatre Royal in 1764. Monuments signed by a James Paty of this time, such as those in Christ Church, are presumably his work. When he died on 1st February 1779, his son John Paty took over the business. Succeeding issues of *Felix Farley* from 13th February to 27th March 1779 contain the announcement that —'JOHN PATY, Carver, Marble Mason, &c., Begs Leave to acquaint his FRIENDS and the PUBLIC that he continues the Business in all its Branches of his late Father, JAMES PATY, at his Yard Under the Bank. . . . Monuments, Chimney-Pieces, &c. . . . N.B. Land Surveying and Plans accurately drawn, also Measuring.' John Paty was admitted a free burgess on 7th December 1778.

Thomas Paty

Thomas Paty, perhaps the most talented member of this family, was born in 1718, presumably a son of James Paty (1). Soon after the age of twenty he seems to have been working with equal facility as a mason, statuary, and architect, and his great gifts eventually led him to be more widely employed than any of his contemporaries, this success being achieved despite the fact that he never became a free burgess of Bristol. From 1741–2 he was principal 'Ornament Carver of the Exchange', and from 1740–7 he worked at Redland Chapel and Court as a stone and wood carver, employing Michael Sidnell and William Halfpenny among his assistants there. He supplied the dressed masonry and carved the stonework at Clifton Hill House, built during 1747–50, and the carving at the Royal Fort and at Arno's Court is also his work.

He rebuilt St Michael's Church in 1775–7 to his own designs, and was responsible for some alterations made to St Augustine's, while in 1763 he took over the work of completing St Nicholas' Church to James Bridges' plans and added a tower and spire of his own designing. One of his last works must have been the preparation of plans for rebuilding Christ Church, the work being carried out after his death by William Paty, his son. St James's Market, Union Street, was built about 1775 to Thomas Paty's plans, and he shared with Daniel Hague the task of designing the new buildings for the Infirmary, begun in 1784. During 1788 he reconstructed the Merchants' Hall, recasting the exterior.

In 1763 he was entrusted with the task of carrying out James Bridges' designs for rebuilding Bristol Bridge, and he laid out Clare, High, Bridge, Union and Bath streets, designing as well the uniform elevations for the buildings lining these thoroughfares. College, Park, Great George, Charlotte, and Lodge streets, Berkeley Square and Crescent, and Upper Berkeley Place, were also laid out, and the house-fronts designed by Thomas Paty and his sons, John and William. In all truth it may be stated that the Patys evolved the standard designs that were adopted for most of the terrace-houses built in Bristol during the second half of the eighteenth century. It is also certain that much of the ornamental stonework used by the Bristol house-builders of that time was prepared in the Patys' yard in Limekiln Lane.

Thomas Paty's field of activity was not limited to Bristol, for *Felix Farley* on 17th August 1776 informed its readers that 'The Corporation of Wells have agreed to rebuild the assize hall and market house, after a plan of the Rev. Dr Camplin's, . . . to be completed under the direction of Mr Paty of this city'. His professional standing as an architect and surveyor was so high that he was brought in to arbitrate in the controversy that arose in 1775 over the rebuilding of Bath's Guildhall.

Monuments signed by Thomas Paty are not only to be found in churches in and around Bristol, but as far afield as the West Indies. An elaborate example is that commemorating William Hilliard, erected about 1750 in St Mark's, College Green (see page 13). In this branch of his art he must have influenced not only his sons, but his son-in-law Thomas King, founder of a family of statuaries who flourished in Bath.

Thomas Paty died on 4th May 1789, and the *Bristol Journal* for 9th May contains this notice—'Monday, died in the 77th year of his age, Mr. Thomas Paty, architect; whose extensive virtues, professional abilities, and strict integrity, will in this city ever be rever'd; and we may say, whose paternal affection added a lustre to his character; let those who knew him, those who loved him, speak.' By his will, made 2nd May 1789 and proved 3rd August 1789, Thomas Paty bequeathed to his daughter Elizabeth King the sum of £800; to his son-in-law Thomas King, statuary, of Bath, £250; and to his son John Paty a sum of money equal in value to the house in Park Street given to and settled on Sarah Hickes at her marriage with his second son William Paty. His sons were the executors and inherited the business.

To sum up Thomas Paty's achievements: His buildings are invariably well built and his masonry is of outstanding excellence; his architectural designs are generally good and never less than competent, usually in a Classical style that appears to have been derived from an intelligent study of Gibbs' and Ware's published works. Batty Langley's influence is distinctly traceable in a few Gothic buildings, but is especially noticeable in Paty's monuments. Another manner, reflecting the elegant art of Robert Adam, appears in the later works of Thomas Paty and Sons, for which William was probably responsible.

In his descriptive poem 'Clifton', published during 1766, the contemporary versifier Henry Jones, or Johnes, eulogizes Thomas Paty:

> *Here buildings boast a robe, tho' rich yet chaste*
> *The robe of judgment, and of ripen'd taste*
> *Convenience here is mix'd with manly grace*
> *Yet ornament but holds the second place.*
> *To human frames these structures seem akin*
> *With aspect fair, while reason rules within.*
> *These domes discretion decks, and fancy cheers*
> *PALLADIO's stile in PATTY's plans appears:*
> *Himself a master with the first to stand,*
> *For CLIFTON owes her beauties to his hand.*

On Thomas Paty's death, his sons published the following announcement in the Bristol newspapers—'JOHN AND WILLIAM

PATY, ARCHITECTS and STATUARIES, offer their best thanks to the Public for the many favors conferred on them, during a partnership with their deceased Father, which subsisted twelve years,—They flatter themselves, that unremitting attention, blended with the most scrupulous integrity, will insure a continuance of that patronage, they are truly solicitous to merit.' The new partnership, scarcely begun, was cut short by John Paty's death on 10th June 1789. The *Bristol Journal*, for 13th June, published the following obituary—'On Wednesday last; died at Bath, Mr. John Paty, statuary and architect of this city, a young man of distinguished genius, incorruptible integrity, and the most unaffected manners.' There is little else to tell of John Paty, save that he was one of the three surveyors appointed in 1788 to enforce the rules, directions, and restrictions of the Act of Parliament for regulating building within the City Liberties.

William Paty

The character of William Paty's own work makes it clear that he had been an active and influential partner of his father during the later years of Thomas Paty's life, and that much of the credit for their work carried out during this time should go to this son. Evidences of style and circumstance point to the probability that Royal York and Cornwallis crescents, with many other buildings begun in Clifton during 1790–2, were designed by William Paty. Some fine detached houses in Great George Street are his work, and he was associated with John Nash in designing the Harford mansion at Blaise Castle, built 1795–8. One of his last buildings was the Poor House in St George's Parish, erected in 1800.

Like his father, William Paty was a most accomplished statuary, and examples of his work, delicate Adamesque designs usually carried out in coloured marbles, can be seen in most Bristol churches. He was admitted a free burgess on 9th December 1790, paying a fine of 15 guineas. He died at the age of forty-five, on 11th December 1800, and *Felix Farley*, on 13th December, published this obituary—'Last night died, at his house in College Place, Mr. William Paty, an eminent architect, of this city: His death will be greatly regretted by the public in general, but particularly by his friends.'

[43]

SEWARD, *Henry Hake*

Henry Hake Seward, a London architect and a pupil of Soane, designed the County Gaol that was built in 1820, on a site in Redcliffe now occupied by the railway. He was also architect for the New Hot-well House, containing baths and a pump-room, erected in 1816 and demolished in 1867. This charming building consisted of an octagonal centre, with flanking wings fronted by Tuscan porticoes. Seward was also one of the un-successful aspirants for the commission of building the new Council House, for which he submitted, in 1821, a design with a fine Grecian elevation.

SMIRKE, *Robert*

Bristol has two Greek Revival buildings by Robert Smirke, the first in date being St George's Church, Brandon Hill, completed in 1823 as a chapel-of-ease to St Augustine's. The west front, towards Charlotte Street, is unimpressive, but the east front—which overlooks Great George Street and is approached by a stairway of three flights—has the costly adornment of a fine Doric tetrastyle portico surmounted by a pediment, behind which rises a belfry of one circular stage crowned with a dome. The spacious interior has a gallery round three sides, supported by widely-spaced Ionic columns, and the single-span segmental ceiling is enriched with coffering. Smirke's second building, the Council House of 1824–7, is fully described in this study. His brother, Sydney Smirke, was employed to design the Customs House on the north side of Queen Square, when it was rebuilt after the riots of 1832.

STOCKING, *Thomas*

Thomas Stocking, by far the best-known of Bristol's eighteenth-century plasterworkers, appears to have begun practising his craft there about 1760. He applied for admission as a free burgess on 29th September 1762 and became one on 20th July 1763, by vote of the Common Council and on paying a fine of eight guineas. This suggests that he was not a native of Bristol, and proves that he was not apprenticed there. The style of his work suggests that he might have come from Dublin, where there was a building slump just before 1760, but on the other hand he might have been influenced by Joseph Thomas, or even by the published designs of Thomas Lightoler. The splendid plaster-work at the Royal Fort, Arno's Court, and St Nicholas' Church, was carried out by Stocking, whose field was by no means limited to Bristol. There are magnificent ceilings by him at Corsham Court and work in his style is often met with in and around Bath, and in isolated examples throughout the western counties. About 1790 he was joined by Robert Harding, who carried on the business when Stocking retired. 'A man greatly esteemed and respected by all who knew him', Thomas Stocking died on 10th September 1808, aged eighty-six, 'having borne with fortitude a lingering and painful illness.'

STRAHAN, John

Research has so far failed to produce any evidence which might throw light on the life and career of John Strahan, prior to his settling in Bristol some time during 1725. From the 1742 edition of John Wood's *Essay towards a Description of Bath* we learn how Strahan 'by printed Bills, offer'd his Services, as an Architect, to the Citizens of Bristol the Beginning of December 1725'. His publicity was evidently successful, for he soon obtained the extensive patronage of some wealthy and in-fluential citizens, such as John Hobbs, a timber merchant who invested largely in building houses in Bristol and Bath. We have it on Wood's authority that Hobbs employed Strahan as architect for the Avon navigation scheme, undertaken about 1726, and for 'laying out some Meadow and Garden Ground on the West Side of the Body of the City of Bath into Streets for Building'. Here it may be remarked that Strahan's work in the Kingsmead area and in Beauford Square, Bath, provides a valuable pointer to the probability of his being the designer of certain Bristol buildings, such as the former Barber-Surgeons' Hall, near the Exchange, and the front of No. 59 Queen Charlotte Street.

The Chandos correspondence in the Huntington Library, California, shows that in 1726 and 1728 the Duke had Strahan under consideration as his architect in Bath, although on each occasion articles were finally signed with Wood. Nevertheless, Strahan was brought in as a surveyor to pronounce on the efficiency of Wood's building, much, we may be sure, to the latter's furious disgust.

[45]

In September 1728 Strahan petitioned the Mayor and Corporation of Bristol, that he might be admitted a free burgess of the City. His petition was granted during the following October, but as his name does not appear in the Burgess Rolls it must be presumed that he was unwilling to pay the £8 fine required for the grant of this privilege. The fact that Wood, in the 1742 edition of his *Essay*, wrote of Strahan as 'deceas'd' shows that he must have died about 1740, presumably at Bristol. This offers proof, in addition to evidence quoted elsewhere in the book, that Strahan was not the architect of Redland Chapel, upon which building his chief claim to fame has rested.

Redland Court, completed in 1735, is the one surviving building in greater Bristol that can certainly be ascribed to Strahan, although he must be credited with Nos. 68 and 70 Prince Street, the twin houses erected about 1728 for John Hobbs, on the evidence of style and date. No. 12 St James's Barton is probably his, and the front of No. 59 Queen Charlotte Street, which closely resembles that of Rosewell House, Bath, in so many of its details. Outside of Bristol there are his houses in Bath, while Frampton Court, Frampton-on-Severn, is so very closely affined in style and date with Redland Court as to leave little room for doubt that Strahan was its unrecorded architect. An example of his draughtsmanship survives in the engraved design for the 'Stone Gallerie and Magnificent Organ of St. Mary Redcliff', erected towards the close of 1726. This no longer survives, neither does the charming front of the Barber-Surgeons' Hall, which had every appearance of being Strahan's work. St Michael's Hill House, also destroyed, was a fine Palladian mansion generally attributed to Strahan, who prepared, in 1725, a design for an additional aisle to St Michael's Church, that was not built.

STRATFORD, *Ferdinando*

Ferdinando Stratford, an engineer and surveyor generally resident in Gloucester, came to Bristol about 1760 to play an important part in the Bridge controversy, for it was his design for a single-arch bridge that John Wallis sought to impose on his fellow Trustees. Stratford was obviously a very competent engineer, and before coming to Bristol he had received high praise for a scheme designed to make the River Avon navigable from Bath to Chippenham. He died at Tidenham, Gloucestershire, in April 1766, from ague contracted while making a survey and report of a navigation scheme for the River Chelmer, which had been proposed by one Thomas Yeomans.

THOMAS, Joseph

Joseph Thomas, tyler and plasterer, was admitted a free burgess on 21st September 1730, being the son of a freeman. During 1748–50 he carried out work at Clifton Hill House to the value of £406. The fine ceilings there, in which Palladian forms are combined with Rococo ornamentation, were probably completed to Ware's instructions, and the clue to Thomas's own style is to be found in some ceilings, if they still exist, at No. 5 Guinea Street. One had a central ornament of a sunburst framed by C-scrolls and *rocaille* ornaments, while each angle contained a Rococo panel introducing birds and squirrels (title page). This house was built for Thomas's own occupation under a Corporation lease dated 5th September 1740, whereby he undertook to pull down an old tenement and erect two new ones. Actually he built three, Nos. 5, 6 and 7, and their uniform fronts are constructed of rubble-stone faced with stucco. The fine decorations of the staircase at No. 15 Orchard Street are also in the style of Joseph Thomas, who died on 6th May 1777.

TULLY, George and William

Although facts relating to George Tully and his son William are few, it is evident that these house-carpenters and surveyors enjoyed a wide practice and high reputation in their time, and that the father played a considerable part in the building development of eighteenth-century Bristol. George Tully was born in Surrey, shortly before 1700, and came to Bristol as an apprentice to John Stibbs. The latter dying, Tully was transferred to John Price, and thus came to work under two of the leading house-carpenters of that time. Having completed his apprenticeship, Tully was admitted a free burgess of Bristol on 17th May 1715. His first important work as a surveyor was undertaken about 1720, when he laid out Dowry Square and Chapel Row on ground leased by him jointly with Thomas Oldfield. King Square, laid out shortly before 1740, was almost certainly

planned by Tully, who built houses there for his own occupation
and for letting. His last important work in this direction was the
laying out of Brunswick Square and the adjacent streets, in 1766.

Dowry Chapel was built by subscription in 1746, to designs
by George Tully, who was also responsible for the Friends'
Meeting House in The Friars, erected 1747–9, and probably the
architect of Wesley's Chapel in Broadmead, of about the same
date. Tully's reputation as a surveyor stood sufficiently high in
1741 for him to be called in, opposite William Smith of Warwick, to report on the efficacy of some repairs that had been
made to the ruinous old church at Tetbury.

In 1741 he was desired by the Exchange Committee to 'propose a plan for building the Exchange'. The Chamberlain's
Audit-Books record that in January 1759 he was paid £42 for
making various surveys and designs for the Corporation. An
examination of his receipt shows that, among other items, the
work included—'Planning ground for the Exchange Buildings:
Ditto for the Shambles: Ditto for Lawford's Gate: Ditto for the
Stone Bridge at the head of the Key: Ditto for the New Street
leading from Orchard Street to College Green: Ditto Foot of
College Green for a publick road thro the Boar's Head ground
up Bullock's Park.'

George Tully's will, made on 24th March 1769 and proved on
3rd March 1770, shows that he left, besides fee-farm rents,
house property in King Square, New Street and College Green,
and his former 'Messuage or Tenement, Stables, Coach House,
Workshop, Carpenters Yard, then in the occupation of Edmund
Workman, standing and being near a place called St. James's
Barton, and nearly opposite to a certain Inn called the Full
Moon'. This last suggests that ill health had caused Tully to
dispose of his business as a house-carpenter to Edmund Workman, an associate who was largely concerned with the building
of Brunswick Square.

John Wallis, when giving evidence during the Bristol Bridge
controversy, often quoted William Tully as one 'whose Knowledge and Experience exceed that of all Mankind', but beyond
this fact there is little information to be gathered. Pre-deceasing
his father, his death was noticed by *Felix Farley* on 19th March
1763, in the following—'Saturday previously, Mr. William
Tully (A Quaker) an eminent Architect, was seized with a Fit of

[48]

Apoplexy, at his house in Stokes Croft, and expired within a few hours. He delivered several ingenious plans for rebuilding Bristol Bridge.'

WALLIS, John

The most powerful opponent of James Bridges, and the strong supporter of Ferdinando Stratford in the Bristol Bridge controversy, John Wallis appears to have held considerable influence in civic affairs. As an architect and builder, however, there are only two works with which his name can now be associated. For erecting 'Wallis's Wall' along the edge of the great ravine on Durdham Down, he was apostrophized as a public benefactor in a verse that was published in *The London Magazine* for 1747, and written, one suspects, by himself. He also designed and built, about 1758, the large structure appropriately called 'The Circular Stables', lying between Stokes Croft and Wilder Street, some fragments of which can still be identified among the later buildings. Wallis was obviously a man of some culture, and when he died on 30th October 1777 *Felix Farley* described him as 'late an eminent architect of this city'. He was buried in Bristol Cathedral, but his monument, with a pompous eulogium of his own composing, no longer exists.

WOODS of BATH, The

Despite the proximity of Bath and Bristol, the latter city has only one building by John Wood the elder, and nothing by his son. It must, however, be observed that while the elder Wood received little or no encouragement from the civic authorities in Bath, those of Bristol had the taste and wisdom to employ him to design the new Exchange, built during 1741–3, and thereby gave their city its finest eighteenth-century building. It has been stated that the elder Wood also designed the Markets and buildings flanking the Exchange, but these are proved to be the works of another. In 1730 the vestry of St Nicholas' sought his advice on ways and means of averting the threatened collapse of their medieval church.

The younger Wood was invited in 1760 to submit plans and proposals for rebuilding Bristol Bridge, but his designs failed to find approval.

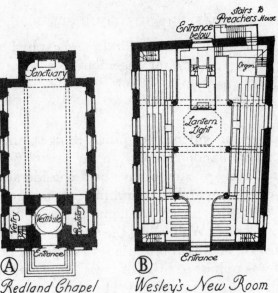

Ⓐ Redland Chapel

Ⓑ Wesley's New Room

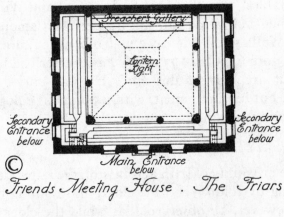

Ⓒ Friends Meeting House . The Friars

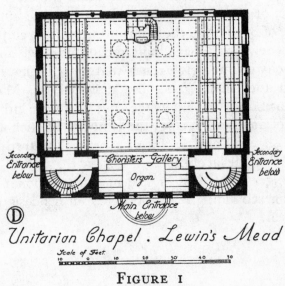

Ⓓ Unitarian Chapel . Lewin's Mead

Scale of Feet.

FIGURE I

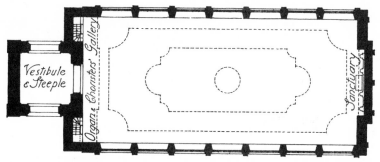

Ⓐ St Nicholas' Church

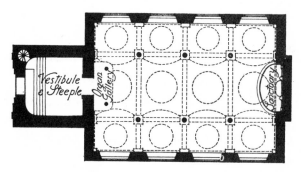

Ⓑ Christ Church

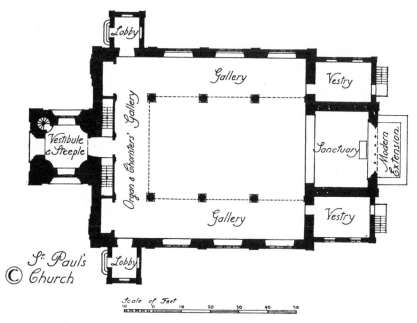

St Paul's
Ⓒ Church

Scale of Feet

FIGURE 2

CHURCHES AND CHAPELS

ST MARY REDCLIFFE, Strahan's Gallery and Organ-Case

The vestry minute-books of St Mary Redcliffe contain the following entries relating to the building of the great organ in 1726–7.

11th October 1726

'We the said Vestry have already contracted with John Harris and John Byfield Organ Builders for the said Organ and that the said Organ may be finished as soon as conveniently may— We do appoint the Churchwardens for the time being and Mr George Whittmow, Capt Edmund Saunders, and Mr John Fisher forthwith to Contract and agree with Workmen to Erect a handsome Ornamental Gallery to contain the said Organ and what shall be necessary to compleat the Same.'

27th March 1727

'At a Meeting of the Vestry It was ordered That the Church-warden Mr Jacob Little shall pay unto Messrs Simpson & Tidway Fifty seven pounds Two shillings for ffreestone and work about the Organ And also that he pay unto Mr Strahan Architect for his Draught of the Organ Seven Guineas.'

Messrs Harris and Byfield circulated a description of their organ, in a pamphlet dated February 1728, wherein they stated that 'Mr Strahan, who drew the Design for the Organ-Case which was lately erected in St. Mary Redclift Church, had it engraved for sale'. From this engraving by Kirkall (Figure 3), and a water-colour drawing by Johnson in the Braikenridge Collection, it is possible to form a complete picture of the splendid Baroque construction that once filled the west end of the nave. The front of the stone gallery formed a triumphal arch, adorned with Corinthian columns that stood in wide pairs on each side of the arched opening, and supported forward

The East Prospect of the Stone Gallerie & Magnificent Organ of S.t Mary Redcliff Bristol
being 53 feet high from the Ground to the top of the Crown pinacle
The great Case about 20 feet Square Contains One great & lesser
Organ the Musical part perform'd by Messieurs Harris & Byfield

FIGURE 3

breaks in the rich entablature. A further break occurring in the centre rested on the acanthus keyblock of the arch. The wooden front of the loft was a panelled pedestal, broken to correspond with the cornice beneath, with carved enrichments to each forward die-panel and a clock case flanked by vases surmounting the middle break. A panelled screen with three arched openings formed the back of the loft, and above this rose the elaborate case. There were three towers, in which the large pipes were clustered to represent the shafts of columns and pilasters, with Composite capitals supporting entablatures. Each outside tower was surmounted by a group of inverted consoles rising to support a ball and mitre. The central tower—wider and taller than the others—had a segmental pediment on which rested angels, supporting a cartouche and holding aloft palm-branches, while behind them rose a finial of inverted consoles supporting a crown. The smaller pipes in each of the connecting bays were framed in an arched opening with an inverted-arch top. From a winged cherub's-head placed at the arch crown rose a finial composed of a cartouche surmounted by a flaming urn.

REDLAND CHAPEL

Redland Chapel, now the Parish Church, was built and endowed at the sole expense of John Cossins, of Redland Court, to serve the religious needs of his household and neighbours. The site formed part of his estate and adjoins Redland Green, which extends round three sides of the small churchyard. The foundation-stone was laid on 1st July 1740, and service was first performed in the completed chapel on 5th October 1743. This is a building of great charm and interest, even though its architectural quality is uneven, and it has remained remarkably free from the disfigurements of later alteration.

All the available evidence now points to William Halfpenny as the architect of the chapel, although until recently it has been generally ascribed to John Strahan, apparently on nothing more substantial than the fact of his having designed Redland Court for John Cossins, about 1732. The first doubt as to Strahan's authorship was cast in the present writer's mind by John Wood's reference, in the 1742 edition of his *Description of Bath*, to certain buildings there being the 'Architecture of one John Strahan, deceas'd', from which, allowing for the interval between writing and publication, it must appear as probable that Strahan had died before the chapel was begun. In addition to this, previous writers have ignored or overlooked the fact that Shiercliff, in his 'Bristol and Hotwell Guide' for 1789, definitely stated that the chapel was built 'in the year 1740, from a design of Mr William Halfpenny, architect'. This guide was published only some forty-five years after the completion of the chapel, and while Redland Court was still possessed by Cossins' heirs, from whom reliable information could have been obtained. Finally, documentary evidence exists to prove that the interior at least, was finished to Halfpenny's designs and under his supervision, and in view of his church-building experience in Yorkshire there was no-one then resident in Bristol who was more likely to have been employed by Cossins for this particular undertaking.

The accounts that have been preserved show that the chapel, apart from its interior finishings and furniture, was built by Richard Williams, a house-carpenter, who undertook to 'Finish ye Whole in a Workman Like Manner' for the sum of £850, except for the 'Foundations and Diging' which were to be 'att ye Expence off Mr Cousins over & above ye Charge as above Mentioned'. The structure must have been completed by 22nd May 1742, the date on which William Halfpenny signed the following agreement:

'I Do Agree With John Cousins Esqr: to Give proper Directions As is Usuall By Architects and Directers of Buildings, to All his Workmen Employ'd At his Chapple At Redland, and to See Said Workmen do their Work in a Workmanlike Manner and See that they Make proper Use of his Materials without Waste, and to See the Whole Compleated for the Sum of ten pounds ten Shillings Sterling

I Said Halfpenny Do Agree to Visit Said Work, Six Days in Evry Week, and for Evry Day Neglect, I Do Agree to Forfit three Shillings, and Sixpence, and to Measure all Said Work When Required both Within and Without.

Wm: Halfpenny.'

The stone-carving of the west front and the interior was executed by Thomas Paty, together with the more elaborate wood-carving and certain of the stucco ornaments. The joiners responsible for the wainscotting and pewing were Thomas Hill and Thomas Utting, of Bristol, while the altar-piece was made by William Brooks, 'Late of London'. All of this work was carried

FIGURE 4
Redland Chapel. West elevation

out in Dutch oak, in accordance with Halfpenny's drawings, although the exquisitely carved enrichments in limewood were

[56]

doubtless designed as well as executed by Paty. The wrought-iron gate at the churchyard entrance was made by Nathaniel Arthur.

The plan form of the chapel is a rectangle, measuring some 56 feet east to west, and 30 feet north to south, with a small chancel projecting from the east end (Figure 1a). The west end of the rectangle is taken up by an octagonal vestibule, placed between small rooms that originally served for the vestry and baptistry, with a gallery over all. The walls are constructed of brick, faced externally with Bath stone above a plinth of Portland. The west front (Plate 4. Fig. 4) is adorned with an engaged portico of the Roman Ionic order, with four plain-shafted pilasters spaced in pairs to carry the entablature, which has a pulvinated frieze and modillioned cornice, surmounted by a triangular pediment. The narrow side intercolumniations are quite plain, but the wide middle one contains the doorway with a niche over it. The door, which is of two five-panelled leaves, is set in a segmental-headed opening with an eared architrave broken by a keystone. This takes the form of a scrolled console, rising through a frieze carved with festoons of fruits and flowers, to support the cornice that breaks forward over the console and back above the narrow rusticated flanks of the doorway. The blocking-course surmounting the cornice serves as a plinth to the niche, which is semi-circular on plan and has a semi-dome head. Its architrave mouldings curve outwards on either side near the base and return inwards to finish in volutes, while the archivolt rises from a moulded impost that returns inside the niche to support the carved scallop-shell that fills the semi-dome. The niche has a wide and plain marginal surround, broken slightly forward from the main face, and a winged cherub's-head carved in bold relief is placed immediately above the crown of the archivolt. In the tympanum of the pediment is a semi-circular window, its enriched archivolt rising from a plinth.

Behind the pediment, and flush with the main wall face, rises the moulded pedestal that forms the square base of the single-stage belfry. At each corner stands a pedestal, supporting a draped vase, from behind which a concave splay rises to intercept the belfry faces and change the plan form from a square to an octagon. Each face is plain except for a circular opening with an architrave surround broken into four equal

[57]

segments by small keyblocks. The frieze and cornice break forward at each angle of the octagon to rest on scroll-consoles, and the stonework finishes with two stepped blocking-courses. The heavily gadrooned cupola of leadwork is an unusual feature, but one which appears in some of Halfpenny's published designs for houses, and it is finished with a ball and cross.

The angles of the west front are rusticated with V-joints, these quoins being returned in alternating long and short courses above the platband that serves for a continuous cill to the four equally-spaced windows in each side elevation (Plate 4). These tall arch-headed openings, which were originally sashed, are framed by panelled pilasters with moulded imposts, and moulded archivolts broken by tall and plain keystones capped with cornices. Below each window is a plain apron, broken slightly forward from the high plain plinth. The main lines of the crowning entablature are carried round the building, but the architrave mouldings are omitted, the frieze is flat, and the cornice is without modillions. The unmoulded pedestal-parapet has blind balustrades placed to correspond with the windows. Halfpenny's all-too-frequent *gaucherie* is displayed in the design of the east end. Here rusticated quoins and the crowning entablature enclose a wall face wherein a tall rectangular sunk panel is surmounted by a length of entablature broken forward at each end, to rest on a boldly carved human-mask and support a moulded archivolt broken by rustic blocks. The lunette thus formed was originally blank but now contains a semi-circular window.

The small vestibule is in plan an octagon with short east and west arms, the cardinal faces being wider than the splayed ones. The chapel is entered through a segmental-headed opening in the east wall, which balances the outer doorway that is now concealed by a screen-door, while smaller openings of similar design lead to the original baptistry on the south, and to the vestry on the north, these openings having busts set on brackets over them. The chapel interior (Plates 5a, b) measures some 39 feet in length and 26 feet in width, while the chancel is 13 feet wide and 10 feet deep. There is a 6 feet high dado of oak on each side wall, formed in small square fielded panels up to the height of the original pewing. Above is a frieze of long fielded panels, ranged between scrolled consoles that are overlaid with cherubs'-heads on folded wings. These support forward breaks in the cornice-capping, providing stops for the window architraves. The wide member of this capping is carved with an Etruscan-scroll (Plate 6b). The three equally-spaced windows are recessed in arched openings that have moulded architraves and archivolts springing from plain imposts, the deep splays being enriched with sunk panels. The small spandrel-panels are decorated with shells and scrolls, modelled in stucco by Thomas Paty, and between each window is a tall rectangular fielded panel moulded in plaster. Each side wall finishes with a simple cornice from whence a deep plain cove rises to meet a moulded beam flanking the flat ceiling, which forms a large plain panel within a moulded surround.

The west wall (Plate 5b) is divided into two stages, the lower containing the centrally-placed entrance-door now flanked by two smaller arches, one opening to the south-west chapel and the other forming a balancing recess. The segmental-headed entrance has an eared architrave, broken by a reeded console-block that rises through a frieze carved with festoons of fruits and flowers, to support a forward break in the bed-mouldings at the base of the triangular pediment. The cornice lines are continued on each side by a fascia that forms a plinth to the upper stage, where there are three openings with arched heads springing from two wide piers and their narrow responds. Each pier contains a sunk rectangular panel framing a small arch-headed niche. Rysbrack's white marble busts of John and Martha Cossins were placed in these niches on 12th July 1762, having remained at Redland Court during their lifetimes. The crowning cornice of the side walls is matched and continued by the imposts to the piers and responds, breaking forward above the niches to rest on acanthus bands. The arched head to the middle opening is semi-circular but that on either side is an ill-formed ellipse; their moulded archivolts are broken by acanthus key-blocks that project below the panelled soffits. There is a blind balustrade in each side arch, and a panelled pedestal in the middle one that provides a background for the pediment above the entrance. The upper part of this wall, like that at the east end, is carried straight up as a plain surface, forming an abrupt stop for the side coves and flat ceiling.

The decoration of the east wall (Plate 5a), although satisfactory in itself, is badly related to the scheme of the side walls. The wide flank on each side of the chancel-arch is adorned with two slightly-projecting pilasters, having moulded bases, fluted shafts and Corinthian capitals, rising from cherub's-head corbels in the wainscot frieze and supporting an ill-proportioned entablature, with a narrow pulvinated frieze. Between these pilasters is a large panel, formed by a raised moulding that returns squarely in at each angle and is surmounted by a winged cherub's-head. The deep reveals of the chancel-arch are adorned with paired pilasters, sunk panels enrich the arch soffit, and the wide moulded archivolt has at its crown a glory of cherubs'-heads. The side and end walls of the chancel are linked by quadrant-curved angles with narrow return faces. An entablature continuing that of the chancel-arch piers breaks round the various wall faces, but across the east wall its frieze and cornice mouldings are modelled in reverse to form a splay below the lunette. The barrel-vaulted ceiling has three rings of octagonal coffers containing paterae of different designs; the arch framing the lunette has a panelled soffit and a wide moulded archivolt; while five winged cherubs'-heads are spaced at equal intervals in the marginal surround. A free-standing figure of an angelic boy stands above the entablature on each side of the lunette, which was originally adorned with a painting but now contains a semi-circular window.

The whole surface of the chancel walls, up to the underside of the entablature, is lined with oak to form an extended altar-piece (Plate 6a). The tall panels on the side and curved faces are lettered with the Lord's Prayer, the Decalogue, and the Apostles' Creed, while the large panel above the altar contains Vanderbanck's copy of a now destroyed painting by Annibale Carracci, of 'The Embalming of Christ'. The panel mouldings are enriched with formalized acanthus-leaves, while the surrounding margins have applied decorations, exquisitely carved by Paty in limewood, of an intricacy that defies description. At the sides are long pendants of ribboned draperies intertwined with olive and other foliage branches, bearing books, musical instruments, and other symbols both sacred and profane, linked above and below the panels by floral garlands or ribboned and tasseled festoons. There is a glory of cherubs'-heads over the altar painting, and below it a dove between two cherubs'-heads.

A modern clothed altar has displaced the Baroque console-table made by Thomas Paty. This now serves for a credence table and has a marble top supported in front by an eagle's outspread wings, and behind by female terminals. Paty's elegant front of carved and gilt wood, forming a hexagonal baluster with a cover surmounted by an eagle lectern, now stands in the vestibule.

WESLEY'S NEW ROOM, BROADMEAD

In John Wesley's Journal, under the date 9th May 1739, is an entry describing how he and a group of followers 'took possession of a piece of ground near St James's Churchyard, in the Horsefair, where it was designed to build a room, large enough to contain both the societies of Nicholas and Baldwin streets, and such of their acquaintances as might desire to be present with them, at such a time as the Scripture was expounded; and on Saturday, 12th, the first stone was laid with the voice of prayer and thanksgiving'. Before nine years had passed this 'New Room' had become inadequate for its purpose, and in February 1748 it was resolved that the building should be enlarged to form the present Meeting House, in which Wesley preached for the first time on 13th September following. No records exists which might point to the designer of this building, but several points of similarity to the Friends' Meeting House in the Friars, rebuilt about the same time, lead to the suggestion that George Tully was probably employed. The fact that Tully was a Quaker made no difference to his building Dowry Chapel for the Established Church, and would not have prevented his employment by Wesley's followers.

Externally the building is almost devoid of architectural interest, for the enclosed site afforded no opportunity for display even had this been desired, but the tactfully restored interior makes an immediate and lasting impression of refined simplicity. The plan takes full advantage of the restricted site and forms a slightly irregular quadrangle with the north end wider than the south, and the east side longer than the west (Figure 1b). There is a wide doorway placed centrally in each end wall, the north entrance opening into a small lobby underneath the upper stage of the two-decker pulpit. The columns that divide the interior into a nave flanked by aisles were introduced for structural reasons, for they give support to the side galleries and carry the two-storied superstructure of the preachers' house. The side galleries advance beyond the lines of the colonnades only in the southernmost bay, and are reached by narrow staircases at the ends of each aisle. On each side of the nave stand three stone columns of the Tuscan order, without pedestals or entablature, equally spaced at wide intervals and ranged parallel with the nearest side wall. These columns carry the beams that cross the width of the room and divide the ceiling into flat plain compartments. The room is well lit by sash-windows set within segmental-arched openings in the upper part of the walls, one centrally at each end, four above the west gallery, and two above the east. Further light is derived from the lantern of octagonal plan that opens out of the ceiling, centrally in the second bay from the north end, and rises through the preachers' house to a roof-light.

This interior derives much of its charm from the extensive use of panelled woodwork. The gallery fronts are formed in fielded panels, ranged in two heights above an architrave and finished with a moulded capping-rail. The seating of low pews and backless benches is also interesting, but the most attractive item of furniture is the two-decker pulpit, placed centrally at the north end of the nave. The two desks are placed one behind the other, and their solid fronts and sides are treated as pedestals, each die face being adorned with a fielded panel in a raised and moulded surround. The stairs, leading down from either side of the upper desk to the lower, have railings formed of turned balusters supporting ramped and moulded handrails, while a railing of similar design encloses the rectangular dais for the communion table, in front of the pulpits (Plate 7a).

THE FRIENDS' MEETING HOUSE, THE FRIARS

The present Meeting House in the Friars was built in 1747–9 to the design of George Tully, on the site and foundations of a building that was erected in 1670 and found to be ruinous early in 1747. The following account of this rebuilding is based on a study of the *Building Book*, and the dates quoted here are given in the old style of reckoning.

On 26.8.1747 a Committee was formed to manage the rebuilding, having among its members such prominent Friends as Thomas Goldney, Mark Harford, and Nehemiah Champion, with George Tully and his son William acting, presumably, as practical advisors. This Committee was desired to meet weekly, or as often as the business required. Their first efforts seem to have been directed towards acquiring certain properties that were necessary for improving the approaches to their enclosed site, but meeting again on 27.8.1747 they resolved that George Tully should survey the ground and 'begin to pull down all the inside of the Meeting and either hire a cellar to put it in or build a shed for that purpose'. The minutes for 3.9.1747 record that 'George Tully having brought to the Committee a Model unfinished for rebuilding the Meeting-House, it was decided to be brought to the next Committee'. This was held on 10.9.1747, when it was resolved that 'the Model for Rebuilding the Meeting-House is Agreed too', provided that 'the Windows over the Preachers Gallery be reduced to the same size as the other Windows and that two more Windows be opened on Each Side of the House, and also that the Pillars have a Pedestal three Feet high'. At the same meeting William Tully was 'desired to go to Bath to take proposals for the Pillars for the Meeting-House, and to know in what time it can be done and make Report to the next Committee'. His report must have been unfavourable for on 17.9.1747 Thomas Goldney and the Tullys were requested 'to Treat with Thos Paty for the Pillars . . . on the best Terms they can'. This resulted in the announcement made on 24.9.1747, that Paty had agreed 'to Erect the Pillars of the Meeting-House for the Sum of Ninety six pounds, of which this Committee approves'. Paty's price 'for Making and Setting the Windows at 24 shillings a Window' was accepted on 5.12.1747, and his estimate of 2s. 6d. per foot for supplying the moulded stone coping to the walls was accepted on 31.3.1748, while on 12.5.1748 it was 'Ordered that a Freestone Frontispiece be Erected at the Front of the Meeting-House agreeable to a Draught put in by Thos Paty'. This, of course, is the pedimented doorway in the centre of the east front.

The most material changes to the original design were those made as the result of certain decisions taken on 19.11.1747. It was then agreed that the intended windows over the Preachers Gallery in the west wall should be omitted as 'they will be inconvenient by letting in the Sun in the Afternoon'. To compensate for this the upper-story windows in the three other walls

[63]

were given increased height, and the pillars had to be lengthened by 6 inches. On 2.12.1747 it was 'resolved that the foundations of the Pillars be fixt with all Expedition', and from a resolution passed on 21.4.1748, whereby the pedestals were to 'have all the corners cut off to an Octagon', it must appear that these were originally made square in plan. On 4.8.1748 the Committee found that it would be necessary to raise a further sum of £600 to finish the building, which was eventually completed and furnished at a cost of £2,050. The new subscription met with every success, for the House was apparently ready for use early in 1749, the first meeting being held therein on 16.2.1749.

In plan the Meeting House is a rectangular building,

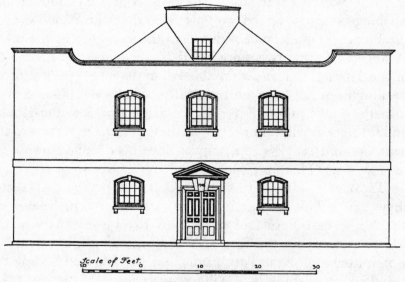

Scale of Feet.

FIGURE 5

Friends' Meeting House, The Friars. East elevation

measuring some 60 feet north to south, and 50 feet east to west. It contains an almost square auditorium with a galleried aisle on its north, east and west sides (Figure 1c). The exterior is built of cement-faced rubble with freestone dressings, simple in design and expressive of the building's purpose. The entrance front faces east, overlooking the old burial ground, and is two stories high. A widely-spaced colonnade of later date partially conceals the low ground-story, which has in its centre Paty's 'frontispiece', a wide rectangular doorway framed by a simply moulded architrave with its head broken by a triple keyblock,

[64]

with flanking pilaster-strips and consoles that support a triangular pediment. On either side, spaced to centre with the internal bay division, is a window of squat proportion, having a moulded architrave that rises from a cill supported on corbels, to a segmental head broken by a plain keyblock. A simple band defines the lofty second-story, where there are three windows similarly dressed to those below, but of taller proportion. The front is finished with a moulded coping that ramps with a concave curve to a higher level at each end (Figure 5). The north and south elevations are similar in character, but there are three windows and a doorway in the ground-story, and four windows above.

The noble simplicity of the interior is most impressive, despite the present dingy colour scheme (Plate 7b). The central space is surrounded on three sides by lofty colonnades, each consisting of three widely-spaced bays formed by Doric columns raised on pedestals, with half-columns against the west wall and triple-shafted piers at the angles. These columns support a trabeation with a plain soffit and an architrave face, from whence rises the slightly splayed margin surrounding the flat ceiling. In the centre of this is a square aperture, now glazed in, opening to a large lantern with a window in each face and a coved ceiling. The gallery front, continued between the columns, is of painted deal and each face contains two long fielded panels placed above a moulded string and finished with a moulded rail. The windowless west wall has no adornment other than the Preachers' Desk, behind which rises a high dado of painted deal, formed into tall panels below a slightly projecting entablature. The fronts of the two-tiered desk are of oak, formed into long panels and capped with a moulded rail. The stair-railings at each end have simply-turned balusters and square newels supporting a ramped moulded handrail.

ST NICHOLAS' CHURCH

Among other improvements, the Act of 1760 for rebuilding Bristol Bridge provided for the removal of St Nicholas' Gate, which formed at that time the low and narrow entrance to the High Street from the Bridge. This gateway was part of the medieval structure of St Nicholas' Church, being underneath its chancel, and the stability of the whole fabric was a constant source of anxiety to the churchwardens. In 1730 they had sought the advice of 'the ingenious Mr Padmore' and the elder Wood was consulted about a year later. When it was certain that removal of the gateway would entail complete demolition of the church, the vestry invited James Bridges to give them suggestions for its rebuilding. His pamphlet entitled 'Four Designs for rebuilding Bristol Bridge', dated 1760, includes several paragraphs addressed to the churchwardens of St Nicholas'. Bridges estimated that to rebuild the gateway and chancel would cost £850, while this sum and the moneys realised on a sale of the old materials, with a further £1,250, would be sufficient to pay for rebuilding the church on a plan similar to one he had seen executed in Pennsylvania. The new building would hold a congregation at least one-fifth greater than that of the old church, and he undertook to complete the rebuilding within twenty-six months, except for the tower 'that stands firm and well, as does the spire also'. Nevertheless, Bridges strongly supported an alternative proposal put forward by the vestry, to build a new church on a site in King Street, after the plan of St Stephen's, Walbrook, which he regarded as representing perfection in modern church design.

Early in 1762 negotiations were concluded between the Bridge Trustees and the vestry, who agreed to demolish the church on condition that the Trustees granted £1,400 towards the cost of the new building. The Bridge Trustees' ledger records the payment of this sum on 7th October 1762 to 'Thomas Bergen, Church Warden of St Nicholas'. Bridges' design was approved by the vestry in May 1762, and during the following August they advertised in *Felix Farley* for 'Persons willing to contract for taking down and building St Nicholas Church to a Model made for that purpose'. The last services were held in the old building on 29th August, and towards the close of 1762 the contractors began their work, having agreed to demolish the old church and erect the new for £2,733.

The new building was far from complete when Bridges left Bristol in October 1763, and the work was taken over by Thomas Paty. Then the wooden spire was found to be very much decayed, despite Bridges' pronouncement that both tower and spire stood 'firm and well'. The vestry first proposed replacing it with a stone lantern and cupola, but taking down the spire served to reveal the equally precarious state of the tower, and

Paty was instructed to prepare designs for a new steeple. All of this caused further delays and expense, for on 22nd December *Felix Farley* reported the purchase of two houses in St Nicholas Street, for upwards of £800. 'When they are pulled down St Nicholas' Tower will be begun, 'till which the Workmen cannot proceed with the Church. 'Tis said the Tower will be built on an Arch of about Ten Feet, and under it will be a commodious Passage from the Back to the Market-Place.'

In February 1766 the unfinished state of the church gave rise to the appearance of a satirical verse in *Felix Farley*, wherein the writer compared the slow progress of St Nicholas' with the rapid building of the new theatre in King Street, thus forcing the conclusion that Man would rather serve the Devil than God. Although the consecration ceremony was announced to take place on 25th August 1767, this event had to be postponed owing to the incompleteness of the interior, and it was not until December 1769 that the church, with its tower and spire, was finished. By then expenditure on the church and tower had amounted to £6,549 5s. while the spire had cost an additional £1,075, and in order to raise these sums it had been necessary to obtain Parliament's consent to levy a special rate.

St Nicholas' was without its spire when Horace Walpole, visiting Bristol in 1766, gave an approving glance and pronounced the church to be 'neat and truly Gothic'. Barrett described it as a 'very fine building, being one broad and lofty room with a flat ceiling, and an elegant raised cornice round it, adorned with mahogany seats and an elegant pulpit'. But this airy Rococo interior was not at all to the taste of late nineteenth-century churchwardens, and in 1882 some £4,000 was needlessly expended in forming a chancel, enclosed by a freestone screen of Gothic arcading, while the organ-gallery at the west end was taken down and the instrument rebuilt in two sections at the east end. The interior was completely gutted during the great air raid of 24th November 1940, but Paty's steeple and the outside walls of the church still stand.

While Paty's tower shows more than a trace of Langley's style, the church exterior designed by Bridges is a fairly successful essay in fifteenth-century Gothic of the Bristol school (Plates 8a, 9a). The old and irregularly formed crypt was encased to provide a rectangular basement for the new building, bringing its floor level with St Nicholas Street and considerably above Baldwin Street. There the long side elevation has the advantage of being raised upon the crypt wall, which forms a high plinth finished with a weathered offset. From this rises the main face, divided by slightly projecting buttresses into seven equal bays and two outside margins of different width. Each bay contains a large window, having a two-centred head and shallow splays that frame an opening divided by mullions into five tall lights, with simple reticulated tracery in the head. The buttresses are rectangular in plan up to the level of the springing of the window arches, above which they continue in diminishing stages of triangular plan. They are linked by a continuous stringcourse running below the window-sills, and by the narrow coved crowning cornice. The parapet is decorated with closely set blind arcading, broken by the terminal stages of the buttresses. The frontage to St Nicholas Street is similar to that just described, while the windowless east wall is vertically divided into three portions, the wide middle one projecting slightly forward from those flanking it. This elevation is adorned, like the others, with buttresses, stringcourses, and the arcaded parapet.

The fine steeple consists of a square tower of two lofty stages surmounted by a spire, built entirely in freestone. The tower projects from the body of the church, in the middle of its west elevation, and when first built it was adjoined by a house on its west side, the porch then serving as a passage between Baldwin and St Nicholas streets. The first stage corresponds in height with the body of the church, and its north and south faces are similar, each containing a moulded and shafted archway with a two-centred head beneath an ogee hood. The archway on the Baldwin Street side has been closed with a traceried window, and the upper part of each face contains a circular foliated window. A plain and slightly projecting pilaster strengthens the exposed angle of this stage, which finishes with two stringcourses continuing the lines of the arcaded parapet of the church. Each face of the second stage has a pair of louvred windows, divided into two tiers of two trefoil-headed lights, with traceried two-centred heads beneath ogee hoods that have pinnacle-like finials. The angle pilasters on each face are adorned with two superimposed trefoil-headed sunk panels, and the tower finishes with an arcaded parapet and a pinnacle at each corner rising from a panelled base. The spire of octagonal plan, its plain faces broken only by two ornamental bands and the loopholes in its second stage, terminates with a weathercock some 200 feet from the tower's base.

The interior (Plate 10) was a first-rate example of the meeting-house type of church favoured by Georgian congregations—a large rectangular auditorium, almost a double-cube, measuring some 95 feet in length, and 45 feet in width and height (Figure 2a). Except for the hood-mouldings to the arched heads of the deep window-recesses, the side walls were left unadorned to provide plain fields for the reception of memorials. The west end was filled with a choristers' and organ gallery, later removed, and the east end contained a shallow recess wherein was re-erected the fine altar-piece from the old church. The arched head to this recess rose from scrolled consoles enriched with acanthus-leaves, the arch-soffit being decorated with square coffers containing paterae of two designs used alternately, while the narrow archivolt consisted of a single moulding enriched with a flowing band of palmettes between foliage-scrolls. Each spandrel was adorned with a cherub, holding aloft palm-branches and wreathed in foliage and floral sprays. The walls were finished with a form of entablature, of which the frieze was decorated with rosettes of spirally-curving acanthus-leaves, placed between swelling consoles that rose from breaks in the lowest moulding and supported the enriched cornice.

The particular glory of this interior was the splendid ceiling, a masterly performance by Thomas Stocking, perhaps working under the direction of Thomas Paty. The flat expanse of plaster-work was most skilfully and economically decorated with cast and modelled ornaments of a restrained Rococo character. Most of the decoration was contained within one large outer panel with incurved corners, formed by a band of enriched chevron moulding fringed on the inside with Gothic ornaments resembling a series of cusped spandrels, and having outside each corner a motif of crossed palm-branches. In the middle of each long side, and at either end, the Gothic spandrels gave place to compositions formed of shells, festoons, foliage and C-scrolls. These approximately triangular motifs extended to join the narrow moulding that surrounded the inner panel. This also

[69]

had incurved corners, but each end was broken outwards in a semi-circle to frame a sun-burst breaking from a cloud whereon floated three winged cherubs'-heads. In the centre of the ceiling was an enriched circular moulding, enclosing a composition similar to that over the staircase at the Royal Fort, where a chandelier-boss is surrounded by three winged *putti* in high relief, on a base of cloud with sun-rays bursting from it.

The altar-piece, constructed for the old church about 1710–12, was the largest and most imposing of the Bristol examples. A handsome design, executed in deal and painted, its principal stage was raised on a panelled pedestal and divided into three bays by a Corinthian order of four three-quarter columns flanked by half-pilasters. The entablature broke forward over the columns and in the centre of the wide middle bay, where it rested on a winged cherub's-head. The side bays were surmounted by profile inverted consoles of carved openwork, flanking the high attic of the middle bay. The face of this was square and contained a circular panel, framed by Corinthian columns, smaller than those below, with an entablature surmounted by a triangular pediment on a pedestal. Lower pedestals over the column-entablatures were crowned by flaming vases. Besides this altar-piece, there survived from the old building an unusually fine brass chandelier with a wrought-iron stay; a pair of beautifully wrought iron gates, probably made by Edney; and the finest sword-rest in the city. This last has most fortunately been salvaged from the ruin that overtook all else within this most interesting of Bristol's eighteenth century churches.

ST MICHAEL'S CHURCH

Early in the eighteenth century the vestry of St Michael's were faced with the problem of enlarging their church to accommodate an ever-growing number of parishioners. The church-wardens' accounts show that in 1729 they paid John Strahan five guineas 'for a Draught of another Isle to ye Church', but nothing appears to have been done to put his plan into execution. The question again arose in February 1758, when the vestry ordered estimates to be obtained, and on 10th June following *Felix Farley* was able to report a proposal to enlarge the church by 'rebuilding, and adding a new Isle on the North Side', for which purpose a subscription had been opened. Sums amounting to £1,000 had already been given or promised, but the vestry decided that no work should be undertaken until at least £2,000 had been received. Subsequently, James Paty was employed to prepare a plan and elevation for the proposed new aisle, for which the vestry paid him £1 11s. 6d., in 1766, but this scheme, like Strahan's, was abandoned.

In August 1774 the rector and churchwardens circulated a pamphlet, stating that the church had been carefully surveyed by Thomas Paty, who had found it in a generally ruinous condition. Reparation was thought to be inadvisable as Paty had estimated that 'a roomy, elegant, and convenient new Church' could be built for £1,800 to £2,000, and subscriptions towards this end were now solicited. A generous response from the parishioners, and contributions of £300 from the Corporation and £150 from the Merchants' Society, brought the fund to £2,400, and the vestry ordered the work to proceed. The last services were held in the old church on 14th May 1775, and its demolition began on the next day. The tower had been thoroughly repaired in 1739, and being in sound condition it was retained for incorporation in the new building. The foundation-stone was laid with some ceremony on 4th July 1775, and the completed church was opened on 22nd June 1777. The final accounts showed that the rebuilding had cost £3,175 1s. 9d., instead of the £2,000 originally estimated by Paty.

By combining a Gothic exterior with an interior where Classical elements predominate, Thomas Paty aroused the censure of later critics who might, remembering the taste of the time in which he worked, more justly have praised him for showing considerable sensibility. For although Paty's Gothic details are poor and thin, he produced an exterior reasonably in keeping with the medieval tower, while the interior was more perfectly suited to eighteenth-century usage than any attempt at a pure Gothic reconstruction could have been.

In plan the church is a rectangle, some 77 feet long by 62 feet wide, divided to form a wide nave of five bays with aisles. The old tower stands forward from the middle of the west front, and a short aisleless chancel forms an eastern extension. The exterior is built of local rubble-stone, matching that of the tower, with a sparing use of freestone dressings (Plate 9b). While the west and east fronts are plain to baldness, each side elevation presents an agreeable composition. The basement wall forms a slightly projecting plinth that is finished with a plain stone band. Above this rises the rubble wall face, unbroken by buttresses but pierced by five windows placed at regular intervals to correspond with the internal bay divisions. These windows have two-centred arches with hood mouldings, and each is divided into two trefoil-headed lights and an elongated quatrefoil head. The westernmost window in each elevation is combined with a doorway that has a flattened arched opening, beneath an ogee head flanked by panelled spandrels. The crowning cornice is a narrow cove and breaks forward in the middle of each pier, to rest on a panelled flat corbel of Gothic design. The surmounting parapet is correspondingly divided into bays by narrow pedestals with panelled dies.

The interior (Plate 12a), an essentially Classical design dressed with Gothic details, cannot be accounted as one of Thomas Paty's best works, but its appearance has not been improved by the loss of its original furniture, nor by the damage sustained during the late war. On each side of the nave are four stone columns, with respondent pilasters on the side and end walls. These columns stand on plain octagonal pedestals of pew-height, have moulded bases and plain shafts, and capitals with a band of fluting above the shaft necking. The base and capital mouldings show by their profiles that these are Gothic columns, although they appear at a first sight to belong to a debased Tuscan order. The intercolumniations of each colonnade are spanned by a trabeation, its soffit decorated with sunk Gothic panels, as are also the cross beams that divide the aisle ceilings into plain flat compartments. These trabeations are faced on the nave side with architraves, from whence plain coves rise to meet a flat ceiling. The east wall contains the two-centred chancel-arch, having a hood-moulding and a panelled soffit, opening to the short and narrow chancel.

CHRIST CHURCH

Although some £1,500 had been spent in 1753 on repairs to the medieval fabric of Christ Church, its state in 1783 was so precarious that the alarmed vestry employed Thomas Paty and

Sons to make a survey and report on its condition. The structure was condemned as ruinous, and the Patys prepared plans for rebuilding on the old foundations, but this proposal was soon discarded in favour of another design, which was contrived to occupy as little as possible of the valuable street frontages, and to permit the long-deferred widening of Wine Street to be carried out. The vestry approved this design, for which William Paty appears to have been responsible, and on 20th May 1786 they advertised for builders to submit prices by 30th June following, for taking down the old building and erecting the new. Meanwhile an Act of Parliament, 25 George III cap III, had been obtained to permit the vestry to raise the necessary funds for rebuilding, and after some changes had been made to the approved design, demolition of the old structure was begun. The foundation-stone of the new church was laid on 30th October 1786, and it was completed in 1790.

A disastrous refurbishing carried out in 1883 resulted in the general removal of Paty's elegant and harmonious furniture, and the replacement of the original sash-windows by ones of coloured glass framed in pseudo-Florentine tracery. Worst of all, a dull and pompous construction in stone took the place of the white and gold altar-piece, that was so perfectly related to the general scheme of the interior, with its Siena-marbled and gilt columns, and white and gold plaster ceiling. Some attempt was made in recent years to remedy this mischief, by re-erecting the architectural frame of the altar-piece to serve as a rood-screen, and by replacing the fittings that had survived destruction.

Since the body of the church was designedly concealed by houses, the only external feature that has an architectural dress is the fine freestone steeple, the ground-stage of which forms the narrow front to Broad Street (Plate 8b). This front breaks slightly forward from narrow margins, and similar surface breaks occur at the angles of each subsequent stage of the tower, where the four faces are identically treated. The pseudo-Florentine doorway is an elaborate anachronism, dating from 1883, replacing the original entrance which consisted of an arch-headed opening set with two concentric marginal recessions of different width in an outer archway, its plain head rising from moulded imposts and each spandrel being adorned with a husk-chain looped over a patera. The second stage is

[73]

underlined by a pedestal-course, and its plain face contains a clock-dial set in a circular architrave-moulding. This clock is now flanked by the Baroque Quarter-Jack figures carved by James Paty (1) for the clock on the Wine Street front of the old church. A bold cornice finishes this stage, breaking forward to rest on consoles and then rising in a segmental curve over the clock, against the high blocking-course that serves as a plinth to the third stage. This begins with a pedestal-course supporting four Ionic plain-shafted pilasters, the two inside ones set slightly forward from those at the angles to form a bay containing an arch, composed of plain piers, moulded imposts, and an archivolt broken by rustic-blocks and a triple key. Slightly recessed within this arch is another, blind and more simply treated. The entablature breaks forward over the bay with a triangular pediment placed against the blocking-course. The fourth and topmost stage of the tower is treated with greater delicacy and on a suitably reduced scale. The pedestal-course carries two pairs of pilasters, with plain shafts and acanthus-leaf capitals, that frame a louvred arch and support an entablature having a modillioned cornice. The angles are plain and only the cornice of the entablature is carried round them. The tower finishes with a stepped parapet and at each angle stands a tall baluster-shaped urn. The spire rises from a high pedestal, both being octagonal in plan. The pedestal-dies have moulded panels, and ornamented bands divide the spire into three stages, the lower two containing an oval loop-hole in each face. A dragon weather-vane rises from the ball-finial.

Although the general scheme of the interior derives at some distance from that of St Martin's-in-the-Fields, its direct prototype is Badminton Church, Gloucestershire. According to *Neale's Views* this church was built in 1785 and designed by an architect named Evans, but the character of its decoration makes it appear probable that the Patys were employed there. The Christ Church interior, however, has a tenuous elegance that is quite individual, and the subdivision of its rectangular space into a nave and aisles of four bays is more apparent than real, so widely spaced are the slender columns of stone that support the elaborate plaster ceiling (Plate 11a, b. Fig. 2b). There are three columns on either side of the nave, with respondent pilasters against the east and west walls. The plain and over-attenuated shafts are raised on high pedestals of octagonal plan, and the capitals are formed of acanthus-leaves in a charming variant of the orthodox Corinthian design. The plain pedestals were originally encased by the oak pewing, and the column-shafts were painted to simulate Siena marble, with gilt bases and capitals. Each column carries a square entablature-block, with a circular patera ornamenting each frieze face. From their cornices spring the shallow segmental arches of the nave arcades; the wide elliptical ones crossing the nave; and those of high segmental form that cross the narrow aisles, each resting on a section of entablature supported by a scrolled console decorated with an acanthus-leaf. The arches have soffits of equal width, decorated with a guilloche band, and they serve to divide the ceiling into oblong compartments. These are formed by a combination of saucer dome and pendentives, but while the nave compartments are much greater in width than in length and have crescent-shaped intersections against the arcades, those of the aisles have greater length than width, and these inequalities have an unfortunate effect in the distorted appearance of surface decoration. Each compartment contains a large circular panel, formed of concentric mouldings ranged at intervals round an acanthus-boss, with spandrel panels of irregular shape, those of the nave ceiling being enriched with delicate Adamesque motifs composed of acanthus-scrolls linked by husk-festoons. The plain side walls are broken by deep segmental-headed recesses, each corresponding to a bay and having a window filling its upper part, originally sashed but now divided into three lights. The west wall is plain except for the elliptical-headed recession that frames the fine three-towered organ-case, while a similar recess in the east wall accommodated the original altar-piece that now serves for a rood-screen.

This altar-piece was executed in deal and painted white with gilt enrichments. Although basically similar in design to the earlier Renaissance examples in Bristol, its details have the tenuous elegance that characterizes the later eighteenth-century work. The principal stage is raised on a pedestal and divided by a pseudo-Corinthian order into three bays that originally contained the customary lettered panels. The wide middle bay is flanked by half-pilasters with plain shafts, coupled to three-quarter columns having fluted shafts spirally wreathed with floral-garlands, while each side bay is terminated laterally by a full pilaster, its panelled shaft enriched with a pendant of flowers, foliage-sprays and ribbon-bows, ending in a chain of bell-flowers. The entablature, which breaks forward to correspond with the varied projection of column and pilaster, has an enriched architrave and cornice, and a frieze adornment of husk-festoons, sprays of bay-leaves, knotted ribbons, etc., with oval paterae placed on the projecting faces. A plain tablet breaks the architrave and frieze centrally over the middle bay. Above each side bay is a high pedestal attic, cut back laterally to a parabolic profile, and finishing on the inside with a pilaster. A motif of acanthus-scrolls linked by husk-chains decorates each pedestal die, while the pilasters are ornamented with bell-flower pendants. The crowning cornice is returned across the middle bay to form an open-bedmould pediment of segmental form, surmounted centrally by a carved mitre and flanked by flaming urns placed on the flat section at each end. The deep tympanum is of painted canvas, but it is open to question whether the present decoration copies the original.

Against the pedestal of the middle bay stood the elegant communion-table of console form that now serves as an altar for the side chapel. This was made in mahogany, painted and gilt, by William and Charles Court, cabinetmakers and mahogany-merchants, whose address was under the Bank. The ensemble was completed by the curved railing of iron-work, a delicate design of interlacing segments between upright bars, enriched with cast paterae and anthemion ornaments. This was made by Walter Swayne, an ironmonger, of Wine Street. The font in the form of an octagonal baluster, with its neck carved in a series of stiff fern-leaves, was designed and made by William Paty, and now serves as a lectern-base.

ST PAUL'S CHURCH

St Paul's Church, Portland Square, was built to serve the new parish created in 1787 out of the eastern extension of St James's Parish. By 1785 it had become obvious that St James's Church could no longer be considered adequate to serve the increasing number of parishioners, and so the proposed division of the parish was approved by the Common Council, who undertook to pay the cost of obtaining an Act of Parliament designed to achieve this end. They also agreed to contribute £400 towards endowing the new living, and subsequently voted a grant of £1,000 towards the cost of building the new church. Representatives of the new parish met in June 1787, when they resolved to erect their church 'in the gardens behind the new tontine buildings in Brunswick Square'.

The Act of Parliament, 27 George III cap III, was obtained, and the Commissioners appointed to attend to the business met on 10th September 1787, when James Allen's design for the new church was approved. Later in the month they advertised in the Bristol journals, inviting estimates for the building. These were to be received on or before 10th October, but on that date it was announced that the matter would be deferred until 7th November, so that further prices could be submitted. The Commissioners then stated that they considered the estimates so far received were insufficiently explicit, and announced a further meeting for 21st November. Their advertisement following this meeting stated that 'the estimates submitted having proved too high, Mr Allen was asked to draw a new plan, upon a smaller scale', which being ready, builders were now invited to submit revised estimates by 5th December. On 7th December 1787, the Commissioners reported that 'Mr Allen's elegant design of the Grecian Order' had been rejected on account of expense, and while they paid fulsome tribute to his ability and promised him full recompense, they had resolved to adopt the 'plan of the Gothic Order, drawn by Mr Hague, an eminent mason'.

As Daniel Hague was concerned in promoting the building of Portland Square, it is probable that corrupt means were used to influence the Commissioners' decision to allow him to supersede Allen. It was also commonly believed at the time that Hague was more acceptable than Allen to Dr J. Atwell Small, the first incumbent of St Paul's, who wished for a consideration say in the design of his new church, and was reputed to have produced the basic idea for the tower. Against this must be set the fact that Hague proudly claimed to have designed the tower after the model of Jerman's Royal Exchange in London.

The foundation-stone was laid by the Mayor, Levi Ames, on 23rd April 1789, and the church was sufficiently finished for services to be held therein on St Paul's Day, 29th June 1794.

[77]

Matthews' Bristol Guide for that year describes the church as 'an elegant structure of stone in the gothic stile. From the door under the tower to the altar, its length is 105 feet, breadth 60. The roof is supported by lofty pillars of stone with rich capitals, and beautifully arched and stucco'd over the middle aile. It has spacious galleries on three sides, and a pulpit in the middle aile at the entrance of the Chancel. The steeple consists of a square tower (for which ten bells are preparing) and two square stages proportionately less, crowned with an octangular pinnacle and vane; it very much resembles that of the Royal Exchange, London, and is 160 feet high. The organ is not yet put up, nor the internal part quite finished'.

This building has been most liberally abused, but its faults are those common to most buildings of its time and style, while critics have generally overlooked or ignored the great merit it has in providing an impressive and entirely suitable climax to Portland Square, its presence doing much to enliven that otherwise dull design. Malcolm's opinion, given in his 'First Impressions' of 1807, is fair and reasonable—'The architect asserts the neat structure thus situated to be in the Gothic, or, if you please, in the antient English Pointed style. I certainly agree with him, and admit that the arches of every description are Pointed; yet, with this concession, he must permit me to add, that the tower resembles a Grecian building at a distance, and, when examined, an attempt to imitate the Pointed style is observable, which it as little resembles as the tower of St Mary Redcliff does the dome of St Paul's, London.'

The plan of St Paul's Church shows the usual Georgian arrangement of a rectangular body divided by slender and widely-spaced columns into a wide nave between narrow aisles, a ritual arrangement adapted to serve structural and decorative ends. The short aisleless chancel, flanked by vestries, has been considerably altered and extended to serve as a ritual choir. The choristers and organ were originally accommodated in the western gallery, while pewed galleries extended over each aisle. The tower projects from the middle of the west end and its ground story forms the vestibule, in plan a square with incurved angles. Beyond this a double-door opens to the middle aisle of the nave, and stairs ascend left and right to the gallery. A further lobby projects from the west bay of each aisle (Figure 2c).

Externally, the church is entirely faced with dressed freestone and the dominating feature of the design is, of course, the lofty steeple, consisting of a three-stage tower, square in plan, and two diminishing stages of the same form, crowned by an octagonal pinnacle (Plate 8c). The first stage embraces two stories, and its front face contains the main doorway, a trefoil-headed opening with an ogee-hoodmould, framed by a moulded arch with a two-centred head. Above this is a three-light window with an ogee-head, framed in a moulded surround. Each side face is similar except that the lower arch is larger and contains a two-light window. The exposed angles are emphasized on each face by slightly projecting pilasters decorated with sunk panels, two tall round-ended ones with a quatrefoil between them. A shallow cornice completes this stage and from a fluted plinth rises the next, slightly offset and proportionately reduced in height. Its west, north and south faces are identical and contain a large unmoulded slightly-sunk panel, headed with a pointed arch and framing a clock-dial that is curiously set beneath an acute gable-moulding and flanked by pinnacled buttresses of triangular plan. The east face is plain except for a small quatrefoil opening, and the angle-pilasters are similar to those below, but for the lozenge panel that replaces the quatrefoil. A Gothic entablature with a panelled frieze finishes this stage. The third stage is also offset from that below, and each face is identical in having a small ogee-headed window of two lights, containing louvres. The panelled pilasters at each angle rise to the narrow crowning entablature, which is surmounted by a parapet with three openwork panels and a pinnacle at each corner. The 'spire' consists of two stages, the first having in each face an ogee-headed window with two lights, containing louvres, flanked by narrow triangular buttresses rising into pinnacles. A panelled buttress projects diagonally from each corner and rises to a pinnacle, and this stage finishes with a decorated cove-cornice that is surmounted by an openwork parapet. Except that the two-light window has a hoodmould formed by two concave curves, the second stage is a reduced version of the first, and from behind its solid parapet rises the octagonal finial, which has an ogee canopy on each face and terminates in a pinnacle, with a vane some 170 feet from the ground level.

The exposed portions of the west front form balancing wings

to the tower. Each face contains a tall and narrow window with a two-centred arched head, divided into two tiers of two lights by a band of solid panels moulded with lozenges. The raking battlement, following the roof slope, stops against a lateral feature composed of a false turret flanked by panelled pilasters. The turret face is adorned with two superimposed blind two-light windows, the upper one divided into two tiers and placed above a quatrefoil panel. The cornice of the turret is surmounted by a square pinnacle that rises above the similar ones terminating the pilasters. The side elevations are identical, and each is divided into four equal bays by panelled pilasters. Each bay contains a large window with a two-centred arched head, set slightly recessed in a narrow moulded surround, and its area is divided by a panelled band into two tiers of three lights. The crowning cornice returns round the pilasters, which are surmounted by square pinnacles. A battlemented parapet extends between them and each end pinnacle is carried up higher than the others. The low porch projecting from the west bay is also finished with battlements and pinnacles, and its front face contains a flat ogee-arched doorway.

The decoration of the interior (Plate 12b) has an elegance more suited to an assembly room than a church, an effect that must have been enhanced by the glass chandeliers that originally hung from the bosses in the nave ceiling. On either side of the nave are three stone columns, with respondent pilasters against the east and west walls. These columns rise from square pedestals and have moulded and fluted bases, plain and attenuated shafts, and capitals curiously adorned with stiff acanthus-leaves above and below fluting. Each colonnade supports a trabeation, its soffit relieved with Gothic panels, while each face forms an architrave with its fascia enriched by a simple fret containing a rosette in every compartment. In the aisles this architrave returns round the end and side walls to frame a flat ceiling, but on the nave side they provide the springing for high quadrant coves that rise to join the flat ceiling. Wide soffit-bands, decorated with Gothic panels, divide the nave ceiling into bays, the coved surfaces being decorated with vertical fluting, while each flat compartment has in its centre a richly modelled acanthus boss, surrounded by four spandrel panels containing arabesques composed of acanthus-scrolls and floral garlands. The east wall contains the pointed chancel-arch, which rises from fluted imposts above plain piers, the archivolt fascia also being fluted while the arch soffit is enriched with Gothic panels. Each spandrel is charmingly adorned with an arabesque of delicate acanthus-scrolls, flowing from a central stem and linked by floral garlands. The aisle walls are left plain to provide a field for the reception of memorials, and the windows are deeply recessed within plain splays.

The south wall of the chancel has been altered to accommodate the organ, but the west wall shows the original arrangement of two quatrefoil windows, placed high up and deeply recessed in circular splays. The vaulted ceiling of plaster is adorned with wide flutes arranged in bands. The east wall was altered to extend the chancel and the original altar-piece of 'St Paul preaching to the Athenians', painted by Edward Bird, R.A., now adorns the east wall of the south aisle.

THE UNITARIAN CHAPEL, LEWIN'S MEAD

The present Unitarian Chapel in Lewin's Mead replaces one that was erected in 1694 but had no architectural importance. Joseph Glascodine and Daniel Hague were asked to survey this building in February 1785, and they found it to be in a 'very unpleasing State'. On 22nd March following 'Mr Paty was desired to make a Survey' and his opinion must have served to confirm the report already given, for on 26th April a Building Committee was formed and a subscription opened for the purpose of erecting a new Meeting House. The main lines on which the building was to be planned were laid down on 28th February 1786, when the Committee resolved 'that the Front of the House face the Street and be carried back as far as the Ground will well permit. The Street to be the longest Side. That the Building be calculated to hold at least Six Hundred Persons exclusive of the Ailes'. At a Committee meeting held on 4th January 1787, 'Mr Bright made a report that he had applied to Mr Blackburne of London for a plan of a New Meeting'. This, when laid before the Committee on 20th April following, was found to be too large for adoption, and Blackburne was asked to prepare a revised plan for a building on the same lines, but measuring only 70 feet in length and 45 feet in width, in the clear. The recess under the gallery was to be reduced to 5 feet in depth, and the

F

external arcade to between 6 and 7 feet. At the next meeting an external portico was proposed to take the place of this arcade. The revised plans, with an estimate of cost, were submitted on 15th August 1787, and received the Committee's unanimous approval subject to some small alterations which, when suggested, were accepted without demur by the architect.

The final designs were produced and approved on 19th February 1788, when Joseph Glascodine expressed the wish to tender for the work 'on such Terms as should be fixed by Mr Blackburne'. After debate, the Committee decided to revoke their previous resolve to offer the contract for open tender, in favour of inviting Glascodine and one other builder, acceptable to the architect, to submit competitive prices. These were received by 25th March 1788, when the estimate of John Tenteman of Newington, amounting to £1,794, was accepted for the main contract, Glascodine's price amounting to £2,071. For the second contract, relating to finishing and furnishing the interior, Glascodine's tender of £516 was accepted. The old Meeting House was thereupon demolished, and the new building was opened for services on 4th September 1791.

The Meeting House was planned in complete accordance with the general lines laid down by the Committee, and forms in effect a rectangular hall, measuring some 70 feet by 45 feet, having a gallery on each short side and a galleried recess, some 45 feet wide, in the middle of its long south-east side and facing the pulpit. The principal entrance is by way of the portico on the south-east front, and the galleries are served by two staircases of segmental plan, placed in the south and east angles of the building (Figure 1d).

The entrance front, facing Lewin's Mead, is a well composed but poorly detailed design, carried out in dressed freestone (Plate 13a). The rear wall of the galleried recess forms the central feature, with the staircase walls as balancing wings, lower, narrower, and slightly recessed. The ground-story face is rusticated, with horizontal and vertical V-joints, and from its centre projects the portico, semi-circular in plan and consisting of three bays, one wide between two narrow. Two pairs of Ionic plain-shafted columns, with respondent pilasters on the wall face, support the simple entablature of frieze and cornice, which is surmounted by a high blocking-course. The wall face on each side of the portico contains a window with a flat-arched head of three voussoirs, and a blind window of the same design decorates each wing. The cornice of the portico's entablature dies into a platband that finishes the rusticated face and forms a plinth to the pedestal-course of the upper story. The top member, a cornice in the central feature and a fascia in the wings, provides a sill to the windows which are centred over those of the ground-story. The wing and side windows in the central feature are square-headed, the former framed with simple architraves and the latter unadorned. Above them runs a platband which is surmounted by a blocking-course parapet over the wings, and by the low false-attic of the central feature. This band also serves as an impost for the arched head of the large middle window that dominates the composition. This window is divided into a lunette and three lights, one wide between two narrow, by two three-quarter columns with respondent pilasters, having plain shafts and capitals of acanthus-leaves and hart's-tongue ferns, which carry an entablature of frieze and cornice, the last lining up with the impost-band. The arched head is flanked by slightly-sunk oblong panels centred above the side windows, and the central feature is crowned with a triangular pediment ending the low-pitched roof. The side elevations are basically similar in design to the front, but the treatment is much simpler, plain stone dressings being used to frame the windows and form the stringcourses that are set in a cemented face.

The bold and simple decorative scheme of the interior arises most logically from the external design. Much of the detail is identical with both, and the large arch-headed window, divided by columns and entablature into a lunette over three lights, again forms the predominant motif. Three of these windows are evenly spaced out in the long north-west wall, and one, with a rectangular light on either side, is centred in each short wall and in the south-east gallery, where it is concealed by the later organ. The walls are without any adornment other than the flat impost-band that continues between the window arches, and the simple cornice surrounding the ceiling. The side galleries abut rather awkwardly into the walls, and each has a plain front underlined by a dentilled cornice and carried on two widely-spaced iron columns. The south-east wall has in its centre the wide and deep recess containing the gallery for the organ and choristers. The side galleries divide the flanking faces into two stories, each containing a centrally-placed doorway, leading to the angle lobby and staircase, while the face above the impost-band is relieved by a sunk oblong panel. The main cornice is carried across the recess to form the face of a wide beam that has a panelled soffit and is supported by concave-curving trusses, these in turn resting on paired consoles. The flat ceiling is divided into six rows of nine rectangular coffers, generally square, six of those in the central area containing formalized sunflower bosses from which chandeliers were originally suspended. The ceiling over the choristers' gallery is similarly divided into two rows of five coffers. This interior retains all its original pewing, and there is an elegant pulpit, finely constructed in mahogany, with a segmental railing enclosing the communion-table, placed below the middle window on the north-east wall.

ST THOMAS'S CHURCH

The present Church of St Thomas replaced a late-Gothic building that was generally considered to have been surpassed in beauty and interest only by St Mary Redcliffe. On 28th June 1786 the vestry ordered that this building should be repaired and whitewashed, and this work must have revealed some serious flaws in the structure. A report called for from James Allen, an architect and statuary residing in the parish, and 'Mr West the Mason', was read at the vestry's meeting on 8th September 1788, when they learned that 'the roof and party walls were in a dangerous condition'. A second opinion from Allen, supported by West and 'Mr Stock the Carpenter', was heard on 19th February 1789, and it only served to confirm the original report by stating that 'the roof and part of the walls must be taken down'. The vestry then ordered that a faculty should be applied for, and Allen was 'directed to do what was necessary and scaffolding to be erected to preserve the pews and other parts of the Church during the alterations'. It was also decided that no services should be held in the building after 23rd February.

On 15th May 1789 a report was received from William Daniel and Daniel Hague, builders, stating their opinion that the exterior walls 'must be taken down to the floor and the middle walls and arches to the butments of the arches on the pillars'. This meant virtually rebuilding the church, and in consequence designs for a new building were called for. By a majority of the vestry Allen's plans for rebuilding were approved on 18th June 1789, and the cost of this work being estimated at some £5,000, an Act of Parliament was sought to enable the necessary funds to be raised. This Act, 30 George III cap 20, was obtained early in 1790, and empowered the vestry to appropriate a parish fund of £1,470, borrow £700 on security of property, and raise £3,500 on security of a special parish rate.

Apart from furniture that was retained for re-use in the new building the removable materials of the old church were sold, and on 5th May 1791 the vestry advertised for builders to submit estimates, before 24th June following, for taking down the old walls and 'building and completely finishing the New Church'. The Gothic tower, first intended for demolition, was retained with the idea of its being 'raised and modernised' in conformity with Allen's design, but this proposal never materialized. The records show that 7s. 6d. was paid on 16th July 1792 'for a foundation stone and plate on it', and the church was sufficiently finished for services to be held therein on 21st December 1793, although it was not completed internally until some months later.

The church is a spacious structure, consisting of a nave rising above flanking aisles, five bays in length, and a short aisleless chancel. The medieval tower is awkwardly attached to the west end, where it stands forward in line with the north aisle. The west elevation is a wretched affair, in fact the only front of architectural interest is that facing St Thomas's Street, where the almost windowless east wall of the chancel is built in dressed ashlar, with a surface decoration in which a blind Venetian-window provides the dominant feature (Plate 13b). Above the high pedestal, four plain-shafted Ionic pilasters rise in pairs to carry entablatures which span the narrow side compartments. A moulded archivolt springing from the side entablatures frames the arched head of the wide middle compartment, which contains a small window, originally semicircular but enlarged in 1888 to form a traceried wheel-window. The wall face above each side compartment contains a tall rectangular sunk panel, and over the arch is a carved decoration of floral pendants and festoons meeting in a cherub's-head on folded wings. The simple entablature is surmounted by a poorly moulded triangular pediment, containing in its tympanum a plain sunk panel corresponding to the arched compartment of the Venetian-window. From the pediment's apex rises a pedestal with a ball-finial.

The aisle walls are of cement-faced rubble with stone dressings. A plain band forms a continuous sill to the five equally-spaced windows, which have semi-circular arched heads and are simply dressed with plain architrave-bands broken by impost-blocks and keystones. The cornice continues that of the entablature to the Venetian-window feature of the east front, and the parapet returns at each end with an incurved ramp rising to the underside of the entablature crowning the chancel walls. The west doorway and those at each end of the north aisle are identical in design. The plain rectangular doorcase of stone projects slightly from the wall face and finishes with a cornice, the opening having a semi-circular arched head rising from impost-bands. The only decoration is a carved cherub's-head on folded wings placed above the crown of the arch. This motif appears throughout the building, and most probably derives from Allen's training as a statuary.

The interior is a sound and coherent design which, in spite of poor and thin detailing, must have looked well enough before it was subjected to a hideous scheme of stencilled decoration, carried out in 1880. On either side of the nave is an arcade of five equal bays, formed by piers of oblong plan with tall pedestals, moulded bases, plain shafts and Tuscan capitals, which carry semi-circular arches having unbroken moulded archivolts and panelled soffits. At each end of the arcade is a plain-shafted Ionic pilaster, larger in scale than the Tuscan piers, surmounted by its full entablature of which the cornice only continues above the arcade, breaking forward over each pier to rest on a cherub's-head corbel. Above the cornice is a clearstory of segmental-headed windows, corresponding to the arcade below and set in lunettes that intersect the barrel-vaulted ceiling. This is decorated with slightly-sunk panels, arranged in simple geometrical pattern between the transverse arches that spring from the cornice breaks. The aisles have flat ceilings, similarly panelled and divided into bays by shallow cross-beams resting on cherub's-head corbels. The outer walls are simply pierced with arch-headed windows, and there are no responds to the arcade piers. Each side wall of the chancel contains an arched window, and the east wall is almost filled with the splendid altar-piece from the earlier building.

This was erected in consequence of a resolution passed by the vestry on 18th April 1716, when it was decided that 'a fair altar-piece of Flemish oak' should be put up, at a cost not exceeding £170. It was fortunately retained for use in the new church, and despite some alterations and the replacement of the lettered panels by paintings of unusual insipidity, it survives as a splendid specimen of the early eighteenth-century altar-pieces that once adorned most of Bristol's parish churches. This example is designed on customary lines, with a lofty principal stage raised on a panelled pedestal and divided into three compartments, one wide between two narrow, by Corinthian three-quarter columns with fluted shafts, which are flanked by half-pilasters of the same order, while full pilasters terminate the side compartments. The enriched entablature breaks forward over the pilasters and columns, and above the middle compartment it is surmounted by a triangular pediment, also broken forward and having in its tympanum a carving of the pelican in its piety. Above this entablature is a pedestal-course that breaks forward over the pilasters and columns, with dies enriched by carved acanthus-leaves. The attic stage surmounting the middle compartment has been reduced in height, and now consists of an oblong panel framed by panelled pilasters, which are flanked by carved open-work scrolls and support a swan-necked pediment. Baluster-like ornaments, representing the seven golden candlesticks, are placed on the pedestals in front of the attic pilasters; at each end, and in the centre of the swan-necked pediment; and on each of the side scrolls.

The fine organ-gallery of oak, dating from about 1730, was re-erected at the west end of the nave. The gallery is supported by columns and square piers of the Roman Doric order, with fluted shafts and enriched capitals. There are three bays, the middle one broken forward and flanked by columns supporting a corresponding break in the triglyphed entablature, which rests at each outer angle on a pier. This entablature is surmounted in the middle bay by a broken triangular pediment,

[87]

its tympanum containing a circular medallion framed in a wreath and flanked by palm-branches. Draped vases of globular form are placed at each end of the panelled pedestal that rises behind the pediment. The fine organ-case has been removed to fill the east end arch on the north side of the nave.

HOLY TRINITY CHURCH, HOTWELLS

The building of Holy Trinity Church, Hotwells, was made necessary by the great increase in Clifton's population, which amounted in 1828 to nearly 12,000 and was served only by the Parish Church and Dowry Chapel, each having very few free sittings. A spacious site was secured, with frontages to the Hotwell Road and Clifton Vale, and plans for the new church were prepared by Charles Robert Cockerell. The building was begun in 1829 and speedily completed, its consecration taking place on 10th November 1830. The building cost amounted to some £10,000 and was met by public subscription, to which Thomas Whippie gave £6,000. As originally arranged, the interior held 1,654 sittings of which 854 were free, but changes were made later for ritual purposes. During the late war the church was completely gutted, but the exterior has survived with little damage.

In planning the church, which forms a rectangle measuring about 85 feet from east to west, and 60 feet from north to south, Cockerell returned to Wren's methods of space-division. By skilfully placing eight unobtrusive but structurally necessary columns, he created a cruciform interior which had a domed crossing, east and west arms of two bays, and north and south arms of one. Galleries were placed over the aisles, and above the communion-screen was a small gallery for charity children.

The exterior is a fine example of Cockerell's eclectic style. The principal front (Plate 13c) is on the south side and consists of a central feature that is, in effect, a forward extension of the south arm of the cross, with balancing wings formed by the walls of the south aisles. The bold and original central feature contains the doorway, a rectangular opening framed in an architrave-band, with consoles supporting a pediment-head, above which rises an arch-headed window. Door and window are made significant by their niche-like setting, with its wide and deep concave reveal, the surface delicately modelled with three bands of slightly-sunk quadrangular panels, expanding outwards to the framing arch. This is set in a plain face between wide pilasters that rise from the rusticated pedestal-base, and terminate with two super-imposed entablatures of plain frieze and boldly-profiled cornice. The upper entablature is the larger and its cornice is returned above the arched recess to form a triangular open-bedmould pediment. The tympanum is enriched with the symbol of the Holy Spirit, a descending dove that radiates light, finely carved by H. Tyley, a Bristol statuary. From behind this pediment rises the small and elegant belfry, square in plan and consisting of a plain base with the clock-dial, and an upper stage where each face contains a tall arch-headed opening in a plain surround, set between pilasters supporting a simple entablature. The low concave-curving roof rises to a ball-and-cross finial.

The balancing wings are more simply treated, each containing two arch-headed windows that are spaced to conform with the internal bay divisions, and are framed in architrave-bands rising from the rusticated pedestal-base. Wide pilasters emphasise the outer angles, and rise to an entablature that continues the lower one of the central feature. The west elevation is similar in character but divided by pilasters into three bays, corresponding with the nave and aisles of the interior. The pedestal-base is broken in the central bay by three doorways, the middle one wider and taller than the others, all being dressed with architrave-bands and pediment-heads resting on consoles. Over each is a window, the side lights narrow and rectangular, and the middle one arch-headed. Each flanking bay contains an arch-headed window.

PUBLIC BUILDINGS

THE OLD COUNCIL HOUSE

Smirke's Council House has replaced the much smaller building erected during 1701–4, in pursuance of a resolution passed by the Common Council on 23rd October 1699, when 'the house ordered that the Council House shall be Amended and Repayred as the Mayor and Aldermen shall direct'. The Chamberlain's Audit-Books show that the new building cost £1,146 14s. od. to complete, and that Joseph Jones, a house-carpenter, was primarily responsible for its construction. The front, however, was obviously a mason's design, and as payment is recorded of £1 to Thomas Sumsion, of Colerne, and 17s. to George Townsend, of Oxford, it seems likely that alternative draughts were supplied by these masons, who must frequently have undertaken to prepare such designs.

A plan taken in 1823 shows the building to have had a frontage of 54 feet to Corn Street, and a return front of about 33 feet to Broad Street, this same depth continuing through the site. The council chamber was on the first floor, above a common hall used for a court-room, and other offices. The front was entirely built in freestone and consisted of two lofty stories. The centrally-placed doorway was framed by Corinthian pilasters supporting entablature-blocks and a segmental pediment, and on each side were two rectangular windows, with moulded architraves based on sills resting on consoles. Further consoles supported the platband marking the first-floor level, where the five tall rectangular windows were framed with moulded architraves, based on pedestal-aprons and surmounted by plain friezes and cornices. The middle window was flanked by pilaster-strips with consoles supporting a triangular pediment; the cornice of the window on each side was surmounted by carved scrollwork; while that of each end window bore a

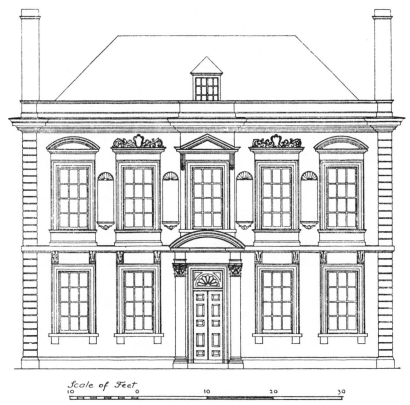

FIGURE 6

The old Council House. Corn Street elevation

segmental pediment. Shell-headed niches were recessed in the
piers between the windows; the angles of the building were
quoined; and the front finished with a deep and richly moulded
cornice (figure 6).

BARBER-SURGEONS' HALL

The Hall of the long-defunct Barber-Surgeons' Company was
situated in Exchange Avenue, originally Cock Lane, and stood
just south of the old Coopers' Hall. The building had a frontage
of some 26 feet to the avenue, and a mean depth of 40 feet. The
hall occupied the principal story, with offices below and an
anatomical-theatre above. After the company's disruption,
about 1745, the surviving members leased the hall for use as a
coffee-house, and as such it remained until well into the nineteenth century, when it became *The Grapes* tavern. During the

[91]

late war its interior was completely destroyed by fire, and the front was soon afterwards demolished.

Among the leading barber-surgeons of Bristol were the Rosewells, Thomas, who died in 1753, and his son John, who was one of the signatories to a mortgage on the hall, dated 1750. It was almost certainly for this Thomas Rosewell that Rosewell House, in Kingsmead Square, Bath, was built in 1736, reputedly from a design by John Strahan. It seems highly probable, therefore, that the Barber-Surgeons' Hall, or at least its front, was rebuilt about the same time from Strahan's designs, for the Exchange Avenue elevation closely resembled Strahan's house-fronts in Beauford Square and Avon Street, Bath.

FIGURE 7
Barber-Surgeons' Hall. Exchange Avenue elevation

The Exchange Avenue front was a simple Classical design, built in dressed freestone, and presenting a plain wall face with two tiers of three openings. The doorway was placed centrally between two windows, each tall rectangular opening being framed with a moulded architrave surmounted by a pulvinated frieze and cornice. The window architraves rose from pedestals of blind balustrading, and the doorway's cornice was surmounted by a segmental pediment. The upper windows were almost square in form, and their architrave frames were slightly eared and shouldered at the sides. The simple crowning cornice was surmounted by a plain pedestal parapet (Figure 7).

THE CITY LIBRARY

The first City Library was housed in a medieval building in King Street, given to the city by Robert Redwood. This structure had become ruinous by 1738 and must have been demolished before September of that year, for the Chamberlain's Audit Book shows that £18 17s. was then paid for 'pulling down the old Library in King Street'. The committee attending to the rebuilding then resolved to erect a new Library that was to measure 38 feet in length and 25 feet in width, in the clear. There were to be cellars below the ground-story, which was to contain the librarian's quarters, and not exceed ten feet in height. Over this was to be the library room, sixteen feet in height, and the front was to be entirely of freestone. The building was erected in accordance with these conditions, and the work appears to have been completed by the end of 1740, at a total cost of £1,301 8s. 1d. The Audit-Books show that three masons were employed—James Paty, Thomas Reynolds, and George Walker—but an examination of the receipts proves that Paty carved all the ornaments, and probably it was he who supplied the design for the elevation. For the Coat-of-Arms he charged £20; for the enriched panels above the first-floor windows—£12; and for the two Ionic (Composite) capitals to the porch—£1 16s.

The front is a Palladian design of some distinction, with beautifully executed details (Plate 14a). The composition is of two stories, with a wide central feature projecting slightly forward from narrow wings. The rectangular windows of the ground story are set, without architraves, in a wall face rusticated with horizontal V-jointing. There is a window in each wing, and one on either side of the rectangular doorway, which is framed by a shallow porch. This is composed of two columns, with respondent pilasters on the wall face, having fluted shafts and Composite capitals. These support an entablature that is recessed over the doorway and surmounted by a triangular pediment, placed above the line of the first-floor platband. The lofty second-story contains five windows, three in the central feature and one in each wing. Each rectangular opening is framed by a moulded architrave that rises from a plain apron and is surmounted by a plain frieze and cornice. A triangular pediment crowns each wing window, and a segmental one that in the centre, but above the cornice of each intermediate window there is a sculptured relief, presenting *putti* engaged in the study of books, the arts and the sciences. This front is terminated laterally by pilasters of V-jointed stones that rise to the underside of the modillioned main cornice. The pedestal parapet breaks against the triangular pediment crowning the central feature, which has in its tympanum a fine Baroque carving of the City Arms and Supporters. The projecting wing on the left flank of the building was added in 1786, with elevations carefully designed to accord with the main front, to which they are suitably subservient.

Internally, there is a good but dilapidated staircase, constructed of oak, with a moulded handrail supported on column balusters. The library room was a noble apartment, with fine bookcases and a magnificent continued chimney-piece that have been refixed in a room of similar design, in the Central Library in Deanery Road. The King Street premises ceased to be used as a library in 1907, and a succeeding period of neglect has apparently made it necessary to remove the pediment, parapet and cornice, and clean off most of the salient mouldings of the front. This drastic surgical operation has ruined the appearance of this building, which is deserving of a thorough restoration.

MERCHANT-TAYLORS' HALL

The Merchant-Taylors' Hall stands on the north-west side of Taylors' Court, Broad Street, and was built in 1740–1 to replace the seventeenth-century hall of this company. The long side of the Great Hall fronts on to Taylors' Court, with an elevation built of freestone but now largely faced with cement. The lofty main story, with its regular range of five tall rectangular windows, is raised upon a semi-basement having a like number of openings. These latter are framed by architrave-bands, but each of those in the main story is dressed with a moulded architrave, based on a moulded sill and surmounted by a pulvinated frieze and pediment, the segmental form alternating with the triangular. A platband marks the hall floor-level, and the front is finished with a moulded coping. That part of the building containing the lobbies and staircase, etc., projects slightly forward from the body of the hall, and has two stories above the semi-basement, each with two windows. These are dressed with architrave, pulvinated frieze and cornice, the lower one on the right being shortened to allow height for the doorway beneath it. Here the double-door is set in a rectangular opening, with a moulded architrave surmounted by a pulvinated frieze and flanked by pilaster-strips. Above these last are carved console-trusses supporting a semi-domed hood of wood and plaster, its lunette modelled with the Merchant-Taylors' Arms and Supporters. The style of this beautiful hood suggests an earlier date than 1740.

The Great Hall was a fine apartment, 56 feet in length and 22 feet 6 inches in width and height, entered through a double-door in its north end wall, from which projected the musicians' gallery. The walls had a panelled dado of about 10 feet 6 inches in height, and the flat ceiling was surrounded by a deep cove. Unfortunately, the interior has undergone conversion into offices, and a floor now divides the Hall into two stories.

THE EXCHANGE

When writing his description of the building of Bristol's Exchange, the elder Wood made only the slightest reference to the events that had preceded his appointment as architect, preferring, no doubt, that his readers should believe that the Corporation never had anyone else in mind for the commission. The story is, however, a long one and introduces the names of several architects and builders who were, at one time or another, considered for the work. It begins early in 1717 with the appointment of a Committee, composed of the Mayor and members of the Corporation, to consider proposals for 'building a more convenient Place than the Tolzey for the assembling of Merchants'. Nothing tangible appears to have been achieved before October 1721, when, acting in response to a petition presented by the merchants of the city, the Corporation applied to Parliament for an Act permitting the building of an Exchange, of which they agreed to pay half the cost. This Act was obtained early in 1722 and a new Committee was formed to carry its provisions into effect, but their efforts were rendered abortive by the sustained opposition of one who had great influence in civic affairs, and it was not until about 1737–8 that events began to move towards a realization of the project.

William Halfpenny was probably the first aspirant for the

commission of designing the Exchange, and the earliest of his several schemes was published in *Perspective made Easy* and most probably dates from about 1728. It is a poor composition in a pseudo-Palladian manner, perhaps derived from Strahan's front to Redland Court, with a pedimented centre and a somewhat exuberant skyline (Plate 14b). Another design, made about the same time, was for a building with a tower of several stages, bearing a startling resemblance to the courtyard tower of Burghley House. Halfpenny prepared at least four more schemes, during 1738–9, for building on the site of the present structure, all with more or less naïve elevations projected from plans of freakish ingenuity, but most fortunately for posterity not one of these designs met with the Committee's approval (Plate 15). It is, however, worth observing that these plans were produced to meet a programme that must have been laid down by the Committee, and was adhered to by others who later submitted proposals for the building. On 28th April 1740 it was resolved 'that Mr Halfpenny be paid ffive Guineas in part for the trouble he has been at in drawing Plans for the Exchange and Markets', and a like amount was paid to him 'in full' during 1741.

In June 1740 the Committee had under consideration a plan that had been prepared by John Jacob de Wilstar, the surveyor generally employed by the Corporation, but this, not meeting with approval, was returned to him for amendment. It was again submitted, but apparently without any positive result, for the minutes of a meeting held on 19th September 1740 record that 'sundry plans have been laid before us neither of which we have come to a resolution upon'. On 26th September it was reported that a member of the Committee, Alderman Jefferies, had corresponded with a London alderman and thereby obtained the services of George Dance, to whom the Committee now wrote asking 'what are his usual Terms in case his Plan is approved, also whether he will undertake the whole building of the Exchange'. The reply received from Dance was not satisfactory to the Committee, who resolved to write him for a 'more explanatory account of his designs'.

John Wood began to move into the picture on 15th December 1740, when Mr Jefferies and Mr Smith were 'desired to go to Bath to treat with Mr Allen or any other persons that will undertake the whole building of the Exchange'. On 9th January 1741, it was resolved that 'Mr George Tully be desired to propose a Plan . . . and Mr Jefferies be desired to write by tomorrows post to his correspondent in London to stop Mr Dance's coming down'. Tully's plan was produced for inspection on 23rd January, when it was 'referred for further consideration', but on 30th January the Committee decided that 'a letter be sent to Mr Wood to desire him to attend this Committee on Monday, Thursday or Friday next'. The rest of the story is best told in Wood's own words, even with all his elaboration of detail.

'On my attending there, upon Thursday the Fourth of February following, they Agreed with me to be their Architect; giving me, at the same Time, proper Instructions to enable me to form DESIGNS for their intended WORKS, which they desired might be done upon the strictest Rules of Oeconomy.

'ACCORDING to these Instructions, I was to contrive a BUILDING round an AREA, proper for about Six Hundred People to assemble in, in such Manner, as that it should have the outside Appearance of one Grand Structure; and this was to be divided into all the useful Rooms that was possible, in order to make the most of the Ground to be built upon. This Fabrick, now called the EXCHANGE of BRISTOL, was to be set so far back, as to make the Street before it two and forty Feet broad; and the Committee assigned the Front Part of the Building for two Taverns; the side Parts for little Tenements, for Insurance, or other Offices, and the Back Part for an Arcade, i.e. Arc-Ædes, with Rooms over it; the former to serve as Part of the Market; the latter for Additions to a Tavern, at the South-East Corner of the EXCHANGE.

'These Directions. . and the confined Situation of the Ground to be built upon, (. . . no more than one hundred and ten Feet in Breadth . . .), soon suggested to my Thoughts an Egyptian Hall, as the properest Center for an august Building; and the most convenient Place for Men of Business to assemble in: So that the Design which I offered the Committee the next Day for this Structure, had, for the Place of Exchange, an Egyptian Hall, in the Corinthian Order, of eighty Feet square, surrounded with a high Building, divided into a great Number of Rooms.

'This Design so far met with the Approbation of the Committee, that they resolved to proceed with the Work, con-

G

[97]

formable to it:' but 'While the Foundation was about, it was debated in the Committee, Whether the Place of Exchange should be Lofty, and Covered at Top, as I had design'd it; or Low and Open, to comply with the Opinion of the Citizens in General, then startled with the Novelty of a covered Place to meet in upon Mercantile Affairs? At length it was resolved, That the Publick shou'd be gratified in that Part of the EXCHANGE which was intended for their Convenience: So that the Committee, waiving the private Interest of the Corporation, and the grand Appearance of the whole Building, not only ordered the Place of Exchange to be made Low and Open at Top, but the Area to be increased ten Feet in Length, to make the North and South Portico's more capacious than those on the Sides, and thereby give the Company the better Opportunity of enjoying the Benefit of the Heat of the Sun.' Here it might be remarked that had Wood's Egyptian Hall been built, his arcaded court would have been spared the disfiguring second story of caryatids and the iron-and-glass roof that were added late in the nineteenth century.

The site had been cleared of buildings before Wood was appointed architect, and work on the foundations for the new Exchange advanced so quickly under his able direction that on Tuesday morning, 10th March 1740–1, the foundation-stone was laid by the Mayor, Henry Combe, in the presence of a large concourse that included members of the Corporation and of the Merchants' Society. This stone, a large block weighing about 2 tons, was placed at the north-east corner of the building, and on its uppermost bed was cut a long and flowery inscription in Latin, afterwards published with an English translation. The accounts show that on 8th May 1741, Thomas Paty was paid £1 for cutting this inscription.

Forms of tender, beautifully printed by *Felix Farley*, were sent out to various competing tradesmen, and prices for the work were 'accepted and agreed to by the Committee'. The freestone was largely supplied by Ralph Allen, and among those employed on the building were—William Biggs, freestone-mason, of Comb near Bath; Samuel Glascodine, house-carpenter; John Griffin, plasterer; Benjamin and Daniel Greenway, carvers and vase-makers, of Widcombe near Bath; Robert Parsons, freestone-mason, of Widcombe, 'House Carver'; and Thomas Paty,

'Ornament Carver'; while David Lewis was the clerk of the works. William Halfpenny submitted a *Proposal for the Carpenter's Works*, but without success. The building proceeded with such expedition that by the beginning of August 1743 Wood 'was enabled to name the Twenty-first of the ensuing Month, as the Day, whereon it shou'd be ready to be opened. The Committee upon this, came to a Resolution to open it, in a Grand and Solemn Manner, upon the Day I had named.' Wood's *Description* contains a fully detailed account of the elaborate ceremonies which took place on 21st September 1743, when the Exchange was opened by the Mayor, Sir Abraham Elton, Bart. The Committee's Accounts show that for designing the building and superintending its erection Wood was paid sums to a total of £833 12s. 11d.

The ground-story plan (Figure 8) of the building as erected is taken from Wood's *Description*, and the following account is to a large extent based on that work. The principal front, on the north side, faces Corn Street, and the centrally-placed doorway leads directly into the room marked A, which is twenty-eight

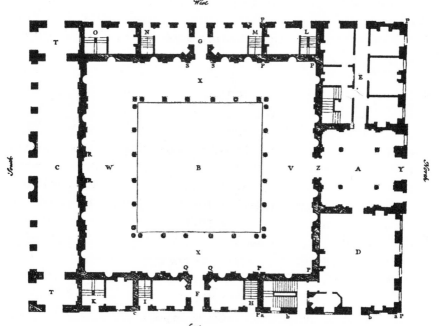

The Principal Plan of the Exchange of Bristol as it is now Erected A.D. 1745

FIGURE 8

[99]

feet square and forms 'a Tetrastyle Hall' of the Corinthian order, executed in freestone. This room is the principal entrance to the 'Place of Exchange', as well as to the Coffee-House and Tavern. 'The Place of Exchange', marked B, is a peristyle of the Corithian order, ninety feet in length and eighty feet in breadth, and south of this is a long room C, with an open arcade on the south side, designed to form the 'chief Edifice of the General Market'. This, like the peristyle, is also built in freestone. The large room marked D, west of the entrance hall, was 'The Exchange Coffee-House'. Wood complains that its walls were 'Wainscotted in a common Manner, but, if my Opinion had prevailed, this Room should have been finished in the highest Taste, as it is the only Place of general Resort in the City, for Gentlemen'. The rooms enclosed in the corresponding rectangle to the east, marked E, formed a 'House intended for a Tavern'. F and G are the vestibules for side entrances to the peristyle, and H to O are individual tenements built for letting as insurance or other offices or to tradespeople.

The north part of the building, marked on Wood's plan with the letters PPPP, is carried up three stories above ground level and crowned with a balustrade, the total height being forty-nine feet, while the rest of the structure is of two stories and thirty-four feet high. As Wood states—'The Whole is fronted with white Freestone, in as ornamental a Manner as a Building, with any Propriety, can be dressed, and yet there is Nothing in it could be properly omitted'.

The north front to Corn Street is a splendid Palladian design, with a central feature, three bays wide, broken forward from balancing wings, each of four bays (Plate 16. Fig. 9). The lofty ground-story has a rusticated face 'composed of regular Stones; some with chamfered Edges, some with plain', in which the rectangular windows are set without architraves, their heads being formed of three voussoirs with the key projecting slightly. The wide arch-headed doorway frames the original doors, their flush faces of wood being adorned with a pattern of nailheads. The ground-story finished with the customary platband, above which is a pedestal course. This is broken forward below the columns and pilasters of the Corinthian order which embraces the two upper stories. A plain-shafted order is used , with pilasters in the wings and four three-quarter columns in the central

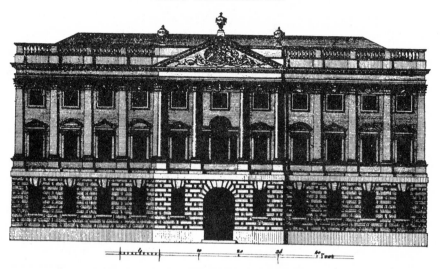

The ELEVATION of the EXCHANGE of BRISTOL, as it fronts North to Corn Street

FIGURE 9

feature, these last being spaced so that the middle inter-
columniation is wider than the others. The windows of the
principal story are dressed with 'rich Tabernacles', that is to say
they are framed by Corinthian pilasters that rise from the
pedestal to support a pedimented entablature, the segmental
form alternating with the triangular. The middle bay contains
a Venetian-window, its side lights framed by pilasters supporting
entablatures from which springs the moulded archivolt of the
middle light. The square windows of the attic-story have architrave frames, the top members coinciding with a moulding that
continues the astragal between the shafts and capitals of the
order. The wall spaces between the capitals 'are filled with
Festoons, which represent Great-Britain and the four Quarters
of the World, with the chief Products and Manufactures of every
Country'. The fine entablature is surmounted over the wings by
a balustrade, having pedestals placed to correspond with the
pilasters, while the central feature is crowned with a triangular
pediment, its tympanum containing 'the King's-Arms' carved
in the Baroque style by, presumably, Thomas Paty. Apart from
the removal of glazing-bars from all the windows, and the
insertion of a clock-face over the Venetian-window, this front
has been spared alteration, and the fine acroterial vases still
ornament the skyline. Wood's comment on the scale of this

[101]

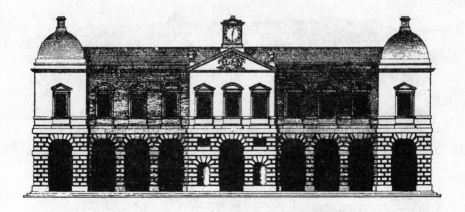

The ELEVATION of the EXCHANGE of BRISTOL, as it fronts South to the General Market.

FIGURE 10

elevation is worth quoting, for it shows his great sensibility in such matters. 'The several Parts whereof this Front is composed are Small, which must be attributed chiefly to the narrow Street wherein they are to be viewed.' How extraordinary it is, therefore, to find this very sensibility stigmatized as a fault by Blomfield, who dismisses Wood's buildings in Bath, where the scale is also most carefully related to the width of streets and squares, as 'rather small and almost weak in design'.

The east and west elevations are more or less identical, and their design has a simplicity fitting to the narrow thoroughfares which they face. The three-storied returns to the north front are each five windows wide, the middle three being contained in a feature that is broken slightly forward and was intended to finish with a triangular pediment. The south front 'is a more perfect Work, it being quite regular' (Figure 10). It is composed of a central feature and narrow end pavilions, broken slightly forward from the connecting wings. The ground-story is an open arcade built in rusticated masonry, the piers finishing with plain impost-bands, and the semi-circular arches rising to projecting keystones. The single archway in the centre is flanked by wide piers, each containing a semi-circular niche with a corresponding oblong recess placed above the impost. Each wing has three arches with narrow piers, and each pavilion one arch between

[102]

wide piers. The second-story begins with a pedestal-course, broken forward below the windows, which have tabernacle frames and are placed to centre over the ground-story arches, one in each pavilion, three widely spaced in each wing, and three in the central feature. This front is finished with a simple cornice, having a blocking-course over the wings, while the central feature is crowned with a triangular pediment, its tympanum carved with the City Arms. A simple clock-turret, with a low dome and a pineapple finial, rises behind the apex of the pediment, each end of which is adorned with a terminal vase. Each pavilion is roofed with a dome, square in plan and finished with a pedestal chimney-stack.

The tetrastyle hall is a fine apartment, wherein each wall-face is similarly divided into three bays, one wide between two narrow, by pilasters responding to the four plain-shafted Corinthian columns that support the coffered cross-beams dividing the ceiling into plain compartments. The wide middle bay of each face contains a 'Corinthian Gate', that is, an arch-way flanked by paired pilasters with entablatures from which the moulded archivolt rises. In the north arch are the entrance-doors; in the south are wrought-iron gates 'made after one of Tijou's Draughts', placed in front of glazed doors leading to the peristyle; while in the partially walled up arches to the east and west are set the architraves framing the rectangular doors to the Coffee-House and Tavern. Each archivolt has a carved mask decorating its key. 'Mercury's Head is next the Coffee-House; Bacchus's Head is next the Tavern; and the Head of Dea Pecunia of the Antients is next the Place of Exchange'.

By discarding Wood's proposed Egyptian Hall in favour of making the Place of Exchange an open court surrounded by porticoes, the Committee adhered to the traditional planning of bourse buildings. In spite of his disappointment, Wood rose to the occasion and created a peristyle of great beauty, the original effect of which can now be studied only in contemporary delineations, although his chaste colonnades remain to offer a dignified contrast to the vulgar superstructure of 1869 which they now support. On each side of the court is an order of plain-shafted Corinthian columns, spaced to form seven intercolumni-ations, the middle one being wider than the others, while that at each end is extremely narrow. These columns support an entablature, originally surmounted by a blind balustrade with vase-crowned pedestals placed above the columns. The rear wall of each portico is similarly divided by responding pilasters, and each bay contains a niche except the middle one, where a doorway occurs. The pilaster capitals are linked with a stucco frieze of masks and rich festoons, and cross-beams with coffered soffits and moulded fascias divide the plaster ceilings into plain compartments. The principal entrance, in the north portico, is a Corinthian archway, and similar arches provide the setting for the rectangular architrave-framed doors on the south, east and west sides, the lunettes above them being filled with stucco ornaments symbolizing Asia, Africa and America. The porticoes were originally covered with lead roofs, sloped upwards from the front balustrade to a second balustrade crowning the rear walls. Behind the north portico rose the rear elevation of the main block, 'so contrived as to appear a distinct Work of Itself'. This has narrow projecting wings, and a central feature crowned with a triangular pediment, its tympanum carved with the City Arms (Figure 11).

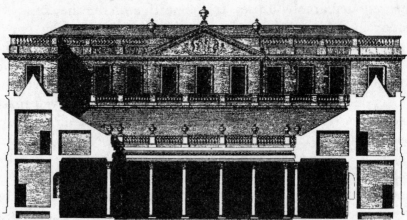

The ELEVATION of the EXCHANGE of BRISTOL, as it fronts South to the PERISTYLE of that Structure.
Together with
The SECTION of the Building on each side the PERISTYLE

FIGURE 11

By way of concluding this account of the Exchange—which from the time of its completion has always been considered the finest of Bristol's eighteenth-century buildings—we would quote Wood's profession of the principles that guided him in preparing the design. 'CONVENIENCE was the predominant Principle required in the EXCHANGE of BRISTOL; to which every other Principle, and every other Precept of ARCHITECTURE, naturally became subservient. The Perfection therefore aimed at in that Structure was in reconciling the Conveniencies required to such Rules of Art, as I conceived wou'd have the best Effect, when executed.'

COOPERS' HALL

The Coopers' Hall in King Street was erected during 1743–4, to replace the company's old hall in Cock Lane, which was demolished in clearing the site for the Exchange. After some hard bargaining, the Corporation agreed to grant the King street site, together with £900, in return for the surrender of the Cock Lane site, and as William Halfpenny had acted as surveyor during these negotiations he was employed to design the new hall. His draught for the King Street front was engraved and published during 1744, and later reproduced in Barrett's *History of Bristol*. During August 1744 *Felix Farley* reported the accidental death of a stone-mason employed in building the Hall. After a varied career as an assembly-room, sale-room, exhibition-hall, and Methodist chapel, the building has now descended into use as a fruit-exchange and warehouse.

The building occupies a site on the north side of King Street, with a frontage of 65 feet 9 inches, and an irregular depth averaging about 40 feet. The front is entirely built of dressed freestone, to a debased Palladian design that exhibits Halfpenny's house-carpenter's architecture in all its aspects (Plate 17b). The low ground-story, which may have been altered, presents a face rusticated by horizontal and vertical V-jointing, with the windows and doors recessed in segmental-headed openings, three equally spaced in the slightly-projecting central portion, one in the left flanking bay, and two narrow openings in the right. This rusticated base is finished with a cornice instead of the usual platband. The principal story is extremely lofty and contains five tall rectangular windows centred over the ground story openings. Each is dressed with a moulded architrave, based on a blind balustrade and finished with a pulvinated frieze and a pedimented cornice, the triangular form alternating with the segmental, while a plain oblong panel is recessed in the wall face above. The three middle windows are placed in the intercolumniations of an engaged colonnade, formed by four Corinthian plain-shafted three-quarter columns, without pedestals, that rise to support the appropriate entablature. This is returned at the ends of the colonnade and continued across each flanking bay, to break slightly forward above the long and short quoins that finish the front laterally. Above the colonnaded centre rises a high attic-story, containing three square windows with architraves rising from plain sills. This attic is surmounted by a steeply-pitched triangular pediment, its tympanum containing the Arms of the Coopers' Company, finely carved in the Baroque style. Each lateral bay has a pedestal-parapet with a blind balustrade corresponding in width with the window below. On each outside die was placed a tall-necked vase of the type used by Vanbrugh at King's Weston, while from the inside ones rise massive inverted scroll-consoles, buttressing the attic-story.

The hall on the first-floor is excellent in its proportions and has four windows on its long side, overlooking King Street. This room still retains its fine modillioned cornice, from which a deep cove rises to meet the flat ceiling, but, this apart, little of interest remains within the building.

THE MARKETS

The Markets behind the Exchange were not designed by John Wood the elder, to whom attribution has been made in the past, but by Samuel Glascodine, the house-carpenter and surveyor, who was sent by the responsible committee to London and Oxford, to view the markets recently erected there, before submitting his proposals. On 20th April 1744 Glascodine was instructed to prepare a design for the High Street front, and this was approved by the committee on 4th May following, but before building was begun the design had to be amended to meet the demands of adjoining property owners. The Markets were opened on 28th March 1745, Glascodine being the carpenter, and John Gibbon the mason employed in their construction.

The most interesting architectural feature of the Markets is the High Street front (Figure 12), a narrow but monumental structure of dressed freestone, which, though badly disfigured by

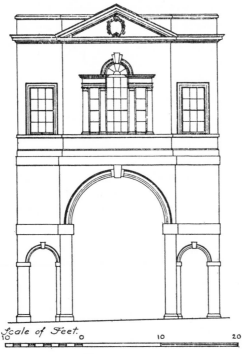

FIGURE 12
The Market. High Street elevation

advertisements, has generally escaped alteration. This somewhat ill-proportioned Palladian design is composed of a central
feature projecting slightly forward from narrow wings, and consists of two lofty stories. The first contains the arched entrance to
the Markets, formed by narrow piers with impost-bands, and a
moulded archivolt broken by a triple-key. In each wing is a
small doorway of similar design, above which the main impost-band is carried. This first story terminates with a platband
below the pedestal-course underlining the second-story windows.
In the centre is a Venetian-window, with Doric pilasters supporting entablatures over the side lights, the moulded archivolt to the middle light being broken by a triple-key. Each wing
has a rectangular window framed by a moulded architrave. This
story is finished with a cornice, the central feature being surmounted by a triangular pediment with a cartouche in its
tympanum, and each wing has a plain parapet. The entrance-
way into the Markets has a plaster cross-vault ceiling, originally
with moulded bosses at the intersections. The open market halls

[107]

were of simple design, with low-pitched roofs of timber construction carried on arcades and Tuscan colonnades, but these buildings have suffered greatly from later alterations and additions.

THE OLD POST OFFICE

The old Post Office, the right-hand building of the two that flank the Exchange, has been mistakenly ascribed to Wood the elder, whereas all the evidence proves that the design, like that for the Markets, was produced by Samuel Glascodine. On 7th March 1745–6 he was instructed by the Corporation to prepare a design for a building to accommodate the Post Office, on a site flanking the Corn Street front of the Exchange. His plans were approved on 18th April 1746, and the contract was signed on 14th May following. The building was erected by Glascodine, with Daniel Millard as the mason. The corresponding building on the left of the Exchange was erected in 1782, from plans by Thomas Paty and Sons, who closely adhered to Glascodine's elevations.

The same design was used for both the front and return elevations, which are three stories high and built in dressed freestone. In this composition of three bays, the middle one projects slightly from those flanking it, and each is one window wide. The arcaded ground-story has plain piers, a deep impost-band, and moulded archivolts broken by keystones that die into the first-floor platband. The rectangular windows of the two upper stories are framed by architraves that rise from plain sills resting on corbels, and the first-floor windows have, in addition, plain friezes and triangular pediments. The angles, and the breaks to the middle bay, are emphasized by long and short quoins with chamfered arrises. These continue to the underside of the main entablature, which is surmounted by a high pedestal-parapet that rises behind the triangular pediment crowning the middle bay (Plate 17a).

THE ASSEMBLY ROOM, PRINCE STREET

Several assembly rooms were opened in Bristol and near the Hotwell during the course of the eighteenth century. The first room in the Pithay was abandoned when the centre of fashion moved to Queen Square, and the assemblies were more conveniently held in the halls of the various companies. There was also a converted playhouse near St Augustine's Back, which served for a time as an assembly room and later became Lady Huntingdon's Chapel. Then there were the upper and lower Long Rooms near Dowry Square, and the rooms in the York Hotel, but all of these were surpassed in splendour and importance by the 'New Musick Room', or Assembly Room, in Prince Street.

The Corporation's Bargain Book shows that on 13th December 1753, Cranfield Becher, John Heylyn, Morgan Smith, William Barnes the younger, and John Curtis, all prominent and wealthy citizens, agreed to surrender on or before 25th March 1768, the leases they held of four small tenements fronting on to Prince Street and Crane Lane. In return, and on payment of a fine of £400 and a yearly rent of £5, a new lease was to be granted them, renewable every 14 years on payment, after the first renewal, of a fine of £100. They in their turn covenanted to demolish the tenements 'and erect a substantial building, which building shall contain one large room with proper conveniencies for an Assembly Room and such like Publick meetings, with a covenant that the Mayor and Burgesses and Commonalty, their successors and assigns, shall have free use of the said room with all conveniency and Appurtenances thereto belonging for the space of six days in every or any one year when the same shall be wanted for the entertainment or accommodation of any of the Royal Family that may come to this City'.

The capital required to build the new Assembly Room was raised by means of a tontine subscription, of 120 shares at £30 each. These were allotted before 23rd June 1754, when the body of proprietors thus formed signed formal deeds of assent to the scheme. The site having been cleared, the new building was erected with all possible speed, being completed by the end of 1755. On 14th January 1756, 'The New MUSICK ROOM opened with the Oratorio of the Messiah. Between the Acts a Concerto on the Organ by Mr Broderip, and a solo on the Violin by Mr Pinto.' For the rest of the eighteenth century, and during the early 1800s, this Assembly Room was the social centre of Bristol, and during the winter season a ball was held there on each alternate Thursday, conducted by a master-of-ceremonies in strict conformity with the prevailing etiquette of Bath. Fashion deserted the Prince Street room when the Clifton Assembly

[109]

Rooms were opened in 1811, and a new use was sought for the older building. It was then 'fitted up in a most elegant stile as a Theatre, at the expense of near £2,000' to 'contain about 2,000 spectators', and the lease was offered for sale on 23rd April 1812. The building opened as the Regency Theatre, which met with strong opposition from the proprietors of the Theatre Royal and closed its doors in 1813. The vicissitudinous career of the building was almost at an end when it passed, by a lease dated 11th March 1909, into the hands of the Great Western Railway Company, who covenanted with the Corporation 'to pull down and rebuild the premises' within a period of seven years. In pursuance of this agreement the Assembly Room was demolished to the level of the first-floor, leaving the mutilated ground-story still standing.

While there is no conclusive evidence as to the architect of the Assembly Room, circumstances and many points about the design suggest that Halfpenny was employed, at least to prepare draughts. During July 1754 he advertised his *Perspective made Easy* in the Bristol journals, which suggests his presence in the city at that time, just when the building was about to be erected. This year saw also the publication of *The Modern Builder's Assistant*, wherein the brothers Halfpenny had collaborated with Robert Morris and Thomas Lightoler, and it must be remarked that the Rococo designs contributed by the last were closely affined to the stucco ornaments in the Assembly Room, although these were probably executed by Joseph Thomas.

The building occupied a rectangular site, with a frontage of some 40 feet to Prince Street on the east, the same to Narrow Quay on the west, and about 120 feet to Assembly-Room Lane on the south. The ground-story accommodated a coffee-room at the west end, a tavern in the middle, and at the Prince Street end was the small entrance lobby containing the staircase to the great room on the first-floor. At the east end of the great room was a gallery, approached by a secondary stair from the main landing, and at the west end were two doors—one leading to the coffee- and card-rooms, and the other to the withdrawing-rooms and a staircase leading to the Narrow Quay.

The walls were strongly built of rubble-stone, the long side elevation being dressed with freestone, while the east and west fronts were entirely faced with ashlar. The Prince Street

Curas Cithara tollit

Scale of Feet.

FIGURE 13
The Assembly Room. Prince Street elevation

elevation was a bold and somewhat uncouth design, its com-
pound of Palladian and Vanbrughian motifs almost proclaiming
Halfpenny's authorship (Plate 32, Figure 13). The ground-
story face, rusticated with horizontal and vertical V-jointing,
was raised on a high plinth and finished with a platband. The
entrance was placed centrally in the wide middle portion that
broke forward from narrow flanking bays, each containing a
small segmental-headed window. A short flight of steps rose to
the arched doorway, recessed within a shallow porch composed
of two widely-spaced Ionic columns, with respondent pilasters
against the wall, supporting an entablature surmounted by a
blocking-course. The lofty principal story was underlined by a
pedestal-course, broken forward across the centre to support the
two pairs of Corinthian plain-shafted three-quarter columns

[111]

that framed the middle bay and supported projecting sections of the main entablature, and of the triangular pediment crowning this central feature. The middle bay contained a Venetian-window, dressed with Corinthian plain-shafted pilasters that rose from a plain and heavy sill on corbels, and supported entablatures from which sprang the moulded archivolt of the middle light. Over this window was a shaped tablet, finished with a cornice-capping and bearing an inscription in raised letters of lead—'Curas Cithara tollit'. In each side bay was a tall rectangular window, placed in too-close proximity to the columns. Each was dressed to accord with the Venetian-window, but the entablature was surmounted by a triangular pediment, and the wall face above had an unmoulded oblong recess placed in line with the inscribed tablet. The fine entablature had a modillioned cornice, and was surmounted by a pedestal parapet dying against the central pediment and containing blind balustrades placed to correspond with the side windows.

The great room measured 84 feet in length, and 34 feet in width and height. The rubble walls were battened, then lathed and plastered, and it was this form of construction allied to the excellent proportions that gave the room its outstanding acoustical quality. The general scheme of decoration was designed on broad Palladian principles, and a considerable use was made of Rococo ornamentation, superbly executed in stucco. Interest was focused on the west wall, where an arched central feature was created by two slightly-projecting pilasters that were based on the pedestal-dado and supported a continued impost with a moulded archivolt rising therefrom. Most of the moulded members were enriched with the appropriate ornaments, and the pilaster-shaft panels enclosed pendants composed of fruits, flowers, masks and musical instruments, tied up with ribbons and descending from fauns' heads. Within the arch lunette was a clock-dial, elaborately framed with acanthus and *rocaille* ornaments, while the spandrels on each side of the arch were similarly adorned. The rectangular field below the impost contained a motif of fruit and floral garlands, festooned from a central basket and ending in pendants. Under this motif was placed a mirror, in a carved and gilt frame of Chinese Rococo style. On each side of the arched feature was a six-panelled door, framed in an eared architrave surmounted by a

FIGURE 14
The Assembly Room. Interior

plain frieze and broken triangular pediment. On the wall face above each door was a tall rectangular panel, formed by a raised moulding with its upper angles incut, and over this was a modelled drapery festoon (Figure 14).

The south wall contained six arch-headed niches of semi-circular plan, evenly spaced and framed by plain pilasters and moulded archivolts, these rising from imposts that continued inside each niche. Above was a clerestory of six windows, deeply recessed in segmental-headed openings, their narrow moulded surrounds rising from shaped aprons. These windows were placed at this height in order 'to prevent the company from being overlooked'. On the north wall were two fireplaces, originally adorned with fine chimney-pieces and surmounted by Chinese Rococo mirrors. A range of blind window recesses corresponded to the clerestory opposite. The east wall contained the musicians' gallery and organ, and all the walls were finished with an entablature having an enriched modillioned cornice. From this rose the quadrant cove, terminating in a deeply projecting moulding surrounding the flat ceiling. This was ornamented with modelled rosettes from whence hung the chandeliers, consisting, according to Shiercliff's account, of 'a large beautiful glass lustre in the centre of the room, . . . two that are smaller, and one over the orchestra'.

BRISTOL BRIDGE

The story of the events that preceded the rebuilding of Bristol Bridge is worth relating in some detail, if only to show how private intrigue, public controversy, and official procrastination could combine to impede the progress of an urgently needed improvement.

By the middle of the eighteenth century the medieval bridge had become altogether inadequate to serve as a main thoroughfare, and the Corporation was frequently petitioned to undertake the necessary work of improvement. The four-arched structure was sound enough, but the narrow roadway could only be widened by removing some thirty houses then lining it. As their acquisition from many different hands presented a host of difficulties, the Corporation tended to let the matter lapse. On 15th October 1754 *Felix Farley* optimistically reported— 'We hear for a Certainty, that either our old Bridge will be made more commodious, or an entirely new one built over a different part of the River', but it was not until about the middle of 1757 that a prominent citizen named Daniel Shewring took the initial step of commissioning a design for rebuilding the bridge, for which he paid James Bridges 10 guineas, repaid later by the Corporation.

At long last, on 28th October 1758, the Corporation appointed a Committee to invite and consider plans and estimates for the improvements, and to propose ways of raising the necessary funds. The Committee presented a report to the Common Council on 23rd January 1759. First mentioning the assistance given by 'Mr Bridges, Mr Tully, and other able and experienced persons', the members declared their unanimous resolve 'that it would be most advantageous to build a new bridge of three arches on the old foundations, agreeable to Mr Bridges' plan marked A and his proposals marked B'. During the following February this scheme was exhibited in the Guildhall for public approbation, but sufficient dissent was voiced to warrant the appointment of a committee of twenty-four citizens, representing the various wards, to confer with the Bridge Committee.

The rest of the year passing in fruitless debates, the Corporation called another public meeting on 28th December 1759, when it was generally resolved—'That a temporary bridge be erected beside the old, before any work on it is begun, and that a permanent stone bridge of one arch be built from Temple side to the opposite shore, to guard against any accident by fire or flood that might happen to the temporary bridge.' In the light of later events it must appear that this scheme was advanced by John Wallis, an architect-builder who had considerable influence in Bristol. This sound but costly solution of the problem was laid before the Common Council on 10th January 1760, when there was general agreement on the expediency of building a temporary bridge, but division on all else. Nevertheless, a Bill was framed to carry out the improvements, proposing that they should be paid for by a coal duty, a rate on houses, wharfage charge, and a five-years toll on the temporary and rebuilt bridges.

Those in favour of one scheme now voiced strong criticism of the other, objection to the coal duty was general, the merchants protested against the wharfage charge, and the citizens' committee threatened to ask Parliament for powers to carry out the improvements themselves. In a notice that appeared in *Felix Farley* on 26th January, the Bridge Committee expressed hope that all objection might be overcome in time for the Bill to pass during the current session, and the dissentients were invited to send representatives to a conference on 31st January. This meeting was reported by *Felix Farley* as a failure, but another committee, chosen out of the Corporation, was appointed to meet the Bridge Committee on 4th February, 'when it was hoped this grand, useful, and necessary Work will be happily determin'd on.' The report ended with this comment—'It is justly observ'd, that no Method hitherto advanc'd by several scheming Gentlemen have any Ways equall'd the first propos'd in the Report; and the Patrons of the New Bridge at Hawkin's Lane, begin to be more and more sensible of the Impropriety of that or any other, before the Old one, except the Temporary Bridge there, which is allow'd necessary; and they will know, the Alarm of Fire or Floods was advanc'd only to serve a Purpose.'

[115]

Further paragraphs appeared a fortnight later, advocating re-building the old bridge and declaring that to erect a second stone bridge would provide 'a lasting Monument to the Folly and Contention of the present Times'. The writer went on to suggest that the warm advocates of the one-arched bridge should turn their attentions towards constructing one from Durdham Down to that opposite, and 'not disturb the good Intentions of the Corporation and the Bridge Committee'.

The Bill was presented to the Commons on 22nd February 1760, in its revised form, with the coal tax omitted and the money proposed to be raised by a tax of 6d. in the £ on houses, a wharfage charge, and a toll on the bridges lasting until the debt was discharged. On 8th March *Felix Farley* printed a note directed at Wallis and his friends, saying that 'the Opposition of the Few would be found to proceed rather from Self Interest, Private Pique, Opinionated Obstruction, Disappointed Ambition, or the Insinuations of a vain busy Intermeddler and his Associate (who is endeavouring all the while to serve himself, or by his thwarting Schemes to prevent a Public Good) than from any reasonable Argument against the propriety of the Scheme'. At the same time, many members of the Bridge Committee, finding themselves opposed by the Corporation committee, published their intention to resign 'rather than obstruct or pro-tract so necessary an undertaking', while reserving their rights to vote on any scheme that might be proposed for execution.

By the beginning of April it was assumed that opposition to the original scheme had been largely overcome, and the Bill providing for its execution was passed early in May. Meanwhile plans and estimates for carrying out the various suggestions had been commissioned from James Bridges, John Wood the younger, and Ferdinando Stratford, each of whom published his proposals.

Bridges' pamphlet is dated 1760 and entitled *Four Designs for rebuilding Bristol Bridge, wherein are explained—I, A Design of three Semicircular Arches on the old Foundations: II, A Design of three Elliptical Arches, also on the old Foundations: III, A Design of five Segment Arches on a new Foundation: IV, A Design of an Arch 130 Feet Cord, and Altitude 29.'* Bridges must have gone to a con-siderable amount of trouble and expense to put forward schemes which he hoped would secure his appointment, for he had prepared elaborate plans and detailed estimates, besides models to demonstrate the methods proposed to be used in carrying out the work of piling, etc. He stated that his first concern with the question of the Bridge was about the middle of 1757, and during the following year he was called into service by the Bridge Committee.

John Wood, the younger, published his *Second Letter to the Commissioners*, written from Wells and dated 20th August 1760. He had submitted various designs, but strongly recommended building a bridge of 'one Elliptical Arch of 110 Feet span, to rise 39 Feet'. He referred to his building experiences in Bath, alluded to his father's great reputation, and stated that he did not submit detailed estimates because of his preoccupation with other work.

Ferdinando Stratford, an engineer and surveyor of Gloucester, was the 'associate' of Wallis referred to above. His published letter was dated 1760 and entitled *A Short ACCOUNT of the Manner proposed for Re-building BRISTOL BRIDGE*. He, of course, advocated building a single-arched bridge, but had also prepared a design and estimate for a bridge of three arches on new foundations.

The Trustees, or Commissioners, appointed under the Act, soon became divided into two apparently irreconcilable groups. One advocated the three-arched bridge utilizing the old piers, as proposed by Bridges, while the other, led by the persuasive Wallis, favoured the employment of Stratford or Wood to build a single-arched structure. Each group found its public supporters who addressed pamphlets to the Trustees and letters to the press, which grew more vituperative as the controversy waxed. During November 1760 a considerable majority of the Trustees elected Bridges to serve as their surveyor, and he was voted £100 for his past services. He at once set to work preparing for the construction of the temporary bridge, the 'cassoon' for which was sunk into position early in May 1761, and during the same month the materials of the old houses were offered for sale. The temporary bridge was opened at the beginning of 1762, and during the following months the Trustees advertised for masons willing to demolish the old bridge and build a quay wall, to Bridges' instructions.

In spite of Bridges' appointment and his obviously satisfactory conduct of the work, any decision to proceed with his scheme for rebuilding the bridge was opposed at every turn by Wallis and his associates, who continued to press for a single-arched bridge on new foundations. At length the Trustees appointed Mr John Phillips to act as arbitrator, and on 30th August 1762 he examined, in their presence, 'Mr Wood's designs A, B, C, and his proposals, but it plainly appeared that the designs of the other competitors were so much preferable, that he thought, with submission, to take no further notice of them.' On the following day he examined Bridges' three designs and accompanying proposals, and Stratford's two plans. He found that the latter were very accurate and showed the avenues proposed to lead to the bridge. He did not recommend the single-arch scheme of either competitor, owing to risks that might arise during construction, although both had expressed their confidence in finding workmen to undertake their designs.

The publication of this report led to the appearance of *A Letter by a By-stander*, a pamphlet that fully endorsed the findings and censured those who continued to oppose the employment of Bridges to carry out his first design. Wallis, or some member of his party, then countered with *A Reply, to a most Partial Pamphlet*, written by 'A Citizen' and published in Bath. Declaring that Phillips' report had been most partial to Bridges, the writer contended that Wood's hastily prepared plans were far superior to Bridges' designs, which had taken three years to prepare and were now exhibited in all the panoply of gilt and glazed frames. Wood's scheme for raising the levels of the streets approaching the bridge, in order to give increased height to the arches while maintaining more or less level highways, had been strongly criticised on grounds of expense, but it was pointed out that the initial expenditure would lead to increased revenue from the vaults and warehouses below the buildings and streets. 'As to Mr Stratford's Plan, tho' the By-stander ludicrously compared it to a Turkey Carpet, yet it is such a masterly piece of Work, that Mr WOOD would not be ashamed to own it, . . . and by it, Mr Stratford has shown himself an excellent Draughtsman, and by his Letter an excellent Engineer.' 'Citizen' roundly declared that Bridges' report was compounded of plagiarisms and gave quotations to prove that it consisted largely of extracts from the various proposals for Westminster Bridge, submitted by

Labelye, Batty Langley, and others. Concluding, he stated that 'Stratford, from his Infancy had been bred an Engineer', while Wood had received 'the advantages of a liberal Education, and the Instruction and Experience of one of the most celebrated Architects of his Time, I mean his Father', whereas Bridges was but a 'Carpenter and Joiner, whose well known travelling Employment cannot entitle him to equal Authority, in matters of Science, with those Gentlemen, nor ever give him a Claim to the Stile of Architect'.

In an effort to end the dispute and satisfy both parties, the Trustees met on 18th December 1762 'when it was agreed that the Bridge should be built on three Arches, and on new Foundations. Mr Bridges and Mr Stratford, Architects, to have the Execution thereof'. For Bridges' opponents, however, this agreement was a compromise to be set aside at the first opportunity. Early in 1763 they spread a rumour that he had misled the churchwardens of St Nicholas' into believing that their church could be safely rebuilt upon the old foundations, whereas these were unsound, but an examination by a number of Bristol's leading masons proved the falsity of the report, which had been circulated to injure Bridges' reputation with the Trustees.

The following advertisement, first published on 27th August 1763, made it clear beyond any doubt that the Wallis-Stratford party had neither relinquished their aims nor lost influence:

'The Estimates for re-building Bristol-Bridge, already delivered, appearing to the Trustees to be vastly too large, Notice is hereby given, To all Persons inclinable to undertake the Building such Bridge, and who can give good Securities for the Execution of the Contract. That the Trustees . . . will at their General Meeting to be held at the Guildhall on Monday 3rd Day of October next . . . be ready to receive further Plans and Estimates, for Building the following Sorts of Bridges over the River Avon, viz:—A One Arch Bridge of 125 Feet Span, and a 32 Feet Altitude from Low Water Mark; A three Arch'd Bridge upon the Old Foundations; and also a three Arch'd Bridge upon New Foundations.'

This must have proved the final blow to Bridges, who resigned his post a few weeks later. On 22nd October 1763 his departure from Bristol was made generally known by the following letter, printed by *Felix Farley:*

[119]

'To the Mortification of many *good* Men, and to the Reproach of some, that are *not good*, Mr James Bridges quitted this Town, and sailed for the West-Indies last Week. No Man was ever better beloved, and no Man more deserved it, and consequently in his Turn, no Man more envied, no Man more maletreated. But this is no wonder, and it only serves to show, that the World is not worse now, than it was Seventeen Hundred Years ago, which Horace to his Lyre laments, when he says, *that we are so very envious, and overwicked: That we bear an implacable Hatred to good and great Men, whilst they are with us, yet so unaccountable is our Conduct, that when they are gone, we pursue them with Regret, and talk of them with Tears;* and I don't doubt, but that many, who treated him *ill* some Months ago, would some Months hence be pleased at his Return; he was, as Shakespear says, *take him for all in all, I know not where to see the like again;* besides his being well hackney'd in the Ways of Men, that is, he had seen the World, he was a sincere Friend, and a pleasing Companion: As to his Business, that of an ARCHITECT, his Buildings are elegant and sound; that the finish'd Edifice of the Fort, with which every one is delighted, and that religious one, now raising on the Bank of the Avon in Bristol, whose Beauty and Regularity will be the Object of our Admiration when finish'd, speak greatly to his Advantage. But to crown all, notwithstanding the united Force of his Enemies, his Plan for the Bridge upon the Old Foundations of the three Arches, will to succeeding Times, shew the Man, when his Enemies are forgotten. . . .

As to the COMMISSIONERS or Trustees of the Bridge, Gentlemen who were absorb'd in Trade, and were not idle enough to mind any Business but their Own, These (Mr Bridges says, of THEMSELVES) never used him ILL, but rather the Reverse. But as two or three Men of Great Consequence (as they thought themselves) tho' of little Skill in Architecture; of these he says he has received the basest Treatment. For tho' they knew but very little of the Science, they took the Direction of the Whole upon them, Saucily saying, *in the Kingdom of the BLIND, we that have ONE Eye ought to govern.'*

One week later *Felix Farley* published a strongly worded letter, complaining that although the Trustees had by then held no fewer than seventy-six meetings, all had been adjourned and no fixed decisions had been reached. Had Bridges' proposals been adopted at the outset, as they should have been, the opportunities of favourable low tides would not have been lost, and the citizens would have had their bridge open. The writer then asked—'Whence this Trifling? Why you may imagine from some Malecontents that were constantly putting in their thwarting Oar, and are pleas'd with nothing but what they propose themselves. One of them has been known to draw many pretty Pictures from Palladio Londonensis, which so pleas'd the Ladies, that they told him he was fit to build Bridges or Churches. And Jacky, being too polite to dispute their Judgment, put in for both, but succeeded in neither.' This last was an open reference to Wallis, who was further enjoined to:

> Burn, *JACKY*, Burn, *those plunder'd Plans of thine,*
> *And to some happier HEAD the Bridge resign.*

Scurrilous letters and verses directed against Wallis then followed one another in succeeding issues of *Felix Farley* until 17th December 1763, when the controversy had more or less ceased.

The Trustees met on 7th November 1763 and reached a decision to build a bridge of three arches, deferring the question of whether or not to use the old foundations. At this meeting Wallis defended his attitude of continued objection to Bridges' proposals, saying he had been advised in this by Stratford, who was supported in his opinion by Wood the younger, and the late William Tully. A pamphlet supporting Bridges, entitled *The Opinion of the Masons, touching the foundations of the Old Bridge*, dated October 1762, was dismissed by Wallis as the production of some ill-educated tradesmen, and of no consequence. The offended 'tradesmen' replied with a long letter that appeared in *Felix Farley* on 17th November, and was signed by Robert Comfort, Thomas Manley, William Jones, Robert Gay, William Daniel, and others. They complained that 'as Mr Wallis is a Commissioner, he always has it in his Power to impeach the Knowledge, Judgment and Experience of others, who he well knows, cannot be present to answer for themselves, as the Business of those Meetings is always done in private.' Wallis had quoted the opinions of the late Mr William Tully 'whose Knowledge and Experience (he thinks) exceed that of all Mankind', but he had never taken the least notice of Mr Phillips and

Mr Shakespeare of London, whose views were entitled to the same respect. The writers even went so far as to question the honesty of both Wallis and Stratford.

On 21st November the Trustees met again to study a report that had been received from several eminent masons of Bath—Sainsbury, Ford, Fisher, Seldon, and Jelly—all of whom were unanimous in declaring after inspection that the old piers were well constructed and entirely sound. When the matter was put to the vote 45 were for building to Bridges' design on the existing piers, and 18 against. Thus the absent Bridges was completely vindicated, and Wallis and Stratford discredited, for shortly afterwards the Trustees placed in Thomas Paty's capable hands, the task of carrying out Bridges' design. The foundation-stone of the new structure was laid on 9th April 1764. and the keystone of the middle arch was placed into position on 23rd June 1767. In September 1768 the bridge was opened for foot passengers, and for general traffic during the following November.

An examination of the Trustees' accounts shows that the several architects concerned with the undertaking were paid the following total sums, in varying amounts, for their labours: James Bridges—£650, John Wood—£150, and Ferdinando Stratford—£280. Thomas Paty, as surveyor during the execution of the work, received a yearly salary of £105, while his brother James Paty was paid £14 10s. for making a stone model of the bridge.

The history of Bristol Bridge, subsequent to its completion, is notable chiefly for the serious riots that occurred in September 1793, occasioned by the deplorable dishonesty of the Trustees in continuing to impose tolls after the building-debt had been discharged. The disused toll-houses were later converted into lock-up shops, and existed as such until their removal when the bridge was widened during 1873–4.

Bristol Bridge was built of Courtfield stone, from Monmouthshire, to a simple Classical design that must have been based to some extent on Labelye's Westminster Bridge. The three arches rest on abutments at either bank and on triangular-ended piers that are 10 feet in thickness and 42 feet in width. Each end arch is semi-circular and spans 40 feet, while the middle arch is elliptical, spans 55 feet, and rises higher than

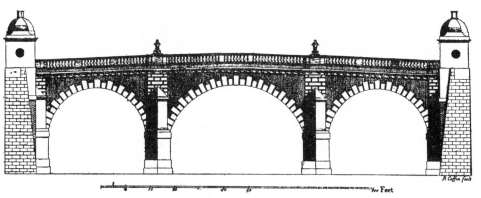

FIGURE 15
Bristol Bridge. Elevation

the others. All are expressed elevationally by a ring of V-jointed voussoirs, alternately long and short. The triangular end of each pier stops level with the crowns of the side arches, and splays back in pyramidal form to meet a rusticated face that projects slightly to support a forward break in the modillioned cornice. This rises with a slight rake from either end to a level section in the middle. Before the alterations of 1873–4, the bridge had a parapet of Portland stone with three balustraded sections to each arch, and the abutments were surmounted by toll-houses, square in plan and roofed with shallow octagonal domes of lead (Plate 18a and Figure 15).

THE THEATRE ROYAL

The Theatre Royal, in King Street, is the oldest playhouse in Britain that has continued in use as such, and despite many minor changes and a partial reconstruction of its auditorium, the building survives to represent for most people the typical town theatre of the mid-Georgian period. For more serious students, it offers a remarkable field for studying the development of theatre design during the second half of the eighteenth century.

This theatre had at least three humble predecessors, the first being a playhouse in St. Augustine's Back, which was opened early in the eighteenth century and became an assembly room shortly before 1742. There was also a theatre in Stokes Croft, conveniently situated and outside the jurisdiction of the City Magistrates. But the most famous and long-lived of these

[123]

playhouses was the Jacob's Wells Theatre, a small and primitive building adjoining the Horse and Groom Tavern. This was opened in 1729 by John Hippisley, the comedian, and so successful was his venture that he was encouraged to promote, in 1747, the building of a theatre in Bath, but both enterprises were cut short soon afterwards by his death.

The proposal to build the King Street theatre was formulated early in 1764, by a group of influential citizens, led by Thomas Symons, Alexander Edgar, William Jones, John Vaughan and Robert Watts. A body of proprietors was formed, with forty-eight members, each subscribing £50 towards the building's cost and receiving in exchange a silver token entitling the holder to 'a sight of every performance'. In addition to this fund, a further sum of £1,400 was raised by admirers of the drama. A house in King Street with a garden in the rear, and ground behind the Coopers' Hall, was purchased as the site for the new building. For this a design was prepared by James Paty (2nd), directly upon that of the Theatre Royal in Drury Lane, as it then existed. On 24th November 1764 *Felix Farley* stated that 'the Workmen are now employ'd in order to lay the Foundation of the New Theatre, in King-street; which would have been done before this Time, had not a Mistake been made in the Calculation, whereby the House would have been built 8 Feet larger in the Clear, than the Theatre Royal in Drury-lane. A Model of that House has been sent for, and the Proprietors seem determined that the Work shall be carried on with great Spirit. The Purchases are made, necessary for the Entrance from King-street and the Rackay; and another way will be made into Baldwin-street'. A week later the same journal reported that 'Yesterday Afternoon (30th November 1764) was laid the Foundation Stone of the new Intended Theatre in King-street, which will be opened the Beginning of next Summer, with a Play for the Benefit of the Bristol Infirmary'. The writer went on to add 'What a melancholy Prospect it must offer to every considerate Mind, to observe with what Facility Buildings of this Kind are erected, and at the same Time the Difficulty with which those set apart for religious Services are carried on'. This refers of course, to the long delay in finishing St Nicholas' Church, and reflects in a small way the considerable opposition that the enterprise met with from the more puritanical religious groups in Bristol.

The construction of the theatre was entrusted to Gilbert Davis, house-carpenter; William Foote, mason; and—Franklin, blacksmith, while the interior painting was executed by Michael Edkins, who appears to have decorated with equal facility such varied objects as coaches, scenery, porcelain and glassware. The work must have been well advanced by the Spring of 1765, for on 17th April of that year the structure was inspected by David Garrick, freshly returned from his tour of Europe. He set the seal of approval on the enterprise by pronouncing the building to be the most complete in Europe, and promised to write a prologue for its opening. The theatre was completed early in the Spring of 1766, having cost some £5,000 to build and equip, but now the proprietors had to face the opposition's threat to invoke the 'rogues and vagabonds' Act of 1757, if any theatrical performances were given. This threat was most artfully countered by billing the first performance, on 30th May 1766, as 'A Concert of Music and a Specimen of Rhetorick'. The building's use as a playhouse was not legalized until 1778, when a special Act of Parliament was obtained and the Royal Licence granted to George Daubeny, as the nominee of the proprietors. The Theatre Royal thus gained its name, and the Royal Arms of the Hanoverian period still appear above the proscenium.

The principal entrance to the theatre was contrived in the lower part of an old house in King Street, and this has been so much altered as to leave nothing of architectural or antiquarian interest. To the old house-front, with its jutted stories and crowning gable, was added a portico consisting of two widely-spaced Tuscan columns supporting an entablature, its cornice rising to form a triangular pediment in front, but this was destroyed to make way for the present tawdry facade.

The theatre proper is a rectangular building, measuring about 120 feet in length and 50 feet in width, with massive outer walls of rubble-stone, and a pitched and hipped timber roof covered with tile. Apart from the segmental wall between the auditorium and the circulation lobbies, and the rear-stage and dressing-room walls, almost the whole interior was constructed in wood. In its first state the auditorium contained a pit with a partially-raked floor, sunk a few feet below the level of the horseshoe-shaped first tier enclosing it. This tier was divided into the circle-and stage-boxes, and evidence of the partitioning still exists. Above was another tier of the same form, containing the gallery and side-boxes. The pit was approached by way of the passages below the arms of the first tier, and the upper tier was probably reached by staircases placed at each end of the ground-floor lobby. The fore-stage projected to the full width of the stage-boxes, framed then, as now, between two giant Corinthian pilasters. It is quite possible, but by no means certain, that two further bays on either side of the auditorium were divided by similar pilasters before the 1800 reconstruction. There was an inner proscenium, of which something still survives in a much altered and useless form, for the doors and balconies over them are now blocked by fire-resisting walls built to flank the proscenium. The ceiling linking the stage-boxes may have followed the same elliptical curve as the proscenium arch, but that over the body of the house was probably a flat and slightly-raked surface.

The auditorium (Plate 19a) was extensively altered in 1800, the original gallery being converted into further boxes, and a large gallery formed over it, while the flat-surfaced ceiling was pitched to accommodate this addition. The new interior is described by *Felix Farley* on 4th October 1800—'Nothing can exceed the elegance and beauty that the present state of the Theatre exhibits—The decorations and ornaments are in the best style of elegant simplicity—the house is a stone-colour, and the pannels a tender green, with gold mouldings and cornices; the columns that support the two rows of boxes are cabled with stone-colour and gold alternately, and have a light and beautiful effect; and the lower boxes are illuminated with a set of new lustres of exquisite taste in their construction, and the former branches whose places they occupy, are removed to the upper tier of boxes.'

Since this reconstruction the auditorium has received few physical changes, but the same cannot be said for the decorations, which are the legacy of all periods in the theatre's history. Thus, the Corinthian pilasters framing the stage-boxes must belong to the original scheme, although the acanthus-scrolls in the shaft panels might be later. The two orders of eight slender Doric columns supporting the upper tiers are certainly Georgian, but their cabled shafts suggest a later date than 1766. It seems most likely that the original shafts were refaced in 1800, when the middle columns of the upper order may have been introduced to carry the new gallery. The three ranges of box-fronts are also Georgian, being treated as simple pedestals—the Victorian overlay probably conceals the panelled dies—above an entablature. It is evident that the present ornament on the frieze of the middle entablature conceals a series of triglyphs, corresponding to the mutules that are interspaced with rosettes on the soffit of the cornice corona. The reference to silvering '90 rosets' in Edkins' account for 1785 proves that this entablature existed before that date. With regard to the plaster ornaments applied to the wooden ceiling of 1800, it seems probable that the surround to the centrepiece, the stars radiating therefrom, the acanthus-scroll panels, and the diaper borders are original work, and that the scrolled cartouches in each corner are later. In general, the Georgian work has been largely overlaid with Victorian gilt and gingerbread, which the present painting in dark green and gold has merely clothed with dull respectability. It may even be questioned whether this colouring is entirely faithful to the original scheme, for, whatever that might have been, there is Edkins' account of 1775 to show that he then charged the proprietors 12 guineas for 'Painting the Theatre Pea Green two Coats in Oil: Silvering, Lacquering, and Painting in Dead White all the Ornamental work.'

There is not the space in this work to attempt a description of the stage and its equipment. It must suffice to say that the old machinery, in its extent and completeness, is probably unsurpassed in this country, while mention must be made of the famous 'thunder-run' in the roof space over the auditorium ceiling.

MERCHANTS' HALL

The first Merchants' Hall to occupy the King Street site was the disused chapel of St Clement, which the Corporation had granted to the Society in 1493. A view in the top margin of Millerd's Plan of 1673 (Plate 1) shows the external appearance of this building, prior to its reconstruction in 1693, when the interior was wainscotted. Further improvements were made in 1701, but what must have amounted to a general rebuilding was begun in 1719. The Great Room and Withdrawing Room were finished in 1720, and shortly afterwards the front and King

Street elevations were rebuilt in dressed freestone. Barrett published a view of this exterior in his *History of Bristol*, wherein the building is described as being 'built of freestone, and consisting of two noble lofty rooms, forming the shape of an L'.

The engraving shows that the small entrance-court was enclosed by a wrought-iron railing, designed in the elaborate style of Tijou, with an armorial gate set between stone piers that were surmounted by carved figures of a Mermaid and Time, the supporters of the Merchants' Arms, while the iron overthrow had a galleon finial. The front was a charming Baroque design, with a lofty principal story of three bays, raised on a low ground-story and surmounted by a false attic. A broad flight of steps with wrought-iron railings led up to the main doorway, an arched opening placed in the middle bay between engaged Corinthian columns, and each side bay contained a tall rectangular window with a panelled apron. This story had quoined outer angles and finished with a simple entablature, broken forward over the columns and quoins. The attic stage was divided into three bays by panelled pilasters, each side bay finishing with an incurved coping and containing an inverted console motif buttressing the middle bay, where a richly carved representation of the Royal Arms was surmounted by a Baroque open-bedmould pediment. The pediment and outer angles were adorned with vases and ball-finials. The long elevation towards King Street was horizontally divided to correspond with the front, and each story contained a range of six windows. The parapet was adorned with a niched central feature.

Another elaborate reconstruction was begun in 1783 under Thomas Paty's direction. This work, which cost some £6,000 to finish, included the complete refacing of the exterior, and the partial remodelling of the interior. Except for the false attic that was added to the King Street elevation about 1880, few changes were made to Paty's remodelled building which, most unfortunately, was completely destroyed during the late war.

Paty recased the exterior in the elegant Classical style of the late eighteenth century, retaining the general form and fenestral pattern of the original building (Plate 18b). The old front was replaced by a purely decorative frontispiece, with a central feature projecting slightly forward from narrow flanking bays with quoined angles. The external staircase, with new railings having scrolled panels alternating with straight balusters, rose to the entrance doorway. This was recessed in an arched opening formed by rusticated piers with moulded imposts, from which rose a moulded archivolt broken by a triple-key. From each pier projected an engaged Doric three-quarter column, bearing an entablature-block of which the cornice only continued above the doorway. In each flanking bay was an arch-headed niche containing a vase, and over it a sunk square panel. Above the doorcase was a platband, broken slightly forward in the centre below an arch-headed niche containing a pedestal with a draped bust of George the Third. The lines of the platband were continued across each flanking bay by a cornice, above which was an attic stage containing a moulded sunk panel. The modillioned main cornice was surmounted by a blocking-course and, in the centre, a panelled pedestal flanked by scrolled consoles. The King Street elevation contained two tiers of six windows, twin casements below and unequally-divided sashes above. The openings of both tiers were framed by moulded architraves rising from plain sills, and a cornice stringcourse was continued above each story, the upper one being surmounted by a parapet with sunk panels placed in correspondence with the windows. The coping rose in quadrant curves at each end to meet the quoined and corniced angle-piers.

Matthews' Guide of 1794 contains the following brief description of the interior—'The access to the principal door is by a flight of steps. . . . The lobby leads into a lofty saloon, decorated (at the upper end) with a large mirror in a richly gilded frame, and with two glass lustres, suspended from the ceiling by gilded chains. On the North of the saloon is the opening into the principal room. These may be occasionally separated by folding glass doors fitted to a lofty arch embellished with carving. This room has (suspended by gilded chains) four beautiful glass lustres, which, with the others, cost £550. Over the chimney the merchants arms with supporters are carved and blazoned. There is here a half-length painting of Edward Colston Esq, said to have been a strong resemblance; from this picture Rysbrack modelled a likeness of his face for his statue in All Saints-church.'

This Great Room was 48 feet in length, 26 feet 9 inches wide, and 23 feet high. The walls were wainscotted with painted deal to their full height, in a scheme of two stages. The first, an unusually high dado, was simply treated with large rectangular fielded panels, and finished with a simple cornice. The upper stage was much smaller in scale and more complex in design, the panels being arranged in three tiers, a small one above and below a tall one, between Ionic pilasters with panelled shafts. This stage finished with an entablature, its frieze adorned by a key-fret and its cornice-mouldings enriched in the conventional manner. Above the cornice a small plain cove rose to meet the flat ceiling, which was unornamented save for the small acanthus roses from whence hung the chandeliers. The fire-place in the centre of the long west side had a chimney-piece surmounted by an elaborately carved representation of the Merchants' Arms, flanked by fluted three-quarter columns of the Corinthian order, rising from carved consoles and supporting a segmental open-bedmould pediment. This motif was repeated with greater splendour in the elaborate doorcase that dominated the south wall. Here the double-door was recessed in a segmental-arched opening, having a panelled soffit and reveals, and a bolection-moulded architrave. The opening was flanked by paired Corinthian pilasters with fluted shafts, rising from panelled pedestals and supporting entablature-blocks. These were linked by the segmental open-bedmould pediment that followed the curve of the arch, over which it was broken back and the tympanum filled with acanthus-scrolling centering on a key-block carved with two cherubs'-heads.

THE CLIFTON HOTEL AND ASSEMBLY ROOMS

The first proposal to build an assembly house in Clifton was made during 1792, but the tontine subscription then opened failed to find the necessary support. A new scheme was offered to the public early in the nineteenth century, by John Lewis Auriol, and on 17th May 1806 *Felix Farley* reported that 'yesterday a meeting of the nobility and gentry of Clifton took place at Sion Hill Pump-Room, for the purpose of considering a proposal for building a New Assembly Room, with Card Rooms, etc. Two plans were submitted, one for erection on Sion Hill, and the other on the Mall'. The latter site was fixed on and events then moved with rapidity, for, on 28th June 1806, the same journal was able to state that 'the Foundations for a new Assembly Room is already begun at the East end of the Mall at Clifton; the design, by Mr Greenway, architect, of this city, does great credit to his abilities, and will be a handsome public building, and will do honour to the liberality and taste of those who have patronised and subscribed to it'. The structure was completely roofed in by January 1809, but during the following May bankruptcy overtook the Greenways, and, as they became involved in a dispute with Auriol, the unfinished structure was offered for sale or letting. The interior cannot, therefore, be ascribed with certainty to Francis Howard Greenway, for the work was completed under the direction of 'Mr Kay' (probably Joseph Kay) who was named as the architect in all notices of the building, which was opened with great ceremony on 21st November 1811. *The Guide to all the Watering Places*, published about 1812, describes the building as 'a spacious and elegant hotel and assembly-rooms'. These last comprised 'a noble reception saloon, and tea-room, a ball-room highly finished and decorated, and a handsome card-room, with convenient lobbies, a billiard-room, &c'. The hotel combined 'every accommodation for both families and individuals, even to sets of apartments, with drawing-rooms, a coffee-room;—a shop for pastry and confectionary, with an adjoining room for soups, fruits, and ices; —hot, cold, and vapour-baths'. The establishment prospered while Clifton flourished as a resort, but becoming outmoded, the Assembly Rooms were adapted in 1855 to form the Clifton Club, while the rest of the building was converted into houses and shops.

The Mall elevation, which is wholly built in dressed free-stone, consists of a central block flanked by recessed wings (Plate 19b, Figure 16). The central block, which is the least altered part of the design, is adorned with an engaged colonnade of six Ionic plain-shafted columns, rising from a low basement of rusticated arches, and embracing two stories. The order consists of half-columns between the three-quarter columns that serve a return bay at each end. The intercolumniations are equal in width and each contains one first- and one second-story window. Those of the first-story have been altered but were plain originally, like those above them. The columns support the appropriate architrave, but in place of the orthodox frieze there

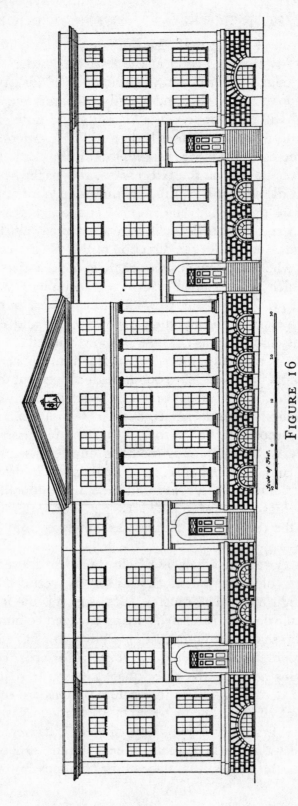

FIGURE 16

The Clifton Hotel and Assembly Rooms
Elevation towards The Mall

is an attic-story with five windows centred over those below. This attic is surmounted by a triangular pediment with a carved shield in its tympanum. Recesses break each wing into two projecting bays that are equal in width but differ in plan. That nearest the centre is rectangular and has two windows to each story, while the lateral bay is segmental and three windows wide. These wings are of equal height with the central block, and the rectangular windows of the three stories were placed without architraves in a plain wall face that terminates with a frieze, cornice and parapet. The basement and first-story have been greatly altered, but the original low basement was arcaded to correspond with that of the central block, while between each bay was a lofty archway opening to a porch with steps rising to doorways in the first-story.

The rooms were planned as an open suite, the centrally-placed ball-room having an ante-recess in the middle of each long side. One opened through a glazed screen to the card-room overlooking The Mall, while the other—now built up—led into the tea-room. The decorations were in a restrained Grecian style and the plasterwork has generally survived, but changing taste has left its dingy evidence to obscure the original colouring, which was carried out by Cornelius Dixon. The most elaborate scheme is that of the ball-room, where engaged half-columns and pilasters divide the walls into bays and support a continuous entablature. A simple Corinthian order is used, one with moulded bases, plain shafts, and capitals formed of acanthus and water-leaves modelled on those of the Tower-of-the-Winds portico. These columns and pilasters were originally marbled with Siena shafts and statuary bases and capitals. Each long wall is formed into three bays by two widely-spaced pairs of half-columns, each pair framing an arch-headed niche and supporting a projection of the entablature. The wide middle bay contains the arch-headed opening to the ante-recess, and in each end bay is a doorway, with a mahogany double-door framed in a moulded architrave with a fluted frieze and cornice resting on consoles. The pilasters divide each end wall into three equal bays, each lateral one containing a shallow arch-headed recess, while in the centre is a mirror of the same form placed above a chimney-piece with console-jambs. From above the entablature rises a deep cove that merges into the flat ceiling. Groined intersections break into this cove in the centre of each short side, and above the entablature projections on the long sides. A large saucer-domed skylight rises from a moulded surround in the ceiling's centre, and the adjacent surfaces were originally painted to simulate coffers with modelled rosettes.

THE COMMERCIAL ROOMS

For some unfathomable reason, Wood's splendid Exchange never found much favour with the Bristol merchants, who continued to meet elsewhere to transact their business, generally in the coffee-houses. Therefore, when a scheme was announced in 1808 for building a new establishment, similar to Lloyd's of London, the proposal was warmly supported. A sum of £10,000 was quickly subscribed, and a site in Corn Street secured. The promotors invited designs from several architects, and selected that submitted by Charles Augustus Busby, then practising in London. On 19th March 1810 the foundation-stone was laid by George Dyer, amid great ceremony. The Commercial Coffee-House, as the building was first designated, opened during September 1811, having cost some £17,000 to complete and furnish.

The site lies on the north-west side of Corn Street, to which the building has a frontage of about 40 feet. As originally planned there were two doors leading from the portico into the great room, which is about 60 feet long and 40 feet wide. At its far end is the buffet, placed centrally between two doors opening to smaller rooms, one allotted for a reading-room and the other for a committee-room.

The Corn Street front is a charming Græco-Roman design, the single lofty story consisting of a tetrastyle portico placed between narrow wings (Plate 20a). The four Ionic plain-shafted columns are equally spaced and the lateral columns are engaged by the wing walls. A triangular pediment surmounts the entablature, this latter being returned on each side of the portico and carried across the wings, each of which contains a rectangular window. This is dressed with a moulded architrave, based on a moulded sill and surmounted by a plain frieze and triangular pediment. Below each window is a panelled apron, flanked by consoles supporting the sill, which continues as a moulding across the wings and inside the portico, where two doors are placed to correspond with the lateral intercolumniations. Each wing is finished with a blocking-course, broken by a plinth bearing a statue. That on the left side represents Commerce; on the right is Navigation; and on a pedestal rising from the pediment's apex stands Bristol, holding a trident and supporting a shield. These figures were carved by J. G. Bubb, a sculptor employed by John Nash. Bubb also executed the long relief panel placed over the doors inside the portico, where Neptune is represented introducing the four Quarters of the World to Britannia. Behind this front rises a plain attic-story, finished with a cornice and blocking-course.

The well-proportioned great room has a simple scheme of decoration, with an attractive ceiling that shows a strong Soanic influence. The walls are plastered to a plain surface and narrow raised mouldings form a series of tall rectangular panels on the side walls, those on the end walls being varied in height and width to suit their respective positions. In the centre of the far end wall is the buffet, constructed of mahogany, with four Ionic pilasters supporting an entablature, and in the long panel above this is a wind-dial. The walls are finished with a simple cornice, from which a plain cove rises to the flat ceiling. This is divided into three compartments by a wide band with fretted panels of scrollwork. The central compartment opens into the square first stage of the elegant lantern-light (Plate 20b). Each face of this stage is formed into a segmental lunette by the spandrels that rise from each corner to effect the transition from square to circle. The spandrels and lunettes alike are adorned with raised mouldings that form panels within marginal surrounds. The upper stage is circular on plan and forms a trellised clerestory, punctuated at equal intervals by the twelve caryatides supporting the shallow saucer-dome. This is also panelled in four quarters, surrounding a central boss of stiff acanthus-leaves.

THE COUNCIL HOUSE

In 1788 the Corporation of Bristol obtained an Act of Parliament for the purpose of 'widening and rendering commodious a certain street called Broad Street . . . and for enlarging the Council House and Guildhall of the said City'. Apparently, it was not until about 1820 that any real effort was made to implement the provisions of this Act, for the earliest design for rebuilding the Council House is one dated 1821, prepared by Henry Hake Seward. His design evidently failed to find favour, and in 1822 the Corporation asked Robert Smirke for plans of a building to replace the old Council House and Guildhall. This plan was then set aside in favour of a proposal to build in the centre of Queen Square, but estimates proved this scheme to be too costly for adoption. Towards the close of 1822 the Corporation decided to rebuild only the Council House, and by including the sites of the next two houses in Corn Street, and that of St Ewen's Church, sufficient ground was provided for effecting the necessary street-widening. Early in 1823 James Foster submitted a plan with alternative elevations, but without success, for Smirke was again asked to provide a design. His plan, which is dated 24th May 1823, was approved, and he was instructed to prepare detailed drawings and specifications. In the following June the Corporation took over the Mulberry Tree Tavern for temporary offices, so that the old buildings could be demolished.

Smirke's plans and specifications were formally approved, with some small amendments, on 29th October 1823, and shortly afterwards a clerk of works, Thomas Brigden, was appointed. The first contracts were signed on 9th February 1824, with Joseph Phillips, mason; William Stock, carpenter; Charles Whiting, plumber; Joseph Grinden, slater; and Underwood & Co., smiths. Further contracts were placed on 28th April following, with J. Crispin, joiner; Joseph Grinden, plasterer; William Edkins, painter; and Henry Payne, glazier.

Smirke and the principal contractors attended the ceremony on 12th May 1824, when the Mayor, J. Barrow, laid the foundation-stone, amid every expression of civic pomp. The work progressed rapidly and the shell of the building was finished towards the end of 1825. The citizens were quick to notice that the Corn Street front was being erected out of alignment with the existing buildings in that street, and this gave rise to an epigrammatic verse, directed against the unpopular close Corporation:

> *Why yonder Mansion stands awry,*
> *Does Bristol wondering seek—*
> *Like to its Councils is its Site,*
> *Oblique—Oblique—Oblique!*

The new Council House was completed by the close of 1827, and opened for business on 12th February 1828, the cost of the whole undertaking having amounted to some £16,000.

Like all of Smirke's buildings, this one is splendidly constructed and the planning is generally good, the faults, such as the poor lighting of the old courtroom, arising out of the site conditions. The entrance is placed in the centre of the Corn Street front, and approached by a short flight of steps. The double-door opens to a wide hall that extends to a light-court at the back of the building. On each side of this hall is a suite of offices, that on the inside containing the old courtroom. At the end of the entrance-hall is the staircase, rising to a half-landing and then returning to finish at the first-floor, where it opens to a transverse ante-room. This serves a suite of offices overlooking Broad Street, the town-clerk's office and two committee-rooms overlooking Corn Street, and the former council-chamber in the north-west angle.

It has been truly said of Smirke that he never feared to repeat himself, and this is confirmed by the obvious fact that the Council House elevations are largely a restatement of the design already used by him for the Trafalgar Square front of the Union Club and College of Physicians building, erected in 1824–5. The Bristol building has the same Ionic order with its ponderous entablature, the same system of emphasis and recession is employed, and the same solecisms, such as the Italian balustrade, appear in this typical Greek Revival design.

The Corn Street front (Plate 21a) is adorned with an Ionic order, consisting of two half-columns and six antæ, embracing the two lofty stories. The antæ are spaced to form a central feature of three bays, and a slightly recessed bay at either end. The wall face in the wide middle bay is set back to admit the two engaged half-columns that flank the entrance and pair with the adjacent antæ. The entrance-doors are recessed in an opening formed by smaller antæ and an entablature that has a carved frieze of anthemia and pateræ. This frieze repeats in each bay to underline the second-story windows, their rectangular openings being dressed with moulded architraves having ears and sides that taper to a slightly increased width at the base. This same treatment is accorded to each lateral window of the ground-story, but that on either side of the entrance has an

[137]

unbroken architrave and a projecting cornice supported by consoles. The deep and massive main entablature has a dentilled cornice, and is broken back over each end bay where a balustrade surmounts it. Above the central feature is a pedestal attic, the die of each side bay containing an oblong panel, one carved with the Royal Arms, and the other with those of Bristol. These were executed by Thomas Clark, sculptor, who was paid £160 6s. 4d. for his work. The central bay of this attic is deeply recessed to accommodate a statue of Justice, carved by Edward Hodges Baily, R.A., a Bristol sculptor and pupil of Flaxman. Baily was paid £210 for this figure, which, being armed with a sword and without a balance, gave rise to further witticisms directed against the Corporation. The return elevation to Broad Street is a simple composition with the emphasis placed at either end. The middle section is three windows wide, and it stands slightly recessed between narrow features flanked by antæ and containing one window of each story. The fenestral dressing is similar to that of the Corn Street front, the ornamental frieze is continued between the antæ, and a balustrade surmounts the entablature.

Internally, the most interesting features are the staircase and the former council-chamber. The staircase itself is of a simple form, but the treads and landings are plated with brass, elaborately cut to Grecian patterns and inlaid with a red composition, while the balustrade is formed of brass Doric columns, placed one to each tread, supporting a massive mahogany handrail. By contrast the walls are quite plain, but the opening between the first-floor landing and the long ante-room is flanked by Doric columns, with respondent antæ, carrying the appropriate entablature. This is continued round the walls of the staircase-hall, below a segmental-arched ceiling of rectangular coffers. The former council-chamber is a splendid room, measuring 38 feet in length by 22 feet in width, and 20 feet in height. Each long side wall is divided by pilasters into three bays, the width of the middle one being equal to that of the room. The pilasters have fluted shafts and capitals of an original design, perhaps based on those of the Lysicrates monument. The wide middle bay is simply decorated with mouldings that enclose three tall rectangular panels, the central one being placed above a black marble chimney-piece, with Doric columns and an entablature. Each side bay contains an arch motif, the half-pilasters bearing an enriched impost that is continued below the moulded archivolt. The entrance is centred in the south-east end wall, the panelled and enriched double-door being framed in a moulded architrave, surmounted by a frieze and cornice supported by consoles. All the moulded members are enriched with conventional ornaments, and the Royal Arms are modelled in high relief over the cornice. On each side of the doorcase is a tall rectangular panel, and the opposite wall contains three similar panels. Beams cross from the pilasters on the side walls and divide the ceiling into three compartments. The narrow side ones are again divided by lesser beams into three sub-compartments, each square in form and containing sixteen square coffers. The large central compartment encloses a circular band of octagonal coffers, surrounding a clerestoried lantern that has a modelled ceiling. The whole of this ceiling is richly adorned with conventional Grecian ornaments, the soffits of the main beams having panels of banded laurel-leaves, while the secondary beams are enriched with frets (Plate 21b).

Smirke's building is adjoined on its south-west side by an extension, also in the Greek Revival style, built to contain a more suitable courtroom than was provided in the main building. The design for this extension was prepared by R. S. Pope and George Dymond, and approved by the Corporation on 31st October 1828, the building being completed in November 1829 at a cost of £1,400.

DOMESTIC BUILDINGS

QUEEN SQUARE

The creation of a suburb in the Marsh area began with the rather piecemeal formation of King Street, laid out against the south side of the old city wall, and following its irregular line. Many of the original buildings in this street were erected during the period 1650–1665, and were wholly medieval in character. Millerd's plan of Bristol, dated 1673, gives a clear picture of the Marsh at that time, showing that, in addition to King Street, some building had taken place alongside the 'Wood Key', now Narrow Quay. The rest of the area was an open space, partly laid out for recreational purposes and partly let as grazing land. A proposal to build on this ground was brought before the Common Council on 1st March 1669, when the following resolution was recorded:

'Upon consideracon of the Citties engagements and the better discharging of debts, and considerable sums owing; It is this day ordered and agreed that it shalbe referred to the Mayor and Surveyor of the Citty lands to view the void ground round about the Marsh and to consider what number of feete may be conveniently allowed, and to lease the same out for the uniforme building of houses there, and to lett and sett the said ground to any person or persons that will covenant to build there and make a good Key of firme stone towards the water leaving soe many foote of ground in length and breadth as the Mayor and Surveyors shall think fitt towards the water for comon and publick use, for halling of vessells, and discharging of goods, in all which Leases there shalbe granted for many foote of ground as the Mayor and Surveyors shall thinke fitt referring for every foote in the front twelve pence in the least, and the terms to be granted to be Ninety Nine years if ffive lives live soe long . . . and if the Mayor and Surveyors shall see fitt the better to encourage

[140]

the building they shall have liberty to give the nominacon of the lives at three years end after the bargaine made.'

This proposal appears to have been left in abeyance for some thirty years, perhaps through fear of arousing the antagonism of the citizens, who would certainly have opposed any scheme which might deprive them of enjoyed amenities. Whatever the reason, the matter was not revived officially until the Council's meeting on 23rd October 1699, when 'Mr Mayor acquainted the house that Dr Reede (The Rev. John Reade, D.D., then Vicar of St St Nicholas') has made a Proposall to build an house on the Marsh and he heares severall other Cittizens are willinge to build on the Marsh. Question was put whether tenures and estates should be granted to persons to build houses on the Marsh. The Mayor and Aldermen Mr Yate Mr Wallis the two sheriffes Mr Towne Clerke and the chamberlain Are Appointed to A Committee to treate with persons thereon seaven of which the mayor being one are sufficient to make Contracts: the same Committee are to take care of Convenient places and methods to lay the soyle and Rubble of the Citty order'd accordeing'.

As the first lease was granted within a few days, it is clear that plans were already evolved, at least in general principles, for building rows of houses grouped round a great public square, probably after the pattern of Lincoln's Inn Fields, a scheme that would presumably have been acceptable to all the interested parties. The central area, measuring some 550 feet square, was planned to be entered by three lanes on its east and west sides, one in the middle of the south side, and two on the north, the positions of these last being largely decided by their being continuations of existing communications. The buildings were thus to be grouped into blocks, two on each side, of which those on the north and south extended beyond the confines of the square. No particular effort appears to have been made to ensure symmetry by deciding beforehand the positions of the single- and double-fronted houses, or by parcelling the ground into regular units.

The Bargain Book for the period 1694–1712 contains particulars of most of the original leases, and records the terms under which Dr Reade was granted, on 27th October 1699, for the term of five lives, his lease of 'so much of the said void ground of the said Marsh . . . as shall contein fforty foot in breadth inwards and to runn of the same breadth down towards the River

Avon in length about One hundred & five foot as it is now layd out allotted and marked by the Citys Officers and workemen . . . under the yearly rent of fforty shillings, being one shilling for each ffoot in front to be payable quarterly cleer of all Taxes and deductions whatsoever to commence from Michaelmas One thousand Seaven hundred. The which ground the said Dr Read hereby agrees to build upon in manner following (vizt.). To have a Court enclosed with a Brickwall the whole breadth of the front of his house of Tenn foot in Breadth from the outside of the Court wall to ye Outside of ye housewall To build the whole front of ye house with Brick ye Quoines of which with ffreestone which is to extend to ye full breadth of the said ground. The whole house to be built of the heighth of fforty foot and all except the front to be built with stone the first and second stories to be eleaven foot in heighth including beams and joists The third story to be tenn foot in heighth and the ffourth eight foot with canterliners also montdellians under the tile over the walls so that the whole front on the inside of the house be in heighth fforty compleat foot That he enclose the whole ground except the said front with Stone wall and have no building towards the River but what shal be for the necessary use of . . . the house such as Back Kitchen warehouses Outhouses Stables and Coach-house but no Tenement to be lett out to any sort of Tenants particularly no Smiths Shopp Brewhouse nor to any Tallow-Chandler or to any other Tradesmen who by noyse danger of ffire or ill smells shall disturbe or annoy any of the Inhabitants who shall build neer it for Compleating which building he is allowed two years from Christmas next and he is at his own charge to Pitch Twelve foot in depth before the front and Tenn foot in depth behind the said house and to continue it Repaired and Amended'.

These conditions governing the heights and number of stories will be found to differ from those under which the houses surrounding Queen Square were built, for although Reade's house was described as 'scituate in the East Corner of that East Row', it stood, not facing the square, but in the south-east angle of Queen Charlotte Street and Little King Street. The second lease to be granted, dated 20th November 1699, was to Francis Fowles, a joiner, who built a house adjoining the south side of Dr Reade's, with a frontage of 20 feet to the East Row.

Most of the void ground bordering the square was leased out and built upon within the period 1700–18, and the Bargain Books record that plots of various sizes were allotted to such prominent citizens as James Hollidge, John Hobbs, Stephen Peloquin, John and Nathaniel Day, Abraham Elton, and Woodes Rogers, all of whom built houses for their own occupation or for letting. House-carpenters such as John Price and Peter Wilkins, both of whom built houses here on their own account, were probably responsible for the design as well as for the construction of the buildings.

The lease granted on 8th December 1702 to Woodes Rogers, the famous mariner, is typical, and gives details of conditions which were imposed upon builders to secure some measure of uniformity in the appearance of the house-fronts, while other restrictive clauses were intended to govern the standard of tenancies. This lease is also the first to make reference to Queen Square, which, hitherto described as 'the Marsh' or 'the Square in the Marsh', had just been named in commemoration of Queen Anne's visit to Bristol on 3rd September 1702.

Woodes Rogers was granted a 52 years lease of a plot with a frontage of 42 feet in the South Row, and an average depth of 118 feet. A peppercorn rental was demanded for the first two years, and during this period the lessee undertook to build 'a substantiall Mansion house' or stand to forfeit £100. For the remaining term a yearly rent of 42 shillings was charged, on the basis of one shilling per foot of frontage. The building conditions demanded that a court, 10 feet deep and enclosed by a brick wall, was to be formed before the house, the front of which was to extend the full width of the site. This front was 'to be made with brick the Quoines with ffreestone', and the top of the wall was to finish with a wooden modillioned eaves-cornice ('Mundilions'). All other walls in the building were to be of stonework; the timber, ironwork, etc., used in construction were to be substantial; and the windows in the roof were to be lucarnes ('Lutharne Lights'). Internally, the first story was to be 11 feet high, the second 10 feet, and the third 9 feet, all clear heights excluding beams and joists. In general, the lessee was enjoined to 'build or erect noe meane sordid buildings to bee receptacles for poor people etc'.

The last leases, relating to some vacant ground remaining in the North Row, were granted during 1725, and all building in the square seems to have been finished by the end of 1727. It was perhaps within a year or so of that date when William Half-penny drew the *North Prospect* which was published separately as well as included in his *Perspective made Easy*, an undated work generally believed to have been first published in 1731. This view embraces the whole of the north side, together with the north blocks of the east and west sides, and in spite of short-comings as an example of perspective drawing, and some obvious lapses in scale, the engraving has great value as a record of those buildings on the north and west sides which were destroyed in the riots of October 1831, and of other houses since altered or demolished (Figure 17).

The houses facing the square were uniformly three stories high with garrets in the roof, and while the number of windows to each upper story necessarily varied with the frontage width, the majority of the single-fronted houses had three, and the double-fronted had five. The elevations were built of red brick dressed with freestone, used not only for the quoins expressing the party-walls, and the stringcourses defining each upper floor level, but for such embellishments as keystones, doorcases, and the en-gaged columns and pediments which served to adorn some of the more ostentatious mansions erected between 1709 and 1711. Some of the larger houses had shallow porches, but most of the doorways were sheltered by hoods of various designs. The sash-boxes were exposed and set almost flush with the building face, in plain openings with flat arches of gauged brickwork. The pantiled roofs were pitched at about 45 degrees above a modil-lioned eaves-cornice of wood, which was carried across the fronts immediately above the arches of the third-story windows, its continuity broken only by the lofty fronts of the Customs House and the Elton mansion in the East Row. The leases of even so late a date as 1725 still specify the use of these 'mundi-lions', although they had been forbidden by the Corporation in the leases relating to Orchard Street, granted during 1717.

Halfpenny shows that the square was dominated by the Customs House, placed almost in the middle of the North Row and adjoined on the east by a range of five single- and two double-fronted houses. The west block continued towards Prince Street and contained eight houses of varying width facing the

FIGURE 17

'Ye North Prospect of Queen Square in ye City of Bristol'
Engraving after a drawing by William Halfpenny

This view, embracing the whole of the north side together with the north blocks of the east and west sides, shows the general uniformity of Queen Square as originally built. The Customs House, just off-centre in the north side, and the Elton mansion, seen on the extreme right, form the only conspicuous breaks in the continuous lines of the three-storied house fronts built of red brick dressed with freestone.

K

square. The north block of the West Row is shown to have been a uniform range with one single- and five double-fronted houses. The East Row extended into what is now Queen Charlotte Street, where the four-storied houses built by Dr Reade and others can be clearly seen. The north block facing the square contained three single- and four double-fronted houses.

The Customs House was erected during 1710–11 at the expense of the Corporation, who then leased the building to the Crown for a yearly rental of £120. The Audit-Books record that sums amounting to £2,525 were paid to John Hollidge 'for materials and labour'. This Customs House was a three-story building of brick, with stone dressings and a wooden modillioned cornice, similar to the houses in the square but superior to them in dimensions and scale. From the ground-story there projected an Ionic colonnade of seven bays, the three middle ones being wider than those on either side. The brick face of the two-storied upper part was decorated with stone quoins, used like pilasters to form one wide bay between two narrow ones, the former three windows wide and the latter two. The windows were spaced to centre over the bays of the colonnade; the usual intermediate stringcourse was omitted, and the middle window of the upper tier was replaced by superimposed panels of stone, one carved with the Royal Arms and the other a sundial.

The central space was laid out in a formal style towards the close of 1716, when lime-trees were planted to form a surround of three close rows, and transverse avenues which divided the greensward into quarters, these being crossed diagonally by gravel paths. The square received its finest ornament during August 1742, when the bronze equestrian statue of William the Third, standing on a simple stone pedestal, was erected in the central position. The Whigs of Bristol, following those of other important cities, raised funds for this memorial, the Corporation contributing £500 and the Merchants' Society £300. Rysbrack and Scheemaker were invited to submit models, and that of the former was chosen. Scheemaker received £50 for his trouble, and Rysbrack was paid £1,800 for producing what must surely be one of the finest works of its class.

Queen Square must have presented a reasonably coherent appearance when it was finished in 1727, although it was never a finely co-ordinated building scheme like its more famous namesake in Bath, where the formal beauty of the architecture expressed the ideals and personality only of its architect-promotor. Nevertheless, the Bristol square originally held great charm and interest, its houses reflecting something of the character of their prosperous burgess inhabitants, and its subsequent spoliation is one of the tragedies of Bristol's architectural history. The destruction of all the original buildings on the north side and most of those on the west, during the 1831 riots, was to some extent compensated by the refinement and uniformity of Henry Rumley's Grecian terrace-houses that replaced them in 1833. The inroads of commercialism have had far more serious effects, for fine houses were destroyed to make way for hybrid monstrosities, while others have been mutilated. The ruin has now been completed by the ruthless manner in which the square has been cut into two triangular halves, by driving a main traffic road across it from the south-east corner to the north-west.

Fewer than one-third of the original houses survive at the present time, and most of these have been considerably altered, at least externally. Features of interest remain, such as the stone shell-hoods at Nos 27 and 28 in the South Row and at No. 55 in the West Row, and there is an unusual and charming use made of stone shell-headed shallow niches in place of the customary quoins to mark the party-wall between Nos 23 and 24, in the East Row. This side also has a well-restored house in No. 17, where the first-floor windows are adorned with pediments. Nos 16 and 22 have imposing stone fronts of later dates, but the former has been deprived of its most interesting feature, an elaborate porch of Doric columns broken with icicle-work blocks, supporting an enriched entablature and a triangular pediment also dripping with icicles (Plate 55a). The original appearance of No. 16 can be studied in Halfpenny's view, where it appears on the extreme right. This house, perhaps the largest and finest in the square, was built between 1709 and 1711 for Abraham Elton, and it was perhaps on account of his elevation to a baronetcy that he caused his house to be remodelled and refronted.

Some of the most interesting and least altered houses are in the South Row (Plate 23a). Although the middle house has been refaced, Nos 36, 37 and 38 form a group of double-fronted houses built about 1703 which retain many original features, such as the long and short stone quoins defining the party-walls; the moulded stringcourses at each floor level; and the wooden modillioned eaves-cornice extending unbroken across all the fronts. The doorcases and window-sashes are, of course, later in date, but the sash-boxes faced with bolection-moulded architraves are original.

FIGURE 18
No. 29 Queen Square. Elevation

The most remarkable of the surviving houses is No. 29, built between 1709 and 1711 for Nathaniel Day, to whom a lease was granted on 25th August 1709, for a plot of ground with a frontage of 44 feet in the South Row, and a depth of 118 feet. The front of this house is built of red brick laid in the customary Flemish bond, and tied in with its neighbours

[148]

by nine-inch stone quoins with chamfered arrises, laid in long and short courses alternately (Plate 23b, Figure 18). The ground-story contains a centrally-placed doorway, which has been altered, and two windows on either side, the fenestral pattern of the two upper stories being similar. The exposed sash-boxes are faced with architrave-mouldings and set almost flush with the building face, in window openings that have flat arches of gauged brickwork with stone keys carved into a variety of grotesque masks. The wooden modillioned eaves-cornice is almost identical with other examples in the square. Thus far the description might be applied to many houses built about this time, but here the builder has chosen to add, in a rather illiterate fashion, ornaments drawn from the Classical repertory. Stone pediments, arranged in the usual sequence of the segmental form alternating with the triangular, are placed above the ground- and first-floor window arches, and engaged columns of the Roman Doric, Ionic and Corinthian orders, superimposed in that relation to the three stories, are used to divide the front into three bays, one narrow between two wide. The pedestals are omitted, and while the Doric and Ionic columns are given their appropriate entablatures, the Corinthian has only its architrave. Scrolled trusses take the place of the Doric entablatures on either side of the doorway, and support a flat stone hood which has a panelled soffit. The fore-court was enclosed by fine railings and an elaborate gate set between richly carved stone piers, all work of about 1750, but the wrought-ironwork has gone and the piers have been truncated.

The plan of No. 29 follows the usual arrangement for houses of this type and period, wherein a wide entrance-hall leads through an elliptical-headed archway into a spacious stair-hall, with the stairs ascending in three easy flights to the next floor. On each side of these halls is a front and back room, the latter leading into a small closet. While the interior is fairly well preserved, and contains a quantity of its original wainscotting and a fine staircase with a railing of turned balusters, it is in no ways remarkable.

ST JAMES'S SQUARE

This is the smallest of the several squares that were formed in

St James's Parish during the eighteenth century, and the earliest in date. Latimer follows Evans in stating that the ground was laid out for building about 1707 and that the houses were finished by 1716, and the evidence of style appears to confirm these dates. The success of Queen Square probably inspired its building, which was promoted by private enterprise.

The square forms an area measuring approximately 140 feet north to south, and 120 feet east to west, entered axially on its south side by an avenue from Milk Street, and by a footway connecting the mews in the north-west angle with St James's Barton. Rocque's plan shows a planted enclosure, but for centuries the area has been cobbled and had at its centre a stone obelisk, raised on a pedestal and bearing a cluster of lamps. The houses closely resemble the contemporaneous ones in Queen Square, having three-storied fronts of uniform height, built of red brick dressed with freestone, finished with a modillioned cornice of wood, and surmounted by a steeply-pitched roof containing a garret-story. The varied disposition of single- and double-fronted houses precluded the imposition of a completely balanced architectural scheme, but the square possessed a considerable degree of homogeneity which suggested that here, as in Queen Square, the builders worked under restrictive covenants governing the general design and construction of the houses, while allowing some latitude in matters of decorative detail.

Despite the conversion of most of its houses into business or club premises, St James's Square preserved its early eighteenth-century character until the 1920s, but thereafter its disintegration was rapid. During the late war more than half the total of houses, including the finest and least spoiled, was destroyed, and only the mutilated and disfigured ranges on the north and east sides remain.

The destroyed west row consisted of three double-fronted houses, Nos 3 to 5, with uniformly designed fronts, each five windows wide (Plate 24a). Pilasters of channel-jointed stones marked the party-walls and divided each front into three bays, one narrow between two wide. Stone was used also for the scalloped shell-hoods of semi-elliptical form, placed on carved and scrolled trusses to shelter the centrally-placed doorways; for the moulded stringcourses defining the two upper floor levels; and for the small keystones to the flat-arched heads of gauged brickwork over the windows. Door-frames and sash-boxes were faced with bolection-moulded architraves of wood, and the same material was used for the crowning modillioned cornice.

The south side contained two single-houses, Nos 1 and 2, on the west of the entering avenue, and a double-house, No. 16, on the east (Plate 24b). Their fronts were treated in a generally similar manner to those on the west side, except that the vertical demarcations were formed of alternately long and short stones.

The surviving north row consists of two double-houses, Nos 6 and 7, and two single-houses, Nos 8 and 9, the last being of later date and less interest than the others. These fronts have suffered greatly in appearance by the partial removal of the crowning cornice, and by the brickwork having been rendered and generally defaced by painted signs. The variations that occur

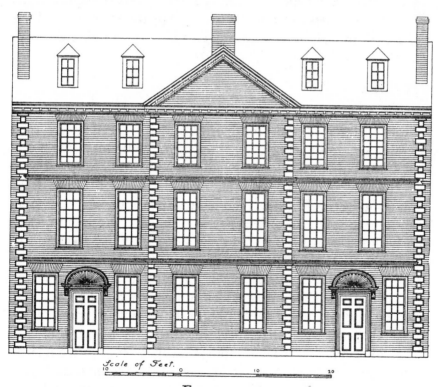

Scale of Feet.

FIGURE 19

St. James's Square
Elevation of two houses forming the central feature of the east side

[151]

in the design and materials of the door-hoods, and in the treatment of window-arches and stringcourse profiles of the different houses, suggest that more than one builder was concerned with their erection. The same is probably true of the six single-fronted houses forming the east row, where only Nos 10 to 13 remain. These three-windows-wide fronts were designed in general accordance with the rest of the square, and the chief interest lies in the treatment of the two middle houses, Nos 12 and 13, where a slight break forward in the building face is defined by long and short quoins, forming a central feature of somewhat gauche design, two windows wide and originally surmounted by a pediment of the same steep pitch as the roofs (Figure 19). The doorways of this pair of houses are sheltered by semi-elliptical shell-hoods of stone, while Nos 10 and 11 have semi-domed hoods of wood and richly modelled plaster (Plate 54a). The windows on this side of the square have wooden architraves of orthodox Classical profile. The angles of the square were left open for access to stable-courts, except the south-east which was closed by the narrow frontage of No. 15, a house that extended some way behind the south row.

ORCHARD STREET

The recorded history of Orchard Street begins with a statement in the minutes of the Common Council's meeting on 17th March 1715, to the effect that 'Mr Mayor acquainted the house that if the garden and orchard adjoining to and occupied with the Hospital of Queen Elizabeth on the College Green were built upon itt would tend much to ye improvemt. of the revenue and thereupon a plan of the ground wch. explains the project of the building was produced to the house'. Whereupon it was 'Ordered that ye Orchard adjoining and belonging to ye Hospitall of Queen Elizabeth or such pt. thereof as shall be allotted by the Committee to be appointed for that purpose, shall be lett out to be built upon'. This, as Governors of the Hospital, the Council were empowered to do. On 20th July 1717 the Committee were able to report that they had 'caused a large wall to be built to seperate the Court of the Hospital and have caused a Comon. Shower (sewer) to be made through the Orchard for accomodating ye Tenants who shall incline to build there and have arched ye same'. They had also successfully concluded the purchase or exchange of certain lands required to make a way from St Augustine's Back to the proposed new street, and had drawn up the following conditions under which it was proposed to grant building leases:

'They (the Committee) have also considered what grants to make to such as shall incline to build in the said orchard and what manner of buildings shall be erected thereon And it is their opinion that Leases of forty years granted with a Clause of Renewal within the 14th year on payment of a certain ffine will be more to the advantage of the Hospital than to grant a term of fifty one years absolute.'

'Also it is their opinion that a ground Rent of 12d p. foot be reserv'd clear of taxes And that the fine to be paid on the 14th year be 12 years purchase of the ground Rent.'

'That all houses built fronting the Street the front shall be built with brick all alike and the walls carried up above the Eves of the houses and no Mundilians or Coves shall be made. That stone walls shall be made betwixt each house and all other the walls (except the front) to be of stone.'

'That no house shall be less than twenty foot in front each house to be three stories above the ground besides ye garrets the first story ten foot and an half the second ten foot and the third nine foot in the clear And with Coffet Joists And that all the windows in the front of the houses shall be sash windows of an equal heighth.'

'And that no dwelling house shall be built on any part of the back ground that is less than twenty foot in front and twenty-eight foot in depth and not less than two stories high above ye ground besides ye garrets.'

The first lease under these terms, granted to William Swymmer on 18th January 1717-18, was for 'Twenty Seven foot of ground in front part of and lying on the Northwest side of the said Hospital Orchard which front is to be and face to a street there intended to be made and called Orchard street (the same street to be and always to continue to be of the breadth of thirty foot three foot whereof on either side the same street is to be allow'd for pallasadoes) And Seventy nine foot in length or depth backwards from the sd. intennded street and front towards ffrog-lane wch. said ground hereby contracted for is now laid out and admeasured and is bounded on the Southwest side by a Lane there intended to be made and called Gaunts Lane And on the North-east side by void ground (part also of the sd. Hospital Orchard) granted or intended to be granted to Peter Wilkins'. Swymmer's house, now No. 10, stands at the corner of Denmark Avenue and the north-west side of Orchard Street, and the four adjacent houses, Nos 11 to 14, were built by Peter Wilkins, house-carpenter, to whom the several plots were leased on 20th February 1717-18. Owing to the previous grant of 27 feet to Swymmer, the frontage of No. 11 was limited to 23 feet, the other plots being 25 feet in width although the houses built on them vary this dimension slightly.

Of the five houses that form the south-east side of Orchard Street proper (Plate 25a), the finest are Nos 27 and 28, with frontages respectively of 20 and 30 feet, which were built for John Becher under a lease granted on 3rd September 1718. No. 29 is also a well-built house of the same date, erected for Andrew Ruddock, but Nos 25 and 26 are inferior structures of a speculative type built by John Price, the house-carpenter, whose lease of 50 feet frontage was granted on 14th July 1722. In Price's lease the prescribed clear internal heights were amended as follows—10 feet for the first story, 11 feet for the second, and 9 feet for the third.

Beyond Orchard Avenue the width of the street was increased to 50 feet by setting back the building-line on the south-east side and forming what was originally named Orchard Square. The finest houses here are the five on the north-west side (Plate 25b), of which Nos 15 and 16 were built for John Worsley, Nos 17 and 18 for Alexander Neale, and No. 19 for William Baker. Neale's lease of 50 feet frontage was granted on 20th February 1717-18, and those of Worsley, for 50 feet, and Baker, for 25 feet, on 22nd July 1718. The south-east side contained the French Protestant Chapel, now replaced by a modern office building with a simple stone exterior, and five narrow-fronted houses, Nos 20 to 24, which closely resemble Nos 25 and 26 and were probably built for speculative letting by John Price.

Several of the houses are built in pairs, sharing common chimney-stacks and consequently having the hall and staircase placed to the right or left hand of the plan, which will be found to vary slightly with every house. In accordance with the conditions of the leases there are three stories, above a basement and with a garret story in the roof. The fronts are of brickwork laid in Flemish bond, with the wall face carried up above the second-floor windows to form a parapet. The party-walls are defined by slightly-projecting pilasters, usually formed of channel-jointed stones, while stringcourses of brick or stone mark the first- and second-floor levels. Where stone is used for these horizontal members, and for the parapet coping, the face is cut to a simple cornice profile and returned round the pilasters. The fenestral pattern varies according to the frontage width, Nos 10, 19, 28 and 29 having four windows to each upper story; Nos 12 to 18 and 25 to 27 have three; and No. 11 has two. The general ground-story arrangement is to have two windows on one side of the doorway, which in the larger houses is flanked by a window lighting the hall. The exposed sash-boxes are faced with wooden architraves and set slightly recessed in rectangular openings, with flat-arched heads of gauged brickwork often centring on stone keyblocks. These are usually plain with chamfered arrises, but those of No. 28 are carved to represent a variety of grotesque masks composed of acanthus-leaves (Plate 25a).

Several of the houses have stone doorcases of coarse Classical design, the most ornate examples being those at Nos 19 and 28, where the rectangular opening is framed by an architrave flanked by fluted Doric pilasters, with scrolled trusses supporting a projecting pediment of broken segmental form, probably intended to accommodate an armorial cartouche or an urn (Plate 54c). The doorcases of Nos 15 to 18 have similar pilasters and trusses supporting triangular open-bedmould pediments. The doorway to No. 14 has a plain semi-domed hood of wood and plaster, while Nos 20 to 26 have wooden flat hoods of the simplest form, with panelled soffits and moulded fascias. Most of the original eight-panelled front doors have survived, but No. 16 has the only surviving example of the wooden wheel-pattern fanlight which must once have been common to many of the houses in this street.

Except for Nos 20 to 24, which have been faced with cement that is coursed to represent stone, the red-brick and stone fronts have been painted a uniform broken-white. The windows have generally been re-sashed with frames having the larger panes and lighter bars of late Georgian character, but sashes of the

original type are to be found in some of the basement and top-
story windows. The fronts of Nos 11 and 12 have been altered
by the removal of stringcourses, and in the last house a large
three-light window has replaced the original fenestration of the
ground- and first-floors.

The interiors are generally well finished in the style of their
period, and contain good staircases of wooden construction, and
full wainscot linings to the principal rooms on the ground- and
first-floors. The main staircase at No. 28 is an admirable specimen of the staircase-hand's craft, and equally noteworthy is the
Rococo plasterwork that decorates the walls and soffits of the
staircase at No. 15, probably the work of Joseph Thomas and
dating from about 1740.

NOS 10, 11 and 12, GUINEA STREET

On the south side of Guinea Street, Redcliffe, are some interesting eighteenth-century houses, perhaps the most remarkable
being the former mansion of Captain Edmund Saunders, built
in 1718 and now divided into three houses, Nos 10, 11 and 12.
The site probably formed part of a close of ground, containing
some four acres, that the Corporation granted to Elizabeth
Gibbs by a lease dated 24th March 1702. Saunders, a merchant
and churchwarden of St Mary Redcliffe, had held this land for
some time before a new lease was granted him on 22nd June
1725, wherein Guinea Street was described as 'new built'.
Eleven other houses in this street, described as 'lately built', were
offered for sale during March 1743, as part of the late Captain
Saunders' estate.

Externally the building has decorative features that link it
with certain houses in Queen Square, Orchard Street, and
Dowry, where the same mason might have been employed. The
wide two-storied front (Plate 26) is built of red brick laid in
Flemish bond, with stone stringcourses immediately above the
ground- and second-story window arches. These strings are
treated as narrow cornices and return round the slightly-
projecting pilasters of brickwork which divide the upper story
into three bays of almost equal width. The plain brick parapet,
extending across the middle and right-hand bays, has a moulded
stone coping that rises in ogee curves to frame a flat-topped
gable surmounting the left-hand bay. Each story contains six

windows, spaced out to form a pair in each bay, and the gable has one. The exposed sash-boxes, faced with wooden architraves, are slightly recessed in rectangular openings with flat arches of gauged-brickwork, those of the upper story being ornamented with curved cutting. All have stone keyblocks which together form the most varied and interesting series in Bristol.

Those of the ground story, from left to right, represent:

1. Two crossed birds (probably eagles).
2. A grotesque male mask.
3. Two crossed dolphins.
4. A parrot's head.
5. A grotesque male mask.
6. A scrolled cartouche, dated 1718.

Those of the second story, from left to right, represent:

1. A bunch of grapes with a vine-leaf.
2. A man seated on a tun.
3. An Irish harp.
4. A flagon with a funnel.
5. A profile head of a man in a woollen cap.
6. A grotesque male mask.

The doors to Nos 11 and 12 are obviously later insertions, but that of No. 10 is original, though perhaps in a changed position. The six-panelled door in the Gothic taste has over it a mutilated wheel-pattern fanlight, and the stone hood, consisting of a projecting triangular pediment with a deeply-recessed tympanum, is supported by scrolled trusses.

In a sale advertisement of 1746, the interior of the house is described as then containing 'four Vault Cellars, two Kitchens, a large handsom Hall, Dining-Room, and Withdrawing-Room, each neatly Wainscotted and Painted, with a Marble Chimney-Piece in Each; three Parlours, two of them with Marble Chimney-Pieces, all neatly Wainscotted, one of them with Cedar and Mahogany, and highly finished; a very neat Mahogany Staircase, handsomly Painted, three Chambers Wainscotted, and a Marble Chimney-Piece in Each; with convenient Presses for Clothes, and three Closets. And six Upper Lodging-Rooms and two Closets, &c'.

DOWRY SQUARE and CHAPEL ROW

The building of Dowry Square was promoted by private enterprise, and most of its houses were erected to provide suitable lodgings for the fashionable visitors to the nearby Hot-well. The ground for the square, and for Chapel Row adjoining, must have been laid out for building soon after 1720, for a deed dated 25–6th March 1721, relating to a plot on the west side, makes reference to 'a certain Square then already agreed on, and intended to be laid out in Dowry aforesaid'. The site of this whole west side, forming part of the Clifton estate of John Power, is described as 'a certain great Splot of ground lately conveyed to Thomas Oldfield and George Tully by the said John Power'. George Tully, a prominent house-carpenter and surveyor, planned the layout of the square and most probably erected some of its first buildings. The original Dowry Chapel, built in 1746, is certainly known to have been his work.

Dowry Square measures approximately 180 feet north to south, and 135 feet east to west. The layout is unusual in that the area is totally enclosed by buildings on its north, east and west sides, and designedly left open on the south. Chapel Row forms a contemporaneous extension of the west side, while Dowry Parade is a later development of the east. The similarity between the earlier houses makes it appear that the elevations were intended to be generally uniform, but the completion of the square was so prolonged that changing taste has given it a most heterogeneous appearance.

The least altered externally of the earlier houses are Nos 5, 6 and 7 in Chapel Row (Plate 27a). The first two are single-fronted and their plans are reversed to share common chimney-stacks, while No. 7 is a double-fronted house. The elevations, respectively three and five windows wide, are three stories high and very similar in general appearance to those in Orchard Street, being built of red brick with stone dressings. Narrow cornices form the stringcourses and coping, and channel-jointed pilasters define the party-walls, but instead of gauged brick, stone is used for the flat arches of the windows, which consist of five channel-jointed voussoirs. The keystones at No. 7 are carved with grotesque masks, but the others are left plain. The rectangular doorways are sheltered by stone hoods of pedimental form, resting on scrolled trusses, that at No. 7 being segmental with a concave tympanum, while those at Nos 5 and 6 are triangular and have recessed tympana.

An advertisement in a Bristol newspaper for 4th February 1727, offering to let 'a large new-built house, with coach houses, stables, &c., in the new Square in Dowry', probably refers to one of the houses now numbered 6 to 9 on the north side, the first to be built in the square. No. 6 is curiously contrived to fill up the north-west angle and has narrow frontages to both sides, while Nos 7 and 8 are single-fronted, and No. 9 is a large double-fronted house (Plate 27b). The elevations are fairly uniform and must originally have presented a very similar appearance to those of the Chapel Row houses. The same stone stringcourses, pilasters, and window-arches appear, but the brickwork has been entirely concealed with cement. Nos 7 and 9 have stone doorcases of Classical design, coarsely detailed, with fluted Ionic pilasters supporting an entablature and broken segmental pediment (Plate 54d). The wooden doorcase to No. 8 has been mutilated, but it originally consisted of an architrave-surround with a plain frieze stopped by consoles supporting a broken triangular pediment. The interior of No. 9, called 'The Dove House', contains a quantity of interesting woodwork of the period, including a fine open-well staircase with a lantern-light above it, and several fully wainscotted rooms.

The other houses on the north side, Nos 10 and 11 (Plate 27b), are obviously later, and were built in 1746 under the terms of an indenture dated 13th April 1745, whereby George Tully conveyed to Richard Matthews, a gardener, 'all that piece or parcel of ground part of a certain late close of ground called Dowry in the Parish of Clifton in the said County of Gloucester laying at the North East corner of the New Square there called Dowry Square and frontest towards and is bounded by the same Square on the South and West parts thereof which said front contains eighty feet or thereabouts and is bounded on the West part with a new built messuage called The Dove House . . . and on the South part by a late new built messuage and stables late of Thomas Oldfield'. Matthews undertook to 'build one or more good and substantial messuage or messuages which said messuage or messuages shall consist of so many storeys and be of such height and outward form or model of building in front as the next adjoining messuage called The Dove House'. Although the elevations of Nos 10 and 11 preserve the general lines and heights of the earlier house-fronts, many differences appear in the details, which are of a coarse Classical character. The frontages differ considerably in width, No. 10 having four windows to each upper story, and No. 11 three. The ground-story is of rusticated stonework, and the upper stories are of brick which has been faced with cement. There are no demarcation features between the houses; the stringcourses are more prominent; and the windows are set in segmental-arched openings having moulded architraves of stone, which rise from corbelled sills and are broken by plain keystones. The stone doorcases are of somewhat similar design to those at Nos 7 and 9 but show greater rectitude of detail, and here the fluted Ionic pilasters support an entablature with a pulvinated frieze, while the crowning segmental pediment is unbroken.

Matthews' estate was advertised for sale during April 1750, when it was described as consisting of 'three extraordinarily well-built good Dwelling-Houses; two of which were built in 1746, and the other just finished'. The last reference is to No. 12, a double-fronted house at the north end of the east side (Plate 27b), which has an elevation of entirely different design to those of the earlier houses, and is markedly similar to Nos 4 and 5 in the west side, the former of which is described below. In general, the east side presents a most varied assemblage of houses with fronts of little interest, and the same must be said of the west side with the exception of Nos 4 and 5 (Plate 33a). The position and dimensions of No. 4 make it clear that this is the house described in *The Bristol Oracle* for 22nd January 1748, in the following sale advertisement:

'A New well-built House, 45 Feet in Front, and 37 deep; situate on the West Side of DOWRY-SQUARE, near the Hot-well, four Stories High, four Rooms on a Floor, the Front of polish'd Brick and Freestone, a large Outlet behind, and a back Door into Green-Street.

N.B. The House is large and commodious, has a Grand Entrance, and Staircase, a Dining-Room forty two Feet by sixteen and an half, four large and necessary Closets, Garrets &c, built on purpose for Lodgings, having below Stairs two large Kitchens, a Servant's Hall, Landry, Cellars, Pantries, both Sorts of Water, and all other Conveniencies, and handsom paved Areas six Feet wide.'

The well-designed elevation is five windows wide and three stories high, and built of red-brick with stone dressings. Pilasters of channel-jointed stones define the party-walls, and long and short quoins emphasize the breaking forward of the middle portion to form a central feature, three windows wide. No stringcourses mark the stories but there is a bold cornice at roof level, and the central feature is surmounted by a triangular pediment with a brick tympanum enclosed by stone mouldings, against which the high brick parapet is stopped. The window openings are without architraves, but have stone sills and segmental arches composed of five voussoirs that increase in height and forward projection towards the keystone. The centrally-placed doorway is now preceded by a porch, apparently of late-Georgian date, with a simple entablature that is supported by fluted columns and antæ, having capitals adorned with fern-leaves.

This house is an early example of the domestic-building style that was to flourish in Bristol for many years, and it is probable that the draughts for many such fronts were made by Thomas Paty, and designed to incorporate the standardized productions of his masonry yard, such as cornices, window-arches, quoin-stones, doorcases, etc.

PRINCE STREET

Prince Street was laid out at the same time as Queen Square, about 1700, and was named in honour of Prince George of Denmark, the consort of Queen Anne. Millerd's plan of 1673 shows that the street existed, in a rudimentary form, as an avenue crossing the Marsh, continuing the lines of Marsh Street and having three groups of houses and wharves between its west side and the Narrow Quay. The first houses to be built in the new street were not remarkable, those that survive having fronts of simple design, three stories high and built of brick dressed with freestone. Greater architectural interest resides in the imposing mansions that were built on the west side, during the second quarter of the eighteenth century.

About the middle of 1725 the Corporation offered on building lease the whole of the west side south of the present No. 50. Sites with frontages of varying widths, for one or more houses, were taken by Robert Yate, John Becher, Noblett Ruddock,

[161]

John Hobbs, John Jelf, and Henry Combe. Most of the houses built for these prominent citizens have been demolished, but Nos 66, 68 and 70 form an impressive surviving group (Plate 28). Nos 68 and 70, which have freestone fronts of identical design, were built for John Hobbs, the deal merchant, under the terms of a lease dated 2nd August 1725, granted by the Mayor Burgesses and Commonalty of Bristol. The site is described as situated in St Stephen's Parish, with a frontage of 60 feet to Prince Street, and a depth of 117 feet extending back towards the Quay. The lease stipulated that 'all houses designed to be built on the said demised voyd ground are intended to be strong lasting uniform and regular'. Each house was to be not less than 25 feet wide and set back within a forecourt 10 feet deep, enclosed by a wall and with only a porch permitted to extend therein. The fronts were to be of freestone—brick was permitted in some later grants—and all windows were to be made sashes of equal height. The internal floor heights were to measure in the clear 10 feet 6 inches for the first and second stories, and 9 feet for the third. For the first three years of the tenure a peppercorn rent was to be paid, and during this period the house, or houses, had to be completed. This was followed by the grant of a fifty-one years lease, at a yearly rent of two-shillings for every foot of frontage.

All the evidence of style and circumstance suggests that these twin fronts were designed by John Strahan, whom Hobbs singled out for special patronage and employment in Bristol and Bath. Each house has a front that is 30 feet wide and composed of a central feature, two windows wide, projecting slightly forward from narrow wings, each one window wide. The ground-story has two arch-headed windows in the centre that are set in plain margins and recessed within rusticated arches, their keystones projecting to support the cornice at first-floor level. The outer wing of each house contains an arched doorway, framed by a moulded architrave and surmounted by a cornice dripmould. The segmental-headed window in each other wing has a moulded architrave broken by a plain keystone. The line of the first-floor cornice is continued by a platband across the wings. The second- and third-story windows are nearly identical in size and uniform in dress, each segmental-headed opening being framed in a moulded architrave, based on a plain sill and broken by a keystone. Pilasters of channel-jointed stones rise through the three stories to mark the party-wall division and the lateral terminations of the fronts, while similar pilasters flank the two upper stories of each central feature. These pilasters are terminated by the plain frieze below the main cornice, which is surmounted by a parapet with a moulded coping. This parapet breaks against the triangular pediment that crowns the central feature of each house, and has in its tympanum a Baroque armorial cartouche carved with two falcons, or hobbies,—a punning reference to the name of Hobbs.

The adjoining house, No. 66, is the survivor of a pair built for Noblett Ruddock, and has an elaborate front of brick, liberally dressed with freestone. While Strahan might also have been responsible for this design, certain mannerisms suggest that it is an early work of William Halfpenny. This front is three windows wide, with a central feature projecting forward from wings that almost equal it in width. The horizontal members continue exactly those of the adjoining houses, and were doubtless common to all in this range, but in other respects the design is dissimilar. The centrally-placed door is recessed in a rusticated surround, with a flat arch of five voussoirs that return horizontally and break forward with successive projections until the key is reached. The channel-jointed courses are stopped by a plain pier on either side, and the voussoired head is surmounted by a cornice, continued by a platband across each wing. The upper stage of the central feature is two stories high and flanked by two Ionic pilasters, with fluted shafts, supporting an entablature. This has a pulvinated frieze and the cornice is surmounted by a segmental pediment, its brick tympanum forming a background to a stone armorial cartouche. The windows, of rectangular form, are uniformly dressed with thin pilaster-strips, rising from a plain sill on brick corbels, and supporting a head of five voussoirs, each successive stone heightened by a brick course and projecting slightly beyond the preceding one towards the keystone. The head of the topmost window in the central feature is brought forward to rest on scrolled consoles, and each succeeding voussoir merges into a fascia of the architrave of the crowning entablature.

No. 12 St James's Barton is a fine mansion of about 1728, built for a member of the Elton family The freestone front has features common to both the Prince Street houses here described, but the design is more probably Strahan's than Halfpenny's (Plate 29a).

REDLAND COURT

The history of the present mansion of Redland Court begins in 1732, when John Cossins, a wealthy retired grocer of London, purchased the Manor of Redland from Gregory Martin, an uncle of Cossins' wife Martha, born Innys. Cossins demolished the Elizabethan house then existing, and commissioned John Strahan to design for him the present building which was completed during the summer of 1735. Various small properties adjoining Redland Court were acquired by Cossins and added to the estate, which his widow bequeathed to her Innys brothers. From them it descended to Jeremy Baker and his son, but in 1799 it was sold to help settle Jeremy Baker's debts. The estate changed hands several times during the nineteenth century, and latterly some streets of small houses were built on tracts of the parkland, but in 1883 the house and part of the grounds passed into the ownership of the Council of the Redland High School for Girls, in whose possession it remains.

The ground has a downwards slope from north to south, and the three blocks of the house are built in an east-to-west line on an artificial platform which extends to form a wide terrace before the south front. The brick retaining-wall is finished with a stone balustrade, and in the middle are steps descending east and west to the lower level of the grounds. The irregular wall surrounding the grounds is broken axially opposite the central feature of the south front, by a wrought-iron screen between stone piers, forming the terminal feature of a long avenue extending southwards across grassland, which partially survives. The monumental piers are rusticated, and the south face of each is adorned with coupled Doric pilasters, the shafts broken by two deep blocks of icicle-work. Each pier is finished with a Doric entablature, which has metopes carved with circles containing heraldic beasts, surmounted by a large and richly decorated stone vase. The iron screen has the form of a wide gate of three equal sections, of which only the middle one opens, with an elaborately scrolled overthrow. The work is generally similar in character to that of the gate before

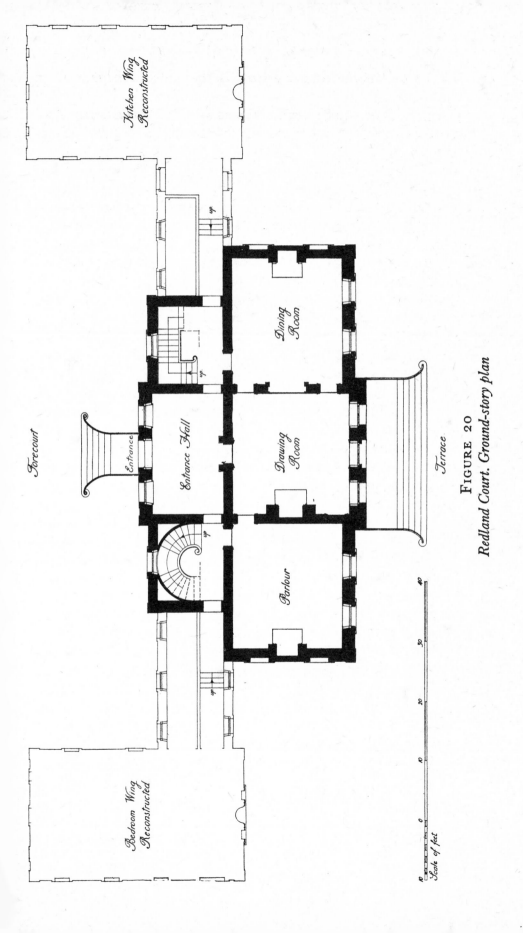

Forecourt

Kitchen Wing
Reconstructed

Entrance

Entrance Hall

Bedroom Wing
Reconstructed

Dining
Room

Drawing
Room

Parlour

Terrace

Scale of feet

FIGURE 20
Redland Court. Ground-story plan

Redland Chapel, and is probably by the same smith, Nathaniel Arthur.

In the notes to Storer's *Delineations of Gloucestershire*, published in 1825, J. N. Brewer states that 'considerable alterations in the building were made by Mr Baker, but much of the fitting-up of the mansion still exhibits the best specimen we have seen, of the ornaments and arrangements of the dwelling of a private gentleman in the first half of the eighteenth century. The gardens and their appendages have desirably been stripped of much of their original formality, by the improving hand of the former proprietor, Mr Seymour, and the present possessor of this seat of dignified comfort, Sir Richard Vaughan'.

The house was planned along Palladian lines, with the reception-rooms and family accommodation in the main block (Figure 20), which is placed centrally and linked by short corridors with the subsidiary blocks housing the offices and staff. These blocks are so related to the main building that they stand forward from the entrance front, facing north, and are recessed from the principal front which faces south. The main doorway, placed centrally in the north front, opens directly into the hall which has on either side an archway leading to a corridor and staircase. The west stair rises in a semicircle to stop at the first-floor, while that to the east is continued in straight flights to the attic-story. The corridors continue beyond the staircases to join with the subsidiary blocks, that to the east containing the kitchen quarters. On the south front are three reception-rooms, arranged *en suite* and each having a door that opens to the hall or to the adjoining corridors. The main building consists of two lofty stories, raised above a basement and surmounted by a garret-story that is largely concealed by the balustraded parapet. The subsidiary blocks are of two low stories, the difference between the floor levels in the three blocks being overcome by the introduction of steps in the connecting corridors.

The fact that the plain surfaces of the main block's exterior are faced with cement, coursed to represent stone, suggests that this part of the building was constructed of brick with a liberal use of freestone dressings, while the subsidiary blocks are entirely faced with freestone. Although the building makes an imposing effect, the treatment of the elevations is unscholarly and there is considerable disparity between the styles adopted for the main and subsidiary blocks. The latter are distinctly Vanbrughian in flavour, whereas Strahan has employed a Palladian manner for the former, using details copied almost directly from such designs of Colen Campbell as that for the garden front at Stourhead. Here it is worth noting that the contemporary mansion at Frampton-on-Severn, which must also be by Strahan, shows to an even greater degree this copying from Campbell and Vanbrugh. All of this makes clear the meaning of John Wood's contemptuous reference to Strahan's 'Piratical Architecture'.

The principal front (Plate 30a), facing south, is composed of a central feature projecting slightly forward from wings that almost equal it in width. A short flight of steps extends in front of the ground-story of the central feature, which presents a rusticated face of V-jointed masonry with three equally-spaced openings, now containing french-windows of early nineteenth-century date. These openings have square heads formed of stepped and projecting voussoirs, the disproportionately tall keystones breaking the line of the first-floor platband, into which the adjoining voussoirs die. This rustic base supports the engaged portico of three bays that decorates the second-story. The four three-quarter columns, and the square-shafted pilasters with which the lateral columns are paired, are without pedestals, and have moulded bases, plain shafts, and Ionic capitals. They stand partially sunk into recesses channelled into the wall face, and support an entablature that has a pulvinated frieze and a modillioned cornice surmounted by a triangular pediment, its tympanum carved in bold relief with an armorial cartouche flanked by standing and kneeling *putti* (Plate 30b). Each inter-columniation contains a square-headed window, that in the centre having a shouldered and eared architrave, while that on either side is unadorned, and all are underlined by a plain and heavy sill. The wings are accorded a much simpler treatment, which is repeated for the return fronts of the block. The basement forms a high plinth, its low windows being heavily framed with rustics, and the angles of the building are slightly emphasized with plain pilaster-strips, broken by the continued sills underlining the windows of each story. Each wing has two widely-spaced windows to each story, those of the ground-floor having moulded architraves broken by rustic-blocks and flat arches formed of five voussoirs which are stepped and projected to break successively into the pulvinated frieze and the various mouldings of the cornice, so that the key rises to meet the top-most fillet. The first-floor windows are more simply dressed with shouldered and eared architraves, finished with pulvinated frieze and cornice. The crowning entablature continues that of the central feature, and it is surmounted by an open balustrade with pedestals placed at the angles, over the piers between the wing windows, and against the pediment. Elaborate stone vases surmount these pedestals and the pediment's apex, four different designs having been used. While there is no evidence pointing to those who were employed on this building, the stone carving has every appearance of being the work of James Paty (1).

The south elevation of each subsidiary block has, in the centre of its ground-story, a decorative feature which is distinctly copied from Campbell's Stourhead design. This is the Venetian-window wherein the arched middle-light is replaced by a semi-circular niche (Plate 31a). The window is raised on a pedestal with blind balustrades below the side-lights and niche. Each of these is framed by a moulded architrave with the frieze and cornice returned inside the niche, to support the carved scallop-shell in its lunette. Rustic-blocks break the vertical architraves and the archivolt, and triple-keystones rise to inter-cept the frieze and cornice-mouldings. On the first-floor and over the niche is a segmental-headed window simply framed by a plain architrave-band. The angles of these blocks are empha-sized with long and short V-jointed quoins, rising from the plinth to meet the plain frieze and crowning cornice. The plain pedestal-parapet is surmounted by Vanbrughian urns placed at each angle. The short connecting corridors have two tiers of two widely-spaced windows, those of the ground-floor having arched heads and architrave-bands broken by triple-keystones. There is no intermediate stringcourse, but immediately above the square-headed upper windows runs a simple cornice which dies into the first-floor window sill of the main building. The plain parapet is surmounted by a ball-finial in its centre.

The north front of the main building is narrower than the south by reason of the incut north-east and north-west angles of the plan, and it is composed of a central feature projecting slightly forward from narrow wings (Plate 31b). In the former is the centrally-placed doorway, closely set between two windows, with three closely-spaced windows to correspond in the upper story. Each wing contains one window in each story. The architectural dress of this front is identical with that of the south-front wings already described, and calls for no further comment except that the doorway is surmounted by a segmental pediment, with a small armorial cartouche in its tympanum. The north elevations of the subsidiary blocks are similar to the south, except that the Venetian-window feature is here replaced by three arch-headed windows, the middle one slightly larger than the others, with architrave-bands broken by triple-keystones. The west elevation contains three similar arched windows and a doorway, now altered to a window, in its ground-story, with four segmental-headed windows correspondingly placed above. From the middle of the west block's roof rises a lantern of simple design and octagonal plan, constructed in wood and roofed with an ogee dome of leadwork.

The most considerable alteration to the building has been the addition of a lofty story to the east block, which has seriously upset the balance of the general composition. The iron-and-glass porch, and the tent-roofed veranda on the south front, date from the early nineteenth century and are charming although slightly incongruous additions, but the wholesale removal of glazing-bars from the windows has had a deplorable effect.

The interior contains much excellent woodwork and some good plasterwork of its period. The entrance-hall is wainscoted, with tall slightly-sunk panels rising directly from the chair-rail above the plain dado. The six-panelled mahogany door to the middle room is recessed in a Doric doorcase, composed of fluted half-columns raised on block-pedestals and supporting an entablature that is surmounted by a broken triangular pediment with a curved pedestal intended to receive a bust or cartouche. The Doric entablature to the walls is of plaster, and its dentilled cornice surrounds a simply panelled ceiling (Plate 57a).

The wainscoting of the reception-rooms is of a more elaborate character, the dado being panelled to match the tall fielded panels above the rail. Generally, each mahogany door is framed by a moulded architrave surmounted by a short scroll-ended frieze and cornice, but the door leading from the hall to the middle room has an architrave flanked by plain pilaster-strips, with acanthus-enriched scrolled trusses that support the cornice.

[169]

Between the middle and east rooms is a four-fold door, set in an opening formed by square-shafted fluted Ionic pilasters, their entablatures supporting an elliptical arch that has a moulded archivolt and a panelled soffit (Plate 62a). The carved capitals with their undercut volutes are particularly worthy of notice. The architraves and friezes of the crowning entablatures vary slightly from room to room, but all have modillioned cornices surrounding the plain ceilings. The marble chimney-pieces are good but simple in design, the best being one in the middle room that has its lintel carved with a lion's mask flanked by drapery-festoons looped over scallop-shells.

Although both wooden staircases are excellent examples of the design and craftsmanship of their period, that to the west of the hall is by far the finer. The first two short flights are set out to conform with the semicircular wall of the well, and the ramped and curving handrail is supported by turnings, with twisted shafts above baluster-shaped bases, spaced two to each winder tread, and three to each straight one, between fluted newel-posts. The railing is complemented by the panelled dado against the wall, which is continued with a balustrade where the landing intercepts the window. The staircase-wall is finished with a fine Doric entablature in plaster, the frieze metopes being decorated alternately with rosettes and ox-skulls. At the junction of the curved and straight walls the entablature breaks forward on ornate consoles, to provide the springing for an arch that divides the semi-dome from its segmental-vaulted continuation. The semi-dome is decorated simply with a radial band of ornamentation; the arch-soffit has square panels with rosettes; and the segmental-vault has five large square panels, each containing a rosette of different design (Plate 60a).

NO. 59 QUEEN CHARLOTTE STREET, QUEEN SQUARE

This house was one of a pair built between 1709 and 1711 by John Price, the house-carpenter, to whom a lease of a plot of ground 'in the East Angle of Queen Square' was granted on 8th July 1709. This house passed by sub-lease to Jacob Elton, to whom the Corporation granted a new lease in 1736, and it was probably about this time that the building was given its impressive stone front. In its Baroque decoration, and the importance given to the third-story, this front has distinct affinities with Rosewell House, Bath, suggesting that they are both the work of the same designer, perhaps John Strahan.

There are four stories including the attic, and each upper story contains four equally-spaced windows. The ground-story has a shallow porch placed just left of the centre, with a narrow window on its left and two windows on its right spaced to correspond with those above them. Moulded stringcourses express the first- and second-floor levels, and the main cornice is placed immediately below the attic windows to give additional height in the third story. These horizontal members are returned round the pilasters forming the lateral terminations to each story, which are decorated in turn with rustics, panels, and fluting, while those to the attic are left plain. The porch of Doric columns supporting a triangular-pedimented entablature has little relation in style to the rest of the front, and might be considered a later addition were it not for the fact that Rosewell House has the same disparate feature. The window openings in the three principal stories are of much the same size and simple rectangular form, and their dress, consisting of a pedestal from which rise shouldered and eared architraves with curved heads, is basically similar although treated with increased elaboration in each succeeding tier. Thus, the pedestals to the ground-story windows are plain and the architrave-heads have simple flattened curves, whereas the pedestals of the two upper tiers break forward with fluted dies below the architraves, which have serpentine-curved heads broken by large plain keystones. In the third-story these keystones merge into wide aprons from whence moulded consoles rise to support the corona of the main cornice. The attic-story has been altered, but it originally contained four square windows, framed in plain architraves broken by keystones, and the front finished with a moulded coping (Plate 29b).

NO. 40 PRINCE STREET

The fine houses built in Prince Street about 1728, by Hobbs, Combe, Becher, and other wealthy citizens, were completely surpassed by the splendour of the mansion that Richard Bayly erected there in 1740–1. The lease of the site, whereon stood the 'Great House' of John Day, had been sold by auction in 1738 to John Bartlett, passing from him to John Rich who in turn disposed of it to Richard Bayly in 1740. In conformity with the terms of the original sale, Bayly rebuilt the front portion of the premises and, having acquired the adjoining ground, he applied to the Corporation for a new lease in respect of the whole property, which had a frontage of 136 feet 6 inches to Prince Street. This was granted for the term of three lives, beginning 10th June 1741, at a yearly rental of £13 12s. 0d., as from 25th March 1740, and a fine of £538 which had already been paid. Bayly died less than two years after the completion of his new house, the contents of which were sold during July 1742. His 'Great House—with a Freestone Front, Marble Chimney-Pieces, wainscotted and very handsomly furnished, with convenient Cellarage, Coach House, both sorts of Water, &c' was offered for sale in March 1743. In recent years the building was used for offices and maintained in good repair, but, unfortunately, part of it was destroyed and the rest demolished during the late war.

The survey plan made for the 1738 sale is preserved in one of the Plan-Books and appears to have been drawn by William Halfpenny. It was probably he who designed No. 40 Prince Street, for its front had several points of resemblance to the Coopers' Hall.

The front was an imposing but not altogether satisfactory Palladian composition, entirely built in dressed freestone (Plate 32, Figure 21). The low ground-story was dominated by the centrally-placed doorway, its rectangular opening framed by engaged three-quarter columns, with plain shafts blocked by vermiculated stones, and Ionic capitals with drapery festooned between the volutes. The straight entablature, with its pulvinated frieze, was surmounted by a segmental pediment. On either side of the doorway were two windows, widely spaced in a wall face that was regularly coursed with V-jointing, the upper joints being returned to form five voussoirs to the segmental-head of each window. A platband marked the first-floor level, a true *piano nobile* where five great windows were evenly spaced, each rectangular opening being framed with a moulded architrave, surmounted by a plain frieze and pediment, two of triangular form alternating with three segmental. The five attic-story windows were almost square in form, and each was completely framed by a moulded architrave, shouldered and eared at the

FIGURE 21

No. 40 Prince Street. Elevation

sides, and broken into an increased width for part of the head. The plain wall face of this upper part was terminated laterally by pilaster-strips of channel-jointed stones, and horizontally by a frieze-band and the boldly-projecting cornice. The high parapet formed a pedestal, divided into bays corresponding with the fenestral spacing, by narrow projections that originally supported fine stone vases. The die of each bay was adorned with an oblong panel of icicle-work. The shallow and slightly-sunk forecourt was once enclosed with an iron railing, the central gate being hung on piers of rusticated stonework, surmounted by heraldic devices of horse's-heads emerging from crowns.

KING SQUARE

The building development of the southern slope of Kingsdown was probably initiated by Giles Greville, a prosperous apothecary of Bristol, who purchased the estate known as 'The Montagues' from representatives of the Dighton family, of St James's Parish. Greville's land was laid out for building during the early part of 1737, and, as a first step, he erected the Montague tavern. The garden ground adjoining on the east was planned for building at much the same time, with King Square as the focal point of the layout, and a series of streets and courts forming parallel terraces along the hillside, linked by narrow and steeply-rising lanes. George Tully, who planned Dowry and Brunswick Squares, was almost certainly responsible for this layout. Two houses in King Square, one built for his own occupation and the other for letting, formed part of his estate and are mentioned in his will, but, unfortunately, they cannot be identified. Matthews' Bristol Directory for 1793–4 shows that several members of the Harford family, to which Tully's wife belonged, were then living in and around King Square.

Rocque's plan of 1742 shows that the ground had already been laid out for the square and its tributary streets, although the only houses then built were those in the south angle of the square and Dighton Street. Little further progress was made with the Kingsdown suburb for many years, but a phase of considerable building activity in and around King Square was the subject of a letter published by *Felix Farley* on 13th December 1760, wherein the writer complains that 'Kingsdown, Delightful Spot! Is already begun to be dug up, and to experience the rude deforming Labour of the delving Masons, contaminated with the Itch of Building'. As a result several newly-built houses in King Square, Duke's Court, and Carolina Court, some erected by Benjamin Probert and others by Peter Prigg, both house-carpenters, were offered for sale during the summer of 1762. One of Prigg's houses is thus described in a sale advertisement:

'A very neat Strong-built House, in the New Square, with two large Arch cellars, two Handsom Parlours, and a large Dining-Room, all neatly wainscotted and ornamented with enriched Cornishes, two curious Marble Chimney-Pieces, with Pattern Tile, and the Entrance panell'd; with stout good Lodging-Rooms, two large Garrets, several Closets, and Pantries, two large Kitchens, both Sorts of Water, an Oven, Clamp-

Kiln, Stew-Holes, and other Conveniences; a large Three-stall Stable, and Coach-House, with Lofts over, and a handsom Garden.'

The north-east row was still unfinished by June 1772, for an advertisement of that time offered for sale some garden ground at the corner of King Square and Jamaica Street, as a suitable site for building three houses.

King Square measures some 270 feet north-west to south-east, and 210 feet south-west to north-east, between the buildings. The south-east side, which continues into Dighton and Jamaica streets, is broken by King Square Avenue in its centre, and the arrangement is echoed on the north-west side, with Duke Street and Carolina Row, and the narrow Spring Hill ascending steeply to Kingsdown Parade. The houses on the south-east and north-west sides were built to conform to level terraces, but those in the south-west and north-east rows were stepped up to accord with the ground's rapid rise towards the north-west. The square has suffered greatly in appearance by the wartime destruction of many of its houses, and by the disfigurement of some that remain. The central space seems to have been laid out at an early stage of the square's development, and was originally planted with a formal surround of lime-trees. These were removed during 1838 when 'the borders were decorated with various shrubs and trees' and the enclosure was surrounded with a 'light and elegant iron palisade'. The wartime removal of the railing has left only the arched lampholders, and the enclosure has become a neglected waste.

The first houses to be built facing the square were Nos 26 and 27, forming the western half of the south-east side. They were erected under the terms of an indenture made on 19th July 1740, between John Dalton, brickmaker, and William Lawrence, house-carpenter, referring to an earlier deed of 1738, whereby the ground was conveyed to John Dalton, Roger Bayly, Henry Bengough, and others, by the co-heirs of George Dighton. Dalton leased to Lawrence 'all that plot piece or parcel of void ground . . . containing in the whole Three Roods and Thirty Perches or thereabouts . . . bounded on the north by a street called or intended to be called Dighton Street and by the intended Square called or intended to be called King Square'.

Lawrence was to 'lay out and spend the full sum of Two hundred pounds of lawfull money of Great Britain in Erecting a good and substantial Messuage or Dwelling house on some part of the ground hereby granted which said Messuage or house shall be of three stories high at least and the front thereof to be made with ffreestone or Brick with ornamental ffreestone And the first floor of the said house shall be at least two ffeet above ground and the front of the said house to be built from the rails of the said Square four and forty ffeet'.

These houses no longer exist, but their fronts merit some description in that they set the standards to which most of the later houses conformed. They were built of brick with freestone dressings, in accordance with the above-quoted conditions, and each front was three stories high, four windows wide, and of similar design. There were no stringcourses to mark the floor levels or to break the strong vertical emphasis given by the narrow pilasters of channel-jointed stones that rose from the plinth to the crowning cornice, and divided each front into three bays, the first and second each one window wide, and the third two. The second bay, containing the doorway, was broken slightly forward and crowned with a triangular pediment planted against the plain brick parapet. Each house had its rectangular doorway flanked by plain-shafted Doric pilasters, with scrolled trusses that supported a projecting pediment, swan-necked at No. 26 and a broken segment at No. 27, the former containing a scrolled cartouche and the latter an urn. The windows were uniform in size and treatment, the exposed sash-boxes being faced with architraves and set slightly recessed in openings that had plain stone sills and segmental-arches of five stepped and projecting voussoirs.

Apart from No. 1, which has been demolished, the whole of the south-west row dates from about 1762. The brick and stone fronts are generally three stories high and three windows wide (Plate 33b). They are more simply treated than those described above, but the stonework details are very similar. Narrow pilasters of channel-jointed stones mark the party-walls between all the houses except Nos 6 and 7, which are treated as one double-fronted house, No. 7 having its entrance-front in Duke Street. The crowning cornice and parapet step up at irregular intervals, the former being broken and returned against the party-wall pilasters between Nos. 2 and 3, and Nos. 4 and 5. In consequence of this arrangement additional height is given to the third story of No. 3, and No. 5 has four stories of reduced heights. The window openings vary in size from house to house, although they all have the same architectural dressing of stone sills and segmental-arches of stepped voussoirs. The rectangular door openings have stone doorcases which appear to be the stock productions of a mason working to pattern-book designs. Those at Nos. 2, 5 and 6 are identical, with a surrounding architrave broken by rustic-blocks and a triple-keystone, and plain consoles supporting a triangular pediment. At Nos. 3 and 4 the architraves are not blocked and the pediments are of the open-bedmould pattern, the tympanum of that at No. 3 being decorated with a panel of icicle-work.

Before the destruction of two houses, Nos. 10 and 11, the north-west side presented a balanced composition, with two groups of four houses, uniform in height and width, each three stories high and three windows wide. These fronts are composed on the same general lines as those on the other sides, and the decorative details are much the same except that here the key-stones of the window-arches are fluted and capped with a cornice-moulding. The north-east side has been destroyed except for two houses at the east end, which are treated architecturally as one. The only feature of interest here is the introduction of a concave-curved ramp in the cornice to join two runs of different levels. The one surviving house on the south-east side, No. 26, has a front of dressed freestone to a Classical design that represents a complete departure from the general architectural scheme of the square.

CLIFTON HILL HOUSE

Clifton Hill House was built during 1746–50 for Paul Fisher, a wealthy Bristol merchant, who employed Isaac Ware to prepare the designs. Ware was sufficiently proud of this house to have had the drawings for the garden-front and the ground-floor plan engraved and published in his *Complete Body of Architecture*, dated 1756 (Plate 34a). Here it may be remarked that, owing to the engraver's direct copying of Ware's drawing, the ground-floor arrangement is shown in reverse to that as built. A note recording Fisher's expenditure on this building shows that

[177]

Thomas Paty was paid more than £2,000 for his work as mason and carver, while other contractors were Samuel Glascodine, house-carpenter, and Joseph Thomas, tyler and plasterer. The payment of six guineas made on 11th February 1747 to Lancelot Dowbiggin, suggests that this carpenter-architect, who designed St Mary's Church, Islington, might have acted as Ware's deputy in setting out the building. Ware's urbane design exerted a considerable influence on contemporary house-building in Bristol, and Thomas Paty's work, in particular, shows evidence of his close association with the building of Clifton Hill House.

In form the house is an oblong block with its greatest dimension running from north to south, to conform with the rapid fall of the ground from west to east. There are three stories, with a basement that is above ground-level on the east front, where the garden slopes away from it. Two short extensions from the north and south sides of the basement were heightened at a later date to provide additional rooms on the ground-floor. The interior is well laid out for convenience and effect, and Ware's very high level of accomplishment is everywhere in evidence. The entrance-door, placed centrally in the west front, opens into the hall that extends through the house to a further door in the east front, opening to the garden staircase. On either side of the hall are symmetrically disposed doors, the first ones opening to cupboards. The second door on the right side leads to the staircase-hall, and thence to the south-west room, while its opposite opens to a short corridor, with rooms leading off and a service stair at the north end. At the far end of the hall are doors that open left and right into the two reception-rooms on the east front. The principal stair rises round three sides of the well and stops at the first-floor landing, while the service stair continues to the second-floor (Figure 22). The vestibule and screen-wall on the west front are of later date, but, like the rooms added on to the north and south sides, they are reasonably in keeping with the original work.

The east and west fronts are identical in design, except that the former is raised on a basement-story and each pediment-tympanum has a different adornment. The east front consists of a central feature, three windows wide, broken slightly forward from wings, each one window wide (Plate 34a, b). The basement-story is of rough-hewn rusticated masonry, the rectangular windows being set in blind arches with plain imposts and keystones. From

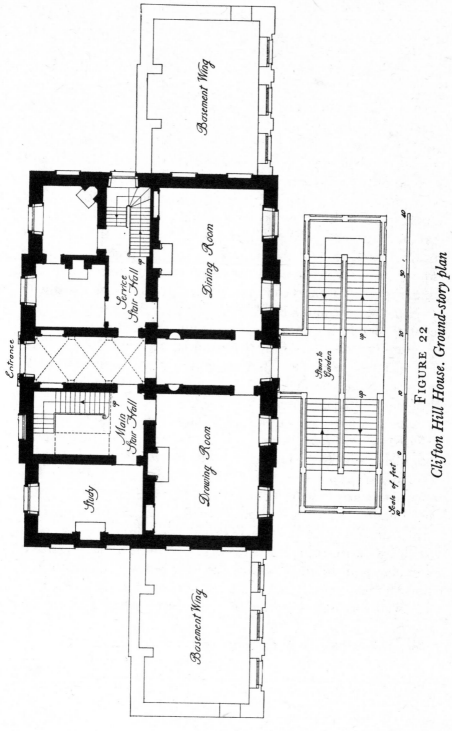

Entrance

Study

Main of
Stair Hall

Drawing Room

Basement Wing

Service
Stair Hall

Dining Room

Basement Wing

Stairs to
Garden

Scale of feet

FIGURE 22

Clifton Hill House. Ground-story plan

the central feature projects the double stairway that leads from the ground-story to the garden. This is also built in rough masonry and finished with a balustrade, while an arched opening adorns the face below the top landing. The basement is finished with a wide platband, forming a plinth to the ground-story face which is rusticated with horizontal and vertical V-jointing. The centrally-placed doorway is framed by a square-headed architrave, broken by rustic-blocks and a triple-keystone, with consoles supporting the cornice. The rectangular windows have heads formed of three voussoirs, the key breaking the line of the head and projecting almost flush with the first-floor platband. The upper part of the front presents a plain face with two tiers of carefully-spaced rectangular windows, those of the first-floor proportioned to a double-square in height, those above being square. All are without architraves, but the first-floor tier is underlined by a plain continuous sill. The front is finished with a simple cornice and a blocking-course over the wings, while the central feature is crowned with a triangular pediment, its tympanum carved with Fisher's armorial shield between floral festoons and pendants. The tympanum of the west-front pediment contains the finely carved monogram of Paul and Mary Fisher, with the building date of 1747.

The interior decorations generally appear to have been carried out to Ware's instructions, for much of the detail can be paralleled with that illustrated in his *Complete Body of Architecture*. As an exception, the Rococo element in the plasterwork is characteristic of local design and craftsmanship. The entrance-hall (Plate 58b) is divided half-way along its length by an arch-way, and the west portion is ceiled with three bays of cross-vaulting, carried out in plasterwork. The vault rises from scrolled consoles, and the intersections are enriched with chains of bell-flowers meeting in bosses. The moulded architrave to each six-panelled door is surmounted by a narrow pulvinated frieze and a cornice.

The stair-hall rises through two stories, and its walls are simply decorated with a scrolled band at the first-floor level, above it being a pedestal-course with a blind balustrade below the single window. The plain walls provide a foil to the wrought-iron railings of the staircase, with its bow-scrolled balusters enriched with fern-leaves, scrolls and foliage sprays (Plate 64c). An

ornamented cornice surrounds the ceiling, which is closely related in design to that shown on Plate 74 of Ware's book, having
an oval panel placed between two oblong ones, all formed by
raised and enriched mouldings (Plate 60b). Within the oval panel
the plasterer has indulged his fancy in an intricate Rococo
composition of shells, C- and acanthus-scrolls, arranged to form
four ogee-shaped motifs extending from an elaborate boss and
linked by floral garlands. A shell with acanthus-scrolls decorates
each of the four spandrels.

The two large reception-rooms on the ground-floor have
similar ceilings, in which the formal Palladian arrangement of
the panels contrasts with the delicate and wayward freedom of
the Rococo ornament within them. The finer ceiling is that in
the north-east room, where the windows have eared architraves
with scrolled sides that rise from pedestals, continuing the lines
of the dado, and the doors are framed in similarly eared architraves (Plate 62b). Each room contains a fine chimney-piece of
white marble, belonging to the class described by Ware as that
'whose sole ornament is sculpture'.

ARNO'S COURT

The interesting Georgian Gothic buildings at Arno's Court, first
named Mount Pleasant, were erected about 1760 for William
Reeve, the Quaker owner of some copper-smelting works at Crew's
Hole, and sometime Master of the Merchants' Society. Reeve improved the grounds and erected a large addition to the existing
house, standing just south of the Bath road which traversed his
estate. On the ground lying north of the road he built a bath-house,
linked by walled gardens to the fantastic court of stables and
offices now called Arno's Castle, which was originally approached through the pompous gateway that was removed in
1912 to its present position in front of the bath-house. While
factual evidence is lacking, the style and circumstances in which
the buildings were erected suggest that James Bridges was the
architect, with Thomas Paty as mason and carver, and Thomas
Stocking as plasterer. Horace Walpole saw the new buildings
when journeying from Bath to Bristol, and that self-appointed
arbiter of Gothic taste was moved to comment on them in a
letter to George Montagu, dated 22nd October 1766: 'Going
into the town, I was struck with a large Gothic building, coal-

[181]

black, and striped with white; I took it for the Devil's cathedral. When I came nearer, I found it was an uniform castle, lately built, and serving for stables and offices to a smart false Gothic house on the other side of the road.'

Reeve became bankrupt in 1774, and during September of that year his estate was advertised to be sold, for the duration of his life. It was then described as 'the Capital Messuage where Mr Reeve lately dwelt . . . in full View of the Turnpike Road, leading from Bristol to Bath; and the Stables, Coach-Houses, Granary, Barn, Gardens and Lawns, with all the Trees, Plants, Pines, Flowering-Shrubs, Statues, ornamental and other Things in the Green-House and Hot-House, and in the Gardens and Walks belonging thereto . . . and likewise about 26 acres of good Meadow and Pasture Ground . . . The Mansion-House, Buildings, Gardens and Lawns are so well known as not to require any particular Description of their Elegance'. After being in several ownerships, the estate was offered for sale in separate lots during May 1821, while the Sisterhood of the Asylum of the Good Shepherd acquired the house in 1850, and subsequently lessened its original charm by building some additions in an unusually sour and forbidding style.

As at the Royal Fort, the new part of the house was planned to provide reception-rooms and living quarters for the family and their guests, in a building of three stories without basement or garrets, these last not being required because the domestic offices and staff were accommodated in the original house. A shallow porch on the south-east front opens into a small fore-hall, with a bay-windowed room on each side. Beyond is the spacious main hall, with two doors on each side, those on the right leading to the large rooms on the north-east front, and those on the left to an ante, giving access to the older house and a service staircase, and to the small library. At the end of the hall was the main staircase, now partially removed, with one flight rising to a semi-circular half-landing, from whence a second flight returned to the first-floor, where there is a similar arrangement of rooms (Figure 23).

Externally the addition takes little cognisance of the older building, which it largely conceals from the road. The elevations are built of dressed freestone and the two principal fronts face south-east and north-east. Seen together they form a charming

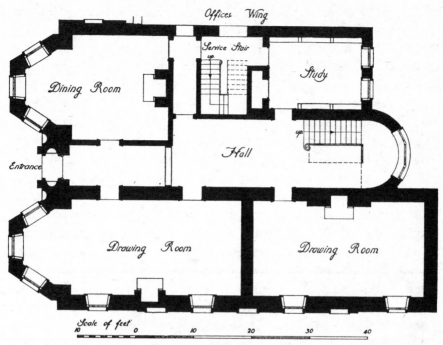

FIGURE 23
Arno's Court. Ground-story plan

composition wherein Georgian Classical formality is piquantly flavoured with Gothic detail. The south-east front is narrower than the other but rendered most important by its assertive treatment (Plate 35b). Two boldly-projecting splay-sided bays, with three windows to each story, rise to the full height of the building and flank a narrow centre, containing the porch and one window to each upper story. The north-east front is seven windows wide, some being false, and these are spaced so that five occur at regular intervals in the slightly-projecting central portion, with one more widely spaced at each end (Plate 35b). The architectural dress of both fronts is similar, though the south-east is additionally enriched by the elaborate decoration of the porch and the window over it.

The ground-story face is rusticated with horizontal V-jointing which is returned into the shallow reveals of the windows. These have flat-arched heads composed of one slightly-projecting voussoir on each side of a keystone that projects further and dies into the first-floor platband. The upper wall face is of plain ashlar, but the rectangular windows of the first-floor are dressed

[183]

with architraves of Classical profile, which rise from plain sills on consoles and are surmounted by false arches of flattened-ogee form, with cusping in their lunettes. The windows in the bays are larger than those on the north-east front, and the finials to the false arches rise from forward breaks in the second-floor stringcourse, which is plain and narrow. The second-floor windows are smaller than those below, and their rectangular openings are simply dressed with narrow moulded architraves rising from plain sills. A Gothic entablature, consisting of a flat stringcourse, plain frieze and cornice, is surmounted by a battle-mented parapet, heightened at each corner by a pedestal adorned with a sunk quatrefoil panel. The porch is a charming hybrid design, with a pointed archway having Gothic mouldings and Rococo spandrels, framed by Doric pilasters with icicle-work blocks and an entablature that breaks into an open-bedmould triangular pediment, its tympanum carved with a Rococo cartouche and foliage (Plate 55b). On each side of the porch is a semicircular niche with an ogee dripmould, and above the entablature is a plain parapet surmounted by a miniature battlement. The first-floor window above the porch has an arched head and a moulded architrave, within a framing of plain pilasters and an ogee-arch adorned with cusping. Several of the windows, including this one, retain their original top-sashes with the bars arranged to form a pattern of interlacing arches.

The interior has suffered from alteration and some features of decorative value have been removed or destroyed. Interest now centres on the two stucco ceilings that remain, one in the dining-room on the left of the fore-hall, and the other above the staircase-well and first-floor landing. The dining-room ceiling has for its centre a floral-knot with eight foliage sprays radiating therefrom. Four of these are linked by garlands which overlay a simple reed moulding forming a panel with four concave sides, lying diagonally on the ceiling. Rococo foliage extends from each apex to join the continuous band of *rocaille* ornaments bordering the main ceiling area and flowing into the bay, dividing this last into two. Each of the six spandrel-fields thus formed is adorned with a flying bird modelled in high relief (Plate 61a). The staircase ceiling is simpler, but no less beautiful. At its centre is an oval boss for suspending a chandelier, closely surrounded by interlacing C-scrolls with icicle- and foliage-pendants, forming a lozenge-shaped pattern that extends outwards to meet the border, a delicate chain of ornaments largely consisting of elongated C-scrolls, some decorated with floral-knots and others with icicles. At each end this border centres on a motif of interlacing foliated-scrolls, which diminish as they extend towards the central ornament (Plate 61b). The halls and principal rooms have enriched cornices, generally modillioned, but there is a Gothic cornice of ogee-spandrels in the fore-hall, and a small cove decorated with foliage-scrolls in the library. The Doric pilasters and elliptical arches in the halls are of wood, with the shafts, arch-mouldings and spandrels enriched with composition ornaments. The simple architraves of the hall doorcases are surmounted by triangular pediments resting on consoles, and the doors generally have six fielded panels. The staircase balustrade, which has been removed, was of wrought-iron and similar in design to that at the Royal Fort.

The Bath-House

Some 200 feet to the north of the mansion stands the Bath-House, described in the 1821 sale advertisement as 'a very elegant building used as a Cold Bath, with Dressing Rooms, having a lawn or pleasure garden in front, with a greenhouse and conservatory 45 feet by 15 feet, and a pinery 63 feet by 16 feet'. It is a small-scale building of one story, built in brick, with an elaborate front of stone designed in the 'improved Gothic' style of Batty Langley (Plate 36a). At each end of the long front stands a square pavilion, its plain face containing a four-centred arched doorway having a moulded splay and a dripmould resting on corbel-heads. Between these pavilions stretches the colonnade of thirteen bays, five being embraced by the segmental-bowed central feature. At the junctions of the straight and curved sections are three closely-grouped columns. The four-shafted columns support an entablature composed of frieze and cornice, the straight lengths of the former being adorned with a trefoil-arcaded motif, continued by a Gothic fret across the pavilions. The simple cornice is surmounted by a pedestal-parapet with openwork panels of various Gothic fret designs placed to correspond with the intercolumniations of the colonnade. Each end

[185]

pavilion is surmounted by a stone dome of octagonal plan and ogee profile, with a ball-finial, while an attic stage corresponding in width with the central bow forms a plain pedestal that rises to conceal the bath-room roof, its face being divided into two bays by narrow projections that are surmounted by three large stone vases of hybrid design. The rear wall of the colonnade is decorated with niches, placed between the shafted responds to the columns, and in the centre is the door to the bath, framed in a trefoil-headed opening with its spandrels containing Rococo ornaments in stucco.

In plan the bath-room is an octagon with two long sides, the entrance and doors to the two dressing-rooms being in the three short sides at the south end. There are three arch-headed niches in each long wall, and one in each short wall at the north end. The plain wall faces terminate in a plaster cornice of coved section, formed of free-standing acanthus-leaves between plain spandrels, the latter rising from half-profile masks of three human characters, used in ordered repetition. A cornice of similar design, but more elaborate in detail, adorns the breakfast-room at Corsham Court. From the cornice springs a high quadrant-cove, decorated with charmingly designed ornaments of Chinese Rococo character. In the middle of each long side is a fantastic architectural landscape, framed by an oval wreath of palm, rising from ripples. This wreath is linked by laurel festoons and pendants to Rococo motifs composed of C-scrolls, dolphins, fountain-jets, shells, masks, etc., placed at either end of each long side and over each short side. A narrow moulding divides the cove from the plain flat ceiling, which is pierced at each end by an octagonal lantern-light (Plate 63a). Unfortunately, years of neglect have had their effect on this delightful and interesting little building, which has now become very dilapidated and must fall into complete ruin unless some protective measures are quickly taken.

The Gateway

The stone gateway now standing in front of the Bath-House was originally the entrance to the Castle forecourt, being linked with its east front by a curving wing-wall. Originally designed to house some statues and other carvings removed from Newgate and Lawford's Gate, which were demolished about the time that

Reeve was erecting his buildings, this hybrid Gothic gateway is obviously a mid eighteenth-century pastiche, and it is incredible that a controversy over its origin should have arisen, as it did in 1911. The lofty wall-like structure consists of a wide central feature, containing the large round-arched carriage entrance, set slightly forward from narrow wings, each with a smaller archway for pedestrians. The middle archway has a coved reveal, boldly decorated and broken by a plain impost that continues across the wings. Each side arch has a plain unbroken architrave and is surmounted by a niche, with shafted jambs rising from the impost to support a decorated ogee-shaped canopy. Above these niches runs a moulding that breaks in the central feature to form an arched surround for a coat-of-arms that was never carved. Immediately over the arch is a plain stringcourse that continues across the wings, where it is surmounted by a parapet of ogee-headed battlements. The central feature is heightened by a further stage, which is decorated with shallow panelling resembling window-tracery, flanking a niche that has an elaborate frame of grotesque *termini* supporting pinnacles and an ogee-arched head adorned with cusps and crockets. A parapet of ogee-headed battlements again provides a finish. It remains to be said that much of the wall surface is lightly decorated with shallow sunk panelling (Plate 36b). The reverse elevation is basically similar in its composition, but here decoration is confined to the horizontal bands that define the various stages, and the plain architraves to the arched openings and niches.

The Castle

Some 350 feet north of the Bath-House stands the Castle, which for all its essential absurdity, and in spite of the changed character of its environment, must be accounted a fairly successful example of an utilitarian building invested with a romantic dress and treated to form a picturesque object in a composed landscape (Plate 37a). This structure was doubtless intended to pass for a medieval fortress, and the builder accordingly dressed it with round and square towers, battlements, and a wealth of Gothic details, but the result is completely of its period and full of naïve charm. A statement in *Felix Farley* for 1st March 1766, reporting that 'fragments from old St Werburgh's Church' had been 're-erected to adorn a gentleman's

[187]

Gothic stable in the neighbourhood', lends support to the probability that Reeve's architect was James Bridges, he having been responsible for rebuilding St Werburgh's between 1758–61.

The Castle was planned to house a laundry, brewhouse, staff bedrooms, and stabling for eleven horses, disposed in the quadrangular building surrounding the courtyard, with two coachhouses in the projecting north-east wing. It is largely built in blocks of slightly iridescent black slag, the waste product of Reeve's smelting-works, freestone being used for dressing the windows and doors, and for the stringcourses, battlemented parapets, and all the ornaments.

The entrance front faces east and consists of a slightly projecting central feature that rises into a square tower, flanked by low and short wings terminated by round towers. Below the square tower is the arched entrance to the courtyard, furnished with elaborately panelled doors and ceiled with a plaster vault. Above the entrance is a smaller arched opening, probably intended for a clock-dial, and over it an arched three-light window with cusped decoration. The tower is finished with a coved cornice, surmounted by a battlemented parapet adorned with Gothic frets, and the original roof was a lead dome of octagonal plan and ogee profile. Each wing contains two widely-spaced arched windows, divided into two lights with cusped decoration in their heads. A plain band of stone, which is continued round the end towers and stopped against the central archway, defines the false attic which is adorned with panels representing two-light windows, responding to those below. The round towers are divided by plain stone bands into three stages, the two upper ones being liberally adorned with make-believe loopholes. Plain battlements form the finish to both wings and towers. The battlemented wing-wall curving forward from the left-hand tower was originally joined by the stone gateway already described. From the right-hand tower projects a short wing with a front of three arches, the high middle one opening through the wing and that on either side framing a coach-house door. The west front has a square central tower of three stages, flanked by two-storied wings, each broken by a small round tower and terminated by a larger one. The decorative details are generally similar to those of the east front.

The courtyard is perhaps the most successful part of the whole

[188]

design. The elements in its composition have been grouped to make their best effect when viewed from the east entrance, and the west side is accordingly treated with much greater elaboration than the others (Plate 37b). The three-stage tower of oblong plan projects forward from balancing wings, which also stand forward from the short walls that form returns to the north and south sides. Massive diagonally-projecting buttresses rise with weathered offsets to die into the angles of both tower and wings, but do not occur elsewhere. The stages of the tower are defined by plain stone bands, the first being broken by the four-centred head of the false archway that answers the opening below the east tower. This false archway, with its plain architrave and a keyblock carved with a man's head wearing a liripipe, frames an arched doorway that has a moulded splay and is surmounted by a Rococo armorial cartouche. High up in the second stage of the tower is an ornamental niche with a cusped ogee-arched head, and the top stage contains a pair of two-light windows with cusped arches. The enriched cove-cornice is surmounted by a battlemented parapet, adorned with interlaced arcading and having a square pinnacle at each corner. Each wing has a two-light window with a two-centred head adorned by cusping, and the false attic story is decorated with two stone panels representing foliated circular windows. The narrow cove-cornice is surmounted by ornamental battlements that stop against pinnacles at the angles. The north and south sides are treated as foils to the elaborate west side, and form identical and balancing compositions, each containing five two-light arch-headed windows that are spaced out at regular intervals. A door is substituted for the lower part of the middle window, and further doors are centred between the two windows on either side. The spandrel-spaces on either side of the middle window are broken by grotesque *termini*, surmounted by panelled pilasters that rise into crocketted pinnacles. These flank a flattened-ogee pediment, which is panelled with a cusped lunette set between two quatrefoils, and has a moulded and crocketted coping. The plain battlement is continued on each side of this feature,

The Castle, which is in excellent repair and appears to be well cared for, has little of interest in its interior beyond the room called 'the Chapel', where the segmental-arched ceiling is formed into panels by richly decorated mouldings.

THE ROYAL FORT

> Long in neglect, an ancient Dwelling stood
>> With tottering Walls, worn Roofs, and perish'd Wood,
> Till gen'rous Tyndal, fir'd with Sense and Taste
> Saw here Confusion,—Ruin there,—and Waste
> Resolved at once to take the Rubbish down,
>> And raise a Palace there to grace the TOWN,
> For Aid,—he, Jones,—Paladio,—Vanbrough viewed;
> Or Wallis,—Bridges,—Patty's Plans pursued;
> No Matter which,—the Fabric soon uprose,
>> And all its various Beauties did disclose.
>
> J. W. SHIREHAMPTON

This rather obsequious verse, probably written by John Wallis, and published by *Felix Farley* on 27th June 1767, celebrates Thomas Tyndall's rebuilding of the Royal Fort, the house held by his family since 1737, under lease from the Corporation. About 1753 he set about acquiring the leases of various fields and properties adjacent to the Fort, some belonging to the Corporation and others to the Dean and Chapter. Tyndall then applied his energies and fortune towards creating a small but beautiful park, designed to form the setting for the house he intended building. The above-quoted verse suggests that plans and estimates were invited from the leading architects and builders then practising in Bristol, and the new house appears to have been completed early in 1761. The Corporation's Bargain-Book contains the following particulars relating to the lease and subsequent sale of the Royal Fort to Thomas Tyndall:

'Thomas Tyndall—holds the above Premises by lease dated 14th December 1757, To Commence from 25th March 1760 for 40 years Renewable at the Expiration of every 14th Year for the Fine of £40 in Consideration of pulling down the Premises and Rebuilding the Tenure altered from 3 lives to 40 years. Fine £80 Rent declaro.

N.B. All the Above Premises Sold to the aforesaid Thomas Tyndall Esq in Fee by Order of Common Council 12th May 1761 for the Sum of £670 as per Deed dated 26th March 1763.'

In 1791, when the rage for building was at its height, Thomas Tyndall sold his house and park to a syndicate headed by T. G. Vaughan, who intended to create a magnificent new residential quarter on this site. The story of this speculation and its failure has already been told (pages 26–7), and it is sufficient to say here that the property reverted in 1798 to Colonel Thomas Tyndall, who had succeeded on his father's death in 1794. Humphrey Repton was now engaged to recreate the park, which had been laid waste by the builders' excavations. He turned these defects to brilliant account in one of his typical schemes, of which, unfortunately, but little survives today. The outlying areas of the park were built over about 1850–60, although the Tyndall family continued to reside at the Fort until 1916. The house now forms part of the University of Bristol, and is well cared for, although it has been almost dwarfed by the towering structure that has replaced the stables. These were contained in a two-storied building with a simple Classical front that had a pedimented central feature, and a cupola with a weather-vane bearing Thomas Tyndall's initials and the date 1760.

The design of the Royal Fort, attributed in turn to Wood the elder, Strahan, and Thomas Paty, is now proved to be the work of James Bridges, by the following items of evidence:

1. The advertisement with which Bridges concludes his pamphlet entitled 'Four Designs for rebuilding Bristol Bridge', published in 1760, wherein he stresses the advantages of having models prepared of intended buildings, and cites the particular success of the model made by him of the Fort, for T. Tyndal, Esq.

2. The valedictory letter written by an admirer of Bridges, and printed by *Felix Farley* on 22nd October 1763, which contains the statement—'As to his Business, that of an ARCHITECT, his Buildings are elegant and sound: that the finished Edifice of the Fort, with which every one is delighted, and that religious one, now raising on the Bank of the Avon in Bristol . . . speak greatly to his Advantage'.

Bridges' model for the Fort still survives in fairly good condition. It is a simple, workmanlike job, built in wood to a small scale and without ornamentation. Its construction in horizontal sections, with the roof and each floor lifting off, enables one to obtain a very clear idea of the internal arrangements (Plate 38a, b).

Miss Tyndall, the last of her family to occupy the house, once stated that its builder was named Gay. This leaves little room for doubt that the mason employed was Robert Gay, who worked elsewhere for Bridges. The other principal craftsmen were Thomas Paty, who carried out the stone and wood carving, and Thomas Stocking, who executed the elaborate stucco decorations.

The new house was designed to provide reception-rooms and living quarters for the family and their guests, in the three-storied building without basement or garrets. These were not required because the older building adjoining on the east was adapted to accommodate the kitchens, offices, and staff rooms. Bridges was an efficient planner and he devised a simple and effective arrangement of well-proportioned rooms (Figure 24). The main doorway, in the middle of the north front, opens

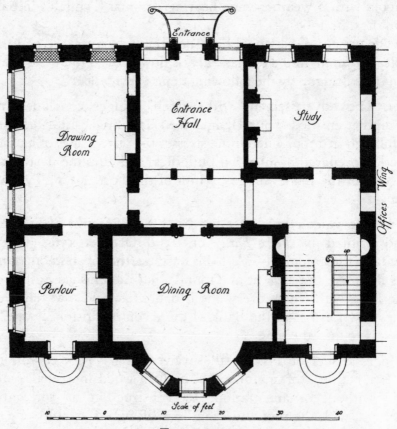

FIGURE 24
The Royal Fort. Ground-story plan
[192]

directly into the spacious hall with its screen of three arches leading to the wide east-to-west corridor. This has doors opening to the drawing-rooms on the west, to the dining-room in the middle of the south side, and to the north-east room, while a wide archway opens to the staircase-hall in the south-east angle, and a smaller archway at the east end gives access to the older building. The main stair ascends to a half-landing and returns to the first-floor level, where the principal bedrooms etc., are arranged on a similar plan. The attic story is approached by a smaller staircase at the east end of the first-floor corridor.

The Fort has three fronts of freestone, which face west, south, and north, and while each differs considerably from the other in composition and ornateness, relationship is maintained by the continuance of their horizontal members round the building. The elevations are typical Georgian Classical designs of an effective but slightly commonplace character, quite obviously the work of no architectural grammarian, but their defects are more than redeemed by the fine quality of the masonry and the beauty of Thomas Paty's Rococo carvings. The west front is the most important and consists of a central feature, three windows wide, set slightly forward from narrow wings, each one window wide (Plate 39). The rectangular windows of the ground-story are unadorned, but those belonging to the central feature are framed by a blind arcade of three arches, formed in rusticated V-jointed masonry with plain imposts and triple-keystones. There is the customary platband at first-floor level, surmounted in the centre by a pedestal-course broken slightly forward below the three windows, each of which is dressed with a shouldered and eared architrave, plain frieze and a triangular pediment. The pedestal cornice-line is continued by a plain sill across the wings, where the windows are similarly dressed except that a cornice replaces the pediment. The square windows to the top story have architrave frames, those of the central feature being shouldered at each corner. The front is finished with a modillioned cornice and a pedestal-parapet, which has balustrades over the wings and stops against the triangular pediment crowning the central feature. The tympanum of this pediment is splendidly carved with the Tyndall's escutcheon surrounded by a wealth of Rococo scrolled ornament.

The south front has for its central feature a boldly-projecting

[193]

splay-sided bay of three equal faces, which rises to the full height of the building and has narrow flanks broken slightly forward from the wings (Plate 40a). This feature also has a rusticated ground-story, the V-jointing being returned into the reveals of the three arch-headed windows in the bay. Central in each wing is a square-headed doorway, dressed with an architrave framed by pilasters and scrolled consoles that support an open-bed-mould triangular pediment, its tympanum carved with the Tyndall's crest amidst Rococo decoration. The platband and plain sill are carried across this front to underline the first-floor windows, which in the bay are without architraves but have flat arches of stepped and projecting voussoirs with female mask keystones. In each wing is a small Venetian-window, its side-lights framed by plain architraves finished with cornices that return into the reveals of the middle-light, which has an arched head with a moulded archivolt broken by a triple-keystone. The second-floor windows are unadorned, and the modillioned cornice and pedestal-parapet, the latter having a balustrade in each face of the bay, form a finish to the front.

The north elevation is the simplest in character, and has a central feature set slightly forward from wings that almost equal it in width (Plate 40b). The most important decorative feature is the centrally-placed doorway, which consists of a Tuscan arch-way framed by engaged three-quarter plain-shafted Ionic columns, with their entablature and a triangular pediment (Plate 56a). The ground-story windows, one on each side of the doorway and two in either wing—those in the right-hand wing were originally blind—are rectangular and unadorned, as are those in the upper stories of the wings. The first-floor platband and sill are continued across this front, but the latter is moulded in the central feature where it underlines a range of three equally-spaced windows, with plain piers, Tuscan imposts, and arched-heads with moulded archivolts broken by triple-key-stones. The corresponding windows on the second-floor have flat arches of stepped and projecting voussoirs, and this front is finished like the others with a modillioned cornice and a pedestal-parapet having three balustraded sections over the central-feature windows.

All the windows have double-hung sashes, properly sub-divided by glazing-bars, and the six-panelled entrance door

[194]

is surmounted by a simple fanlight. The entrance steps are flanked by outward-curving railings of fine design, with scroll-work panels of wrought-iron, and tall standard lampholders that are furnished with link-extinguishers. It is a pleasure to record that these fronts are almost free from alteration, except for such minor changes as the lowered sills of the ground-floor windows on the west front, and the opening-up of two blind ground-floor windows on the right side of the north front.

The Fort's chief attraction lies in the splendid Rococo embellishment of its interior, where the guiding hand was probably that of Thomas Paty, whose work here may owe something to the designs of Thomas Lightoler, published in *The Modern Builder's Assistant*, dated 1754. The ground-floor rooms, and the staircase-hall in particular, are unrivalled in Bristol.

The entrance-hall has a beautifully co-ordinated scheme, where attention is focussed on the screen of three arches that leads into the cross-corridor (Plate 57b). The piers are faced with Doric pilasters, the shafts of those on the main faces being fluted, while those of the reveals, being wider, are panelled. The arches have moulded and enriched archivolts, and panelled soffits, which are broken by triple-keyblocks, the middle ones moulded, while the spandrels are adorned with floral pendants suspended from ribbon-bows. Above the arcade is a Doric entablature that continues round the room, its frieze containing a series of metopes variously composed of bows and quivers, drums, hunting-horns, shields and lances, with occasionally the conventional ox-skull. The soffit of the cornice corona is enriched with paterae placed between the mutules. As a foil to this richness, the side walls are left plain except for the carved Rococo lamp-brackets which project between crossed stems of Indian-corn. The ceiling also is plain but for the central ornament of branches curved and radiating from a boss. The scheme of the hall is continued into the cross-corridor, where the walls are treated with blind arcading (Plate 59a). The elliptical-headed arches at each end, and the one crossing this corridor, have single keyblocks adorned with human masks.

The wide elliptical-headed archway that opens to the staircase-hall is more richly decorated than the others, its soffit panels being filled with scrolled ornaments, while a grotesque mask forms the keyblock (Plate 59b). The staircase-hall is two

[195]

stories high, and its walls are enchantingly decorated with a series of modelled grape-vines, rising in wavering lines to spread their cluster-laden branches in interlacing patterns over the surface. At the foot of each vine is a small pastoral scene, here with a dog, there with a fox, sometimes a group of sheep, and then a pond with ducks, while squirrels and birds rest in the security of the upper branches (Plates 59b, 60c). All of this freely-flowing naturalistic ornamentation is held in check by the architectural forms of the Ionic pilastered Venetian-window above the half-landing, and the richly adorned modillioned cornice that surrounds the ceiling. This has in its centre a chandelier-boss, around which sport three winged *putti*, and behind them is a cloud from which sun-rays are bursting. This motif is enclosed by a heavy wreath of elaborately modelled fruits, flowers, and foliage, knotted with ribbons that flow over the plain surround. Rococo motifs, composed of interlacing C- and acanthus-scrolls, extend diagonally from this wreath (Plate 60d). The very fine staircase railing of wrought-iron is composed of S-scrolled balusters, enriched with hammered leaves and delicate scrolls, and the handrail is of mahogany.

The dining-room walls are wainscoted, with a series of tall and slightly-sunk panels having incurved corners ranged above the chair-rail. The fine chimney-piece of coloured marbles is of simple design, with Doric columns supporting a broken entablature, but the shelf is surmounted by a pediment-like cresting of elaborately carved and modelled ornament in the Chinese Rococo style. The space above, left blank for a picture, is flanked by carved pendant trophies, emblematic of field sports. Pendants in a similar style, but composed of fruits and flowers, are placed in the panels on either side of the wide segmental bow on the south side of the room. Perhaps the most delightful feature in this room is the Chinese Rococo surround to the doorway (Figure 25). The six-panelled mahogany door is framed by an enriched architrave, and on either side stand slender columns with wreathed shafts and foliated capitals, from whence serpentine scrolls extend to meet over the doorway, tracing the outline of a swan-necked pediment. Above this is a painted landscape, perhaps by Michael Edkins, set in a scrolled frame and flanked by wide-flung festoons with ribbon-bows and pendants. The walls are finished with a cornice, its corona being

FIGURE 25
The Royal Fort
Dining-room doorway

supported by Rococo consoles with lozenge-shaped pateræ between them. Chains formed of freely-flowing C-scrolls and other Rococo ornaments form an outer border and a diagonally-placed panel on the ceiling, in the centre of which is a flying eagle, modelled in high relief.

In the two drawing-rooms the walls were intended to be hung with silk or wallpaper, so that the use of decorative plaster-work was confined to the cornices and ceilings. In the larger room there is a narrow cove-cornice, formed of free-standing acanthus-leaves alternating with palmettes between decorated spandrels, while the ceiling has a border and central panel of delicately-modelled and freely-flowing Rococo ornaments. Flying cranes, with their necks and heads modelled clear of the ceiling surface, are introduced into the angles of the border. This room contains a fine chimney-piece of coloured marbles, with terminal-figures of a shepherd and shepherdess supporting the shelf, while a relief of a lamb decorates the central panel of

[197]

the lintel. The mahogany doors have enriched panel-mouldings, so have the window linings and shutters, which are of painted deal. The painted deal mouldings of the architraves, skirting, and chair-rail are also freely enriched (Plate 63b).

ALBEMARLE ROW

No. 5 Albemarle Row was built in 1762, as the date carved in the pediment testifies. An examination of the deeds relating to this house, known as Cumberland House, shows that it was erected for John Webb, a gentleman of Cherstoke, by James Fear, a house-carpenter, in conformity with the terms of an indenture dated 24th June 1762, and all but one of the other houses in the Row appear to have been built about the same time, under similar conditions. The owners of the ground, Christopher and Mary Budge, had granted to Webb by a previous indenture 'all that plot piece or parcel of ground as the same hath been allotted or marked out for him by the said James Fear, lying and being in the Parish of Clifton, in the County of Gloucester, containing in width in the front eastwards, next to a certain street laid out or intended to be laid out called Albemarle Street, 47 feet, and extending itself of the same width backwards towards the west 95 feet'. The ground to the south had been similarly contracted for by one Nathaniel Crook, and that to the north by Fear himself.

Webb undertook to 'lay out and expend the full sum of £500 at least . . . in erecting one good and substantial Messuage or Dwelling House, which shall face Albemarle Street in a regular manner so as to fill up with such wings or buildings for offices as may adjoin thereto the whole front of the said plot of ground hereby granted, leaving an Area in front of the said Messuage, and that the same Messuage shall consist of three stories in height from the level of the parlour or principal floor, and be fronted with freestone or brick ornamented with freestone quoins, arched over the windows, and a cornice and parapet over it, and that the parlour story shall not be less than 10 feet the chamber story not less than 9 feet, and the attic story not less than 8 feet in height in the clear'.

The influence, if not the hand, of Thomas Paty is to be discerned in the design of these houses, and it was probably he who supplied the dressed stonework and carved the monogram set in the pediment of No. 5. Furthermore, the lease stated that Webb's share in the cost of making common sewers, etc., was 'to be apportioned by Thomas Paty, Architect, or in the case of his death, in such proportion as any other architect or master builder of good name and character shall be named by Christopher Budge and his wife Mary'.

No. 1, a small house of about 1780 with a front of little interest, is an extension of the original row, Nos. 2 to 8, which is a uniform range of houses with their fronts stepped up to accord with the ground's steep rise from south to north (Plate 41). Each house contains a basement and three stories, the third varying in height from house to house, with a garret story in the roof. Nos. 2 to 5 are double-fronted, with central doorways and five windows to each upper story; Nos. 6 and 7 are single-fronted, three windows wide and with the doorways on the right-hand side; while No. 8 shares a five-windows-wide frontage with a house that has its entrance-front in Hope Square. The fronts are of red brick with freestone dressings, a bandcourse above the basement, channel-jointed pilasters marking the party-walls, and a crowning cornice that is broken and returned round the pilasters between Nos. 2 and 3, 4 and 5, 5 and 6, and 7 and 8. The wall face of No. 5 is set slightly forward from the general building line to form the central feature, which is three windows wide, defined by long and short stone quoins, and crowned by a triangular pediment against which the plain brick parapet stops. The brick tympanum of this pediment contains an oval stone panel carved with John Webb's monogram and the building date 1763 (Figure 26). All the windows are dressed with plain stone sills and have flat arches of stepped and projecting voussoirs. Nos 2, 3, 5 and 8 have stone doorcases of identical design, with a square-headed architrave broken by rustic-blocks, voussoirs and a triple-keystone, while plain consoles rise from the side pilasters to support a triangular pediment. The doorcases to Nos 4, 6 and 7 are similar, but the architrave is broken only by the triple-keystone (Plate 55c, d). The front doors show different arrangements of fielded panels, and while some fill the doorways others are surmounted by wooden fanlights in Gothic taste. The windows of No. 5 retain sash-bars of the original section, but those of the other houses have generally been replaced by ones of a lighter pattern. The basement areas are

[199]

FIGURE 26
No. 5 Albemarle Row, Hotwells. Elevation

guarded by iron railings, those at Nos 4 to 7 having decorative wrought panels at intervals, sometimes capped with scrolled finials.

These houses were built to serve as lodgings for fashionable visitors to the Hot-well, and their plans show a simple arrangement of rooms which are nearly uniform in size. The double-fronted houses have a wide entrance-hall leading through an arched opening to the staircase-well, with a front and a back room on either side, and a closet opening out of the latter (Figure 27). One such house, offered for sale during August 1785, is described as 'having 2 Parlours, 2 Dining-Rooms, 4 Lodging Rooms on the Ground Floor, 3 Ditto on the Dining-Room Floor, 5 Ditto on the Attic Story, 10 Garrets, 2 large Kitchens, 3 Servants Halls,

[200]

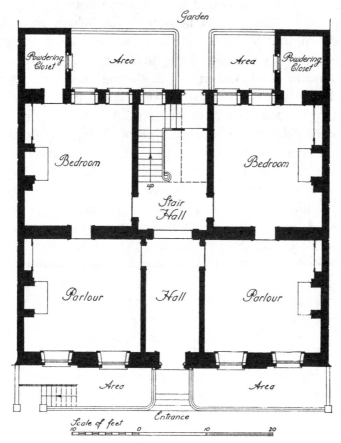

FIGURE 27

No. 5 Albemarle Row, Hotwells. Ground-story plan

good arched Cellars, Pantries, and other proper Offices, with an exceedingly good and pleasant Garden'. The interiors are well finished but contain no decorative features of special interest. The wooden staircases have turned balustrades, and the lodging-rooms are finished with panelled dadoes and simple plaster cornices.

DOWRY PARADE

Dowry Parade, taking its name from the wide paved walk in front of its houses, forms in effect an extension of the east side of Dowry Square. It is a uniform terrace of double- and single-fronted houses, built during 1763–4 by Benjamin Probert, Robert Comfort, and other speculating builders who sought to

[201]

profit by meeting the demand for lodging-houses convenient to the Hot-well. The ground landlords, the Merchants' Society, granted building leases for the term of 39 years 6 months, renewable every 14 years, and beginning 25th March 1762. One of the houses was advertised for sale during September 1764, and described as 'the third house on the New Parade, newly-built, and let at £80 a year'. Another, offered for sale by Robert Comfort in *Felix Farley* for 23rd October 1765, was described as —'A double house containing 43 Feet in front, having a good Hall and Staircase, two Parlours in front on the first floor with three good bed chambers behind same, two large Dining rooms in front, and three good bed chambers behind them, over which are 6 good bed chambers, and over them 9 good garrets, besides good kitchens, servants halls, arched cellars, &c'.

These houses are generally similar to many others built hereabouts during this period, and contain a basement, three principal stories, and a garret story in the pitched roof. The double-fronted houses are five windows wide, and the single-fronted three. The elevations have all the characteristics of Thomas Paty's designing, although they are not necessarily his work. They are built of red brick with freestone dressings, there are the usual pilasters of channel-jointed stones defining the party-walls, and the windows have flat arches of stepped and projecting voussoirs, but the narrow cornice forms the coping and is not surmounted by a parapet (Plate 42a). The use of exposed sash-boxes nearly flush with the building face is a survival of an earlier practice. The single-fronted houses have stone doorcases similar to those in Albemarle Row, with an architrave broken by rustic-blocks and surmounted by a triangular pediment. Similar doorcases were replaced by paired doorways within simply treated arch-headed openings, when the double-houses were subdivided at a later date, probably about 1790. The charming metal fanlights and delicate balconies that grace some of the houses are additions of much the same date.

BOYCE'S BUILDINGS, CLIFTON

Boyce's Buildings were erected in 1763 for Thomas Boyce, a peruke-maker of King Street, to serve as lodging-houses for wealthy visitors to the Hot-well. Boyce spent some £8,000 on the buildings and their furnishings, lost heavily by his speculation,

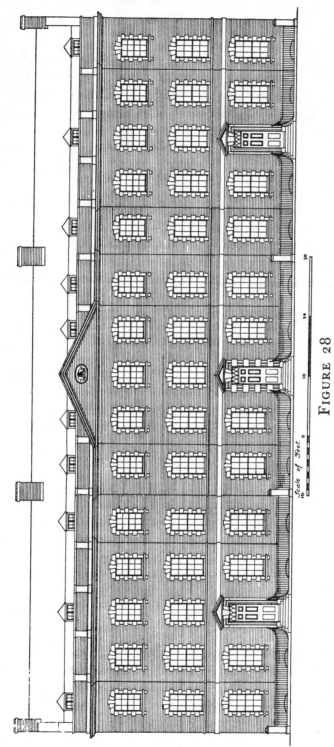

Scale of Feet.

FIGURE 28

Boyce's Buildings, Clifton. Elevation

and was declared bankrupt in November 1772. The property was advertised to be sold by auction on 18th February 1773, when it was described as consisting of '3 capital, substantial and commodious Messuages, having a Terras, or Gravel Walk, extending the whole length of the Buildings: Grass Slopes, Gravel and Grass Walks in Front, a Pavement Walk and Pleasure Garden, 3 Summer Houses, or Tea Rooms: 5 Stables, containing 34 Stalls.'

Before the destruction of the right-hand house of the group and the mutilation of the others, Boyce's Buildings formed a handsome and uniform range of three double-fronted houses, each containing a basement and three stories, with a garret story in the mansard roof. The fronts, which are evidently the work of Thomas Paty, are built of red brick, now faced with cement, and dressed with freestone. Each house-front is five windows wide, the middle three being embraced in a slightly projecting central feature. The ground-story is now hidden by shops that extend over the original front gardens. The rectangular windows of both upper stories are dressed with band-architraves, which rise from plain sills resting on corbels, and are broken by rustic-blocks and keystones. A pedestal-parapet surmounts the main cornice, stopping against the triangular pediment that crowns and emphasizes the central feature of the middle house. The tympanum of this pediment is ornamented with an oval stone panel, carved with Thomas Boyce's monogram and the building date 1763 (Figure 28).

Nearby, on Clifton Green, are two adjoining houses that were designed by Thomas Paty, and built about 1765 for Samuel Worrall. The right-hand house has been considerably altered, but the other, Prospect House, has a front closely resembling those of Boyce's Buildings, except that here the first-floor middle window has an arched head (Plate 42b).

BRUNSWICK SQUARE

The proposal to build Brunswick Square was noticed by *Felix Farley* on 19th April 1766, in a paragraph stating that 'the plan for building a handsom street from just below the Full Moon was put into execution Wednesday last by beginning the first house. The street is to run back through the gardens, and at the further end of it will be built a most handsom square'. The new development was sited partly on the garden of Sir Abraham Elton's house in St James's Barton, but mostly on garden ground belonging to Joseph Loscombe, a merchant who lived in a large house in Wilder Street. Two indentures, dated 9th and 30th September 1766, show that Loscombe agreed to grant building leases of certain plots on the south side of Cumberland Street and on the west side of Brunswick Square to Thomas Manley, plaisterer, and Isaac Manley, mason, who undertook to 'erect and finish substantial messuages of three stories, with fronts of brick ornamented with stone', in accordance with the plans prepared for Loscombe by George Tully. The building of the south row was begun at much the same time by Edmund Workman, a house-carpenter who was closely associated with Tully. The finished houses in the square began to be tenanted during 1771, but by that time the supply of new dwellings in this quarter had far exceeded all demands, and it was not until about 1784 that Workman found support for the tontine subscription raised to enable him to complete the east row. The ground behind the intended north row was demised at an early date to the trustees of Lewin's Mead Chapel, who laid it out as a cemetery, and that might have deterred speculators from erecting houses on this side. The ground was eventually granted to the Congregationalists, whose neo-Greek Chapel, designed by William Armstrong, was opened during 1835.

There is no evidence proving that Tully did more than plan the layout of the square, and perhaps offer suggestions for the elevations, for while they share a material unity and have certain details in common, each row was built to a different design. The houses in the south row are very similar to certain houses in Dowry and King squares, both projects with which Tully was closely concerned, but on the other hand both the south and west rows are closely related in general design and detail with buildings known to be by Thomas Paty.

The area, measuring approximately 250 feet square, is approached by the streets entering at each angle. The central green, now shockingly neglected, is crossed by diagonal paths and was originally planted with elms, but these were removed in 1858 and replaced with the present limes.

The south row contains seven houses, the middle one being double- and the rest single-fronted, while those at each end

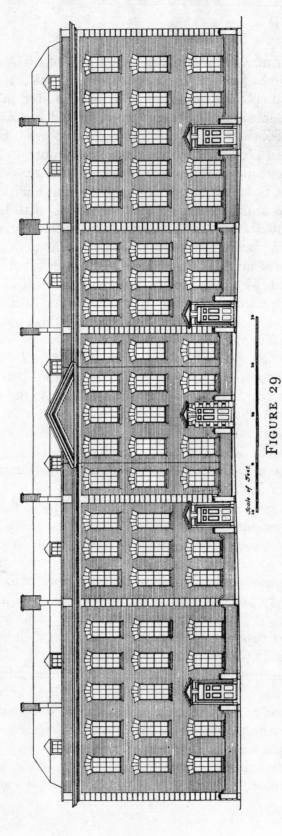

FIGURE 29

Brunswick Square. Elevation of the south side

have their entrances in the return fronts to York and Gloucester streets. The three-storied fronts, built of red brick with free-stone dressings, are combined to form a balanced composition with an emphasized centre (Plate 43a, Figure 29). This design bears a close resemblance to Albemarle Row, to which it is inferior in scale and detail, but superior in having the unbroken horizontal lines due to a level site. The outer angles and the party-walls between the houses are marked by pilasters of channel-jointed stones, these being omitted between the two houses at either end where a double-fronted effect is intended. The middle house is five windows wide, three being contained in the central feature which is formed by a slight forward break in the building face. This break is not emphasized by stone quoins as in the similar houses in Albemarle Row and Dowry Square, but the cornice is surmounted by a triangular pediment of stone with a plain brick tympanum. The adjoining houses are three windows wide, and their doorways are placed against the party-walls of the middle house. The fronts at each end are shared by two houses, so that the five windows are differently spaced in groups of three and two. The window openings have plain stone sills and segmental-arched heads of stepped and projecting voussoirs. The centrally-placed doorway to the middle house is square-headed, with a surrounding architrave broken by rustic-blocks and voussoirs that rise through the frieze to intercept the bed-mouldings at the base of the triangular pediment. The other houses have doorcases of a similar but simpler design, in which the moulded architrave is broken only by a triple keystone, and the triangular pediment rests upon plain consoles.

The unfinished west row contains three houses, with three-storied fronts of brick, uniformly adorned with freestone dress-ings. The frontages are almost equal in width, and Nos 15 and 16 have three windows to each upper story while No. 14 has two, spaced at wider intervals, this house having its entrance-front in Cumberland Street. The party-walls are defined by plain stone pilasters, which rise from the plinth to the parapet coping, broken only by the main cornice which is returned round them. The square-headed entrances to Nos 15 and 16 have similar doorcases to the middle house of the south row, and the rect-angular window openings are uniformly dressed with moulded architraves, which rise from corbelled sills and are broken by rustic-blocks and triple-keystones. The return front of No. 14 is divided into three bays, each one window wide, the central one, containing the entrance, being broken slightly forward and crowned with a triangular pediment. The doorway is arched and framed by engaged Doric columns, their entablature-blocks being united by an open-bedmould triangular pediment. The windows in this front are without enrichments, and the brick-work has been entirely faced with cement.

The east row, which was not finished until early in 1786, is a uniform range of six houses. That at either end has its entrance centred in its return frontage, and the others are single-fronted houses planned in pairs to share common chimney-stacks. The fronts, which are of red brick dressed with freestone, are all three windows wide and generally three stories high, but each end house is treated as a pavilion, projecting slightly forward from the main building line and heightened by an attic story (Plate 43b). The elevational design departs in several ways from the scheme of the earlier houses. The floor heights are greater, and while there are no demarcations between the houses, the strong horizontal emphasis is strengthened by the plain plinth, the platband immediately below the first-floor windows, and the crowning modillioned cornice, all of stone. The windows generally have stone sills and flat arches of stepped and pro-jecting voussoirs, but those in the attics have flat arches of gauged brickwork, and the wall face between them is adorned with plain stone pilasters rising to the moulded coping. The doorways to Brunswick Square are identical in design, the arch-headed opening being framed by plain piers and a moulded archivolt broken by a triple-keystone. Plain consoles rise from the moulded imposts to support an open-bedmould triangular pediment. The doorway to each end house is set in a wide arched opening dressed with a band-architrave broken by rustic-blocks.

The Brunswick Square houses have remained reasonably free from external alterations, but quite recently the fronts have been badly disfigured by painted signs. The interiors have generally been changed and reconstructed for commercial use, but some idea of their original arrangement is given by the following advertisement, quoted from *Felix Farley* for 15th August 1785, offering to let 'a very neat Dwelling-House, situate on the South

Side of Brunswick-Square; consisting of two Parlours, China and Servants Pantry, a genteel Drawing-Room, and convenient Lodging-Rooms with Garrets; two good Kitchens, over which is a spacious Laundry, and plenty of both kinds of Water; also three Cellars, with an outlet to a back-door, with room for Hallage'.

The end house in Gloucester Street and several of those in Cumberland Street have interesting fronts, with bay-windows of wooden construction, dressed with Classical ornaments, projecting from the ground-story, and stone-dressed Venetian or other three-light windows to the upper stories. One such double-fronted house in Cumberland Street, offered for sale by Thomas Manley in *Felix Farley* for 2nd February 1771, is described as 'a new-built Dwelling-House, consisting of a neat Hall and Stair-Case, two large handsome Bow-Parlours to face the Street, with Marble Chimney-Pieces, and Flock Papers; six Lodging Rooms, two large light Closets, two Kitchens, with Plenty of both Sorts of Water, Pantries, Cellars, and all Conveniences. N.B. Rent £21 per Annum, clear of Taxes.'

REDCLIFFE PARADE

The building of Redcliffe Parade was promoted about 1768 by Sydenham Teast, a ship-builder and dock-owner of nearby Wapping, and some of the houses were being offered for sale or letting early in 1771. It was intended to build two balancing ranges, but only the west block of eleven houses and two of the east were finished to this design, and the latter range was completed about 1800 with houses of a smaller scale and different appearance. The situation is splendid despite a north aspect, and the houses front on to a broad terrace raised high above the old course of the Avon, now the Floating Harbour, commanding a view of the whole city.

The fronts are uniformly built, of brick sparingly dressed with freestone, to a simple design (Plate 44a). Each house is three stories high and three windows wide. The rectangular doorway is framed by an architrave, surmounted by a plain frieze flanked by consoles that support the cornice. This is returned into the plain platband marking the first-floor level. The rectangular windows to each story are uniformly framed with band-architraves, rising from plain sills and broken by small keystones.

[209]

The crowning cornice returns round the plain pilasters that define each party-wall, and there is no parapet.

COLLEGE STREET

In 1770 the Bishop of Bristol sought and obtained an Act of Parliament permitting him to let for building development the ground known as Bishop's Park, which lay to the west of his Palace and behind College Green. This site he granted to Samuel Worrall for a term of 90 years, at a yearly rent of £60. An advertisement addressed to builders, published in *Felix Farley* on 29th September 1770, stated that the ground was 'to be laid out for building. The principal street to be 40 feet wide, of which the road level will be 6 feet higher than the level of the houses now in the occupation of Mr Vaughan and Mr Patty. A frontage also to Limekiln Lane, and proper sewers. Builders will be permitted to make cellars under the streets as in the new buildings in Bath'. On 17th November 1770 *Sarah Farley* was able to report that 'this week was finished the main Sewer in the Ground called Bishop's Park, lately laid out for Building'. The streets were planned, and the general lines of the design for the house-fronts were laid down by Thomas Paty and Sons, who were to be closely associated with Worrall's building promotions.

During the late eighteenth and early nineteenth centuries College Street was a favoured place of residence for successful tradesmen. William Paty and Thomas Stocking lived thereabouts, in houses adjoining their yards and workshops in Limekiln Lane. Now the street is depressing and forlorn, its unity having been destroyed by the construction of the Deanery Road viaduct, and the demolition of most of the houses on the east side to make way for the new Council House.

Apart from a few which are double-fronted, the houses are generally of moderate size. The original layout of their accommodation is described in a contemporary sale advertisement—'The Premises consist of Two Parlours, a China Pantry, Kitchen and arched Cellar, with a spacious Outlet or Garden Plot behind the whole; a Dining-Room, Bedchamber, and light Closet on the first Floor, and two Bedchambers in the Attic Story.' The fronts, which are three stories high and generally have two windows to each upper story, are built of red brick sparingly dressed with freestone. This is used for the pilasters that define the party-walls, generally plain but sometimes of channel-jointed stones; for the flat or segmental arches of stepped and projecting voussoirs to the upper story windows; and for the rather insignificant crowning cornice that forms a coping to the walls. Bay-windows of wooden construction, occasionally segmental but usually angular on plan, project boldly from the ground-story, and the doorways generally have surrounding architraves surmounted by triangular pediments resting on consoles.

PARK STREET

The protracted history of Park Street began on 9th August 1740, when the Corporation granted to Nathaniel Day, at a yearly rental of £20, the reversion of certain land near the Boar's Head Inn, to enable him to open up a street 40 feet wide in Bullock's Park, which he already held, 'to lead from College Green up into the road towards Jacob's Well.' An interval of 18 years then elapsed before the project was again brought before the Common Council, who recorded their approval, on 17th July 1758, of an extended design submitted by Alderman Day and George Tyndall, wherein it was proposed to lay out a road from the top of the new street to Whiteladies Gate, where it would join the turnpike road leading from the city via St Michael's Hill.

Shortly before the close of 1758 the Corporation employed George Tully to 'plan the ground at the Foot of College Green for a publick road thro' the Boar's Head ground up Bullock's Park'. In February 1761 builders were invited to lease plots of ground for building, Thomas and James Paty being among the first to erect houses at the College Green end of the new street. These houses no longer exist, but some idea of their character and accommodation may be gained from the following advertisement, which appeared in *Felix Farley* for 27th August 1763:

'A new well-finished House, having two Wainscotted Parlours in Front (which is built with Freestone) several Marble Chimney-Pieces, China and Water Closets, both Sorts of Water, a large dry Arch-Cellar, with a Rolling Way, and several other Conveniences. Enquire of THOMAS PATY, near said House.

N.B. The intended Shop may be appropriated to an Office, Servants-Hall. &c.'

Donne's Plan of Bristol, published in 1773, shows Park Street laid out, but only partially lined with houses up to its junction with Great George Street, beyond which point no building had taken place. The symmetrically treated houses that flank the entrance to Great George Street, and have deep return frontages thereto, must therefore date from about 1762 and belong to the first stage of Park Street's development. These houses have three-storied fronts, designed in Thomas Paty's typical style and built of red brick dressed with freestone. Each elevation has a pedimented central feature, broken slightly forward, and the rectangular windows are dressed with stone architraves, those of the second-story being broken by rustic-blocks.

The building of the upper part of the street was begun during the period of reckless speculation which lasted from 1786 to 1793, and many of the houses here were left in an unfinished state by their bankrupt builders, to remain so until the early years of the nineteenth century. One of the completed houses, offered for sale during July 1786, is described in the following advertisement:

'A new-built Messuage, in Park St, consisting of two parlours and a drawing-room on the ground-floor; a drawing-room and seven bed-chambers besides garrets; a store-room and two kitchens, with plenty of both sorts of water; there is a garden well stock'd with fruit trees; a coach-house, and three-stall stable adjoining, with a rain-water cistern under the coach-house, and every other convenience.

The house is substantially built and elegantly finished, the doors and skirting-boards in several of the rooms and the balustrades of the stair-case are mahogany, there are grates in all the rooms (except the drawing-room and front parlour) book-cases and other fixtures.'

All of these houses were given fronts of dressed freestone, the design being a more-or-less standard one evolved by Thomas Paty and Sons for use in the building developments of the time. Modern shop-fronts of varying design have generally replaced the original ground-stories, but an unaltered example shows a V-jointed rusticated face containing two windows and an arch-headed doorway, the latter framed by Doric pilasters with entablature-blocks supporting an open-bedmould triangular pediment. The upper part of each front contains two tiers of three rectangular windows, set without architraves in a plain wall face, the lowest tier having a continuous sill. The houses step up in succession, to accord with the steeply rising ground, and each front is finished with a sharply-profiled cornice that returns round the heads of the plain pilasters marking the party-walls. Park Street suffered severely during the late war, when approximately one-third of its houses were destroyed.

THE COLONNADE, HOTWELLS

The Colonnade was erected by Samuel Powell, to whom the ground was leased by the Merchants' Society, for the term of 40 years beginning 25th May 1786.The building was designed to meet the wishes of influential visitors to the Hot-well, who complained that no sheltered promenade existed for use in inclement weather. Some form of protected walk had previously existed, however, for in May 1760 a tradesman advertised that his warehouse was situated 'under the Piazzas, near the Pump Room'. This modest 'Colonnade' had its prototype in 'The Pantiles' at Tunbridge Wells, and a splendid successor in Bath Street at Bath.

The segmental building consists of shops on the ground-story with a wide colonnaded walk before them, and a single story of living-rooms above. The elevation is simple and charming, with a Tuscan order of stone columns, spaced to form seven wide intercolumniations and a narrow one at the north end, supporting an entablature that consists of a plain wooden frieze and a stone cornice. In the upper story, which is faced with red brick, are thirteen windows, evenly spaced but unrelated to the colonnade below. These windows are without architraves, but have stone sills and flat-arched heads of five voussoirs, arranged with the usual steps and projections towards the key. Each window is furnished with a low and shallow balcony of ironwork, generally of a simple Gothic design. The crowning cornice of stone is surmounted by a brick parapet (Plate 44b).

The south end of the Colonnade adjoins 'Rock House', a once-fashionable lodging-house of earlier date. The later embellishment of the five-windows-wide front consists of a Doric colonnade of five bays at the ground-story, supporting a wide balcony with a Gothic railing of ironwork, while the third story has a tent-roofed veranda of the same character.

BERKELEY SQUARE and CRESCENT

The site of Berkeley Square forms part of the Bullock's Park estate, and the first scheme for building thereon was that outlined in a notice to builders which appeared in several issues of *Felix Farley* during December 1787:

A CRESCENT

Ground to be lett, for building a CRESCENT, in a field adjoining Park-street, Brandon-hill, and the road leading to Clifton, the Downs, &c. For the Plans, Elevations, and other particulars, apply to THOMAS PATY and SONS.

It is probable that the promotors abandoned their intention of building a crescent and adopted the present layout to exploit more fully the possibilities of this site. The moving spirit in building here was James Lockier, and those associated with him included Davis and Husband, builders; Thomas Rawlings, house-carpenter; and Robert Jones, builder. Their common bankruptcy in 1793 left many of the houses in Berkeley Square and Charlotte Street to remain unfinished until the early years of the nineteenth century.

The houses of Berkeley Square are built round an irregular quadrangle that measures approximately 400 feet on the north side, 320 feet on the south-east, 265 feet on the south-west, and 235 feet on the west. The ground rises sharply from the north-east angle towards the south-west, and not one range of houses has a level frontage. There were originally thirteen houses in the north terrace, ten in the south-west and nine in the west, these last two ranges adjoining. The south-east side was designedly left free from buildings, perhaps in order that the houses on the other sides might have the advantage of an open prospect, but more probably because of the proximity of the intended houses in Charlotte Street. The central garden enclosure is surrounded by a roadway, and two entering avenues flank the north terrace. Berkeley Crescent contains six houses and forms a curious appendage to the north end of the west terrace.

This minute crescent was probably built as a concession to those who favoured the original scheme, for this particular form held an irresistible attraction for eighteenth-century builders and tenants alike.

The houses in the square are large, and most of them are planned with a top-lit open well staircase placed between the front and back rooms, which are nearly equal in size. All have three stories above a basement, and a garret story in the mansard roof. The fronts to the square are faced with dressed freestone and, with one exception, they are almost identical in design. The houses are stepped in successive order, singly or in pairs, to accord with the rise in the ground, and a plain pilaster-strip of slight projection is introduced between each of the fronts, serving to link them and yet provide stops for the rusticated ground-stories, the stringcourses and crowning cornices. The ground-story face of each house is rusticated with horizontal and vertical V-jointing, and the two windows have flat-arched heads formed by a triple-keystone projecting slightly between two voussoirs. The door, with six fielded panels, is surmounted by a fanlight and set in an arch-headed opening. This is framed by Doric plain-shafted pilasters, with triglyphed entablature-blocks supporting an open-bedmould triangular pediment. The upper part of each front contains two tiers of three rectangular windows, set without architraves in a plain face. The tall windows of the first-floor are underlined by an unmoulded pedestal-course. The crowning cornice of each house is returned round the flanking pilasters to stop against the faces of the adjoining houses, so that the pilasters generally bear two superimposed cornices, and the plain parapet is finished with a narrow coping (Plate 45b).

Approximately in the middle of the west side was a double-fronted house, now mostly destroyed, with a front of greater elaboration than the rest of those in the square, of which it was intended to form the focal centre (Plate 45a). Such emphasis was not desirable in an asymmetrical layout on a sloping site, and this particular house-front was singularly awkward and mannered in design. The middle portion of the rusticated ground-story, containing the pedimented doorway centred between two windows, was broken slightly forward and flanked by bays of unequal width, each with one window. The first-floor pedestal-course was broken forward immediately above the side piers of the middle portion, to carry two pilasters that rose through the two upper stories and framed the three middle windows of each. These pilasters had panelled shafts and curious wide-spreading capitals adorned with acanthus-leaves and fluting, and they supported an entablature composed of a fluted frieze and a modillioned cornice, surmounted by a triangular pediment with an oval window in its tympanum. A moulded architrave emphasized the central window in each upper story—that of the first-floor being blind—and a band of Etruscan scrolling formed a stringcourse placed about one foot below the second-floor window sills. The entablature was continued with a plain frieze across each flanking bay, where a plain parapet surmounted the cornice. This house had a good overthrow lampholder, of flattened-ogee form, and similar lampholders still survive at Nos 15 and 28, while there is a good standard at No 11. The area railings differ slightly in design from house to house, some having spear-head terminations and others vases.

The return fronts are faced with red brick dressed with free-stone, the west elevation of the north terrace being a fine and austere composition in which the dominant feature is the centrally-placed entrance. The two-leaf door, each with three panels, is framed by a moulded architrave and surmounted by a large metal fanlight of simple radial pattern, the whole being recessed in an arch-headed opening with a surround of rusticated stonework. The Queen's Parade elevation of the north terrace, also built in brick dressed with stone, was designed to accord with Berkeley Crescent. This contains five house-fronts within a segment that just exceeds a quadrant, and has two straight return fronts. The uniform three-storied elevations were designed by the Patys to incorporate stone dressings of stock patterns which they produced in quantities for use in the extensive building projects of the late eighteenth and early nineteenth centuries. The ground-story of each house contains two windows and a doorway on the left side. This has an arch-headed opening framed by plain pilaster-strips with simple corbels supporting an open-bedmould triangular pediment. In each upper story are three windows, equal in width but suitably proportioned in height, dressed like those of the ground-story with plain sills and slightly cambered heads of five voussoirs, increasing in height and projection towards the key. The party-walls between the fronts are defined by plain and narrow pilaster-strips which rise unbroken to meet the simple entablature of narrow frieze and cornice. This entablature is returned round the pilasters and surmounted by a brick parapet with stone dies above the pilasters (Plate 46a).

The interiors of the houses, particularly those in the square, are well finished. The stock joinery is generally of good quality and excellent design, and the principal rooms have enriched friezes, cornices and ceiling borders of cast plaster, selected from the extensive repertory of the eighteenth-century plasterers. The staircases are generally constructed of stone, and have iron railings formed of plain square-section balusters with interval panels wrought to a design of interlaced segments, delicately enriched with cast lead ornaments, the wooden handrail being veneered with selected mahogany.

GREAT GEORGE STREET

The south-east side of Great George Street contains some fine houses built about 1790, from designs by Thomas Paty and Sons, generally to suit the requirements of individual clients rather than for speculative sale or letting. These houses are detached from their neighbours on one or both sides, and they have fine front elevations built of dressed freestone, similar in general design but differing in details and fenestral patterning. For example, No. 3 is more elaborate than the others, having a blocked architrave surrounding its rectangular doorway,which is placed centrally between two windows in the usual V-jointed rusticated face. A continuous sill underlines the three first-floor windows which are placed, like those of the top story, without architraves in a plain face. This is quoined at the angles and finished with a modillioned cornice, surmounted by an open balustrade with interval dies (Plate 47a).

The best-preserved of these houses is No. 7, now the Georgian House museum, the front of which is more austere than that of No. 3, although the composition is similar. The rusticated ground-story contains two windows, placed one on either side of the arched doorway, which is framed by Doric pilasters with entablature-blocks supporting an open-bedmould triangular pediment. The plain upper face contains two tiers of three widely-spaced windows, without architraves, and it is finished with a simple cornice surmounted by a pedestal parapet (Plate 47b, Figure 30). The house has a rectangular plan, measuring

Scale of Feet.

FIGURE 30
No. 7 Great George Street. Elevation

about 41 feet in front and 52 feet in depth. The interior is arranged so that the principal apartments are at the back, facing south-east and commanding a fine prospect; the secondary rooms overlook the street, while the main and service staircases rise, right and left respectively, to landings between the two groups of rooms. The slope of the site has permitted the inclusion of a sub-basement, with cellars, wood-store, wine-cellar, rain-water tank, and a heating plant. The basement proper contains the still-room, larder, and a cold plunge-bath in the front, and two kitchens, etc., at the back, which is on ground level at this point. The front part of the ground-story has the owner's office on the left, and a powder-closet and pantry on the right of the entrance-hall, which opens to the main hall and staircase. There are two reception-rooms arranged *en suite* at the back. The first-floor has two bed-chambers in front, and

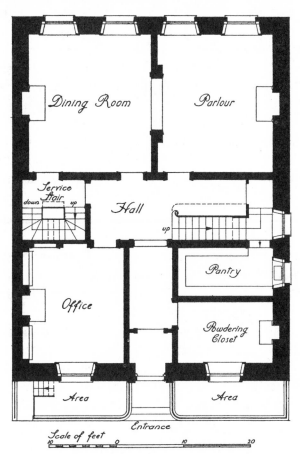

FIGURE 31
No. 7 Great George Street
Ground-story plan

the large drawing-room at the back, with a water-closet and an ante-room on the left side. There are four bed-chambers, with closets, on the second-floor, and above this are the servants' garrets in the double-mansard roof (Figure 31). The rooms are decorated in a style of elegant simplicity, the principal apartments have enriched friezes and cornices of plaster, in the stock Classical designs used at the close of the eighteenth-century. The six-panelled doors—some are of mahogany—are framed in moulded architraves of painted deal, which is used also for the

[219]

skirtings, dado-rails, and the panelled shutters and linings of the windows. The Adamesque chimney-pieces are of wood, enriched with carving or with composition ornaments, and the grates are set within slips of marble or fluospar. In the office the chimney-piece is flanked by built-in bookcases of mahogany, designed in the later style of Chippendale, with glazed doors of geometrical trellis, and broken triangular pediment-heads. The stone staircase has an iron railing of square-section balusters, varied at intervals with panels of interlaced segments adorned with cast lead enrichments, and the handrail is veneered with mahogany (Plate 64d). To serve their present purpose the rooms have been decorated and furnished in excellent taste. The kitchen-quarters are equipped with every device known to their period.

PORTLAND SQUARE

A reference to the intended building of Portland Square was made in a letter, published by *Sarah Farley* on 24th May 1788, wherein the writer commented on the considerable amount of building then taking place in Bristol, and mentioned 'the new streets and square around St. Paul's'. The foundation-stone of this new church was laid in April 1789, and the surrounding area must have been laid out and prepared for building before March 1790, for in that month the Bristol newspapers published the following advertisement, addressed to builders:

'Bristol, *March 24th* 1790

To be sold—Several lots of Void Ground,—with common sewers already and ready to be made, near the site of the new church of St Paul. Plans of which, with the elevations, may be seen at Daniel Hague's, architect and builder, in Wilder Street.'

Hague planned the square to contain thirty-four houses, and the sites for these were allotted to three builders, eighteen to James Lockier, ten to Thomas Pope, and six to Davis and Husband. These speculators soon began building, but when bankruptcy overtook them in 1793 the loose materials on the sites were sold and their houses were left in various states of incompletion until well into the nineteenth century. In *First Impressions*, published in 1807, James Malcolm writes that 'a modern square, dedicated to the Duke of Portland, at the

Northern extremity of Bristol, is a second memento of speculation in freestone, which remains unfinished, and nods in concert
with one or two streets near it'. The square had received its
name in honour of the third Duke of Portland (1738–1809), who
was High Steward of Bristol at the time of its building.

Several of the houses were completed during the second
decade of the nineteenth century, and from the advertisements
of that time it is possible to gain some idea of the original disposition of the interiors. For example, the middle house on the
south side, offered for sale in June 1812, contained 'three arched
under-ground cellars, a servants' hall, housekeeper's room, back-
kitchen, larder, brew-house, and other offices, on the area floor;
An entrance hall, front parlour 20 feet by 22 feet, two back
parlours, and a Garden on the ground floor; A drawing-room
21 feet by 27 feet, and two other rooms on the first story; four
rooms and a water-closet on the attic story; and four rooms on the
upper story.' The accommodation of the north-east corner
house, that was offered to be let or sold during May 1814, consisted of 'a servants' hall, arched cellar, coal house, wine cellar,
and other offices on the area floor; A front parlour 21 feet by 25
feet, entrance hall, back parlour, china pantry, cook's kitchen,
brew-house, garden, and other offices on the ground floor; A
drawing room 20 feet by 25 feet, best bedroom, laundry, store
room and water closet on the first floor; four rooms on the attic
story; and four rooms on the upper story.'

For about a century Portland Square flourished as a fashionable place of residence, but now most of its houses have been
converted into factories or warehouses, their interiors stripped
of all items of decorative interest, and the exteriors generally
disfigured by painted signs. The north and west terraces were
severely damaged during the late war; the central garden is now
a tangled wilderness; and this square—once the finest and most
uniform of Bristol's eighteenth-century building ensembles—
has a forlorn and squalid appearance.

The buildings are disposed in a symmetrical formation round
a rectangular area, measuring some 350 feet from north to south,
and 300 feet from east to west, and having a large enclosed
garden of oval form in its centre. Entering streets flank the
north and south terraces, and another is placed centrally in the
west side, axially opposite to the tall Gothic steeple of St Paul's

Church, about which the whole architectural scheme is balanced (Plate 8c). The east side contains two short blocks, each of four houses, placed on either side of the west front and steeple of the church. The north and south terraces each contain seven houses, built to an identical design composed of a central feature flanked by short wings and end pavilions. The west side consists of two balancing blocks, each containing six houses (Plate 48a).

The houses are three stories high, above a basement, but while each end house and the middle one in the north and south terraces are heightened by a full attic story, the remainder have a garret story in the double-mansard roof. The elevations towards the square are entirely faced with dressed freestone, and most of the houses have fronts of a simple and uniform design, three stories high and three windows wide. This design is generally similar to that used for Berkeley Square, except that here the rusticated ground-story is continuous from house to house, and the dividing pilaster-strips rise from the first-floor platband; the doorcases are more elaborate, the arch-headed opening being framed by Ionic plain-shafted three-quarter columns, supporting entablature-blocks and a triangular open-bedmould pediment, with a modillioned cornice (Plate 56b); and the crowning cornice is also modillioned. The end and middle houses in the north and south terraces have their fronts broken slightly forward from the general building face. Each contains four windows closely spaced in its width, and in the middle house these are placed in bays between five pilasters, with plain shafts and debased Doric capitals banded with acanthus-leaves, which rise through the two stories to support an entablature of architrave, plain frieze and cornice. The attic story is correspondingly divided into bays by plain pilaster-strips, and finished with a simple cornice of slight projection (Plate 49a). The return fronts are generally faced with red brick and sparingly dressed with freestone, like those of Berkeley Square, the door and window openings being framed with band-architraves broken by rustic-blocks.

The front areas are enclosed by iron railings of simple design, but two houses, Nos 18 and 19, have enriched wrought-iron lamp-brackets of scrolled form, excellent in design and workmanship, placed centrally over the arched doorways. The central garden is enclosed by an iron railing, intercepted at each cardinal point by gates hung on standards filled with segmental trellis, which diminish in width as they rise in ogee-curves to end in scrolls and support a lamp-iron. The middle of the garden was once graced with a statue of George the Third, made of Coade's Stone, the sculptor's name not being recorded. This was set up in April 1811, replacing an obelisk erected in October 1810 to commemorate the fiftieth year of the monarch's reign, but during the night of 23rd March 1817 the statue was thrown down by a party of political dissentients, and sustained such damage that it was not re-erected.

THE MALL, CLIFTON

The following item of local news was published in *Felix Farley* on 29th November 1788:

'We hear with pleasure that Clifton and the Hotwells are become the favourite choice of company, as well for winter as for summer residence: . . . New buildings in an elegant style of architecture are still to be erected on the most elevated spot of that beautiful hill, as well as in the immediate vicinity of the Hotwells.'

There can be little doubt that this referred to the proposed building of the north and south terraces flanking The Mall, and the generally similar houses of St Vincent's Parade, down by the Avon and near to the Hot-well House. There is also an item in an account-book of John Eveleigh that appears on evidence to relate to the Mall houses. This entry is dated November 1788 to January 1789, and shows that Eveleigh charged Robert Bayly (perhaps the banker) 15 guineas for the following services:

'Drawing three designs for Buildings at Clifton, taking dimensions and drawing plans and elevations of Offices, and drawing other designs. Setting out ground for line of street, and ground in dispute with Bludson and Baker (lodging-house keepers in Gloucester Place, Clifton) Drawing plans and elevations for range of houses next the road, attending etc, and journey expenses.'

The two terraces on The Mall are more or less identical in design, and each consists of thirteen houses, containing three stories above a basement, and a garret story in the double mansard roof. The fronts are built in dressed freestone, now generally painted, and they form a composition with a central feature and end pavilions, each of one house, broken slightly forward from wings containing five houses (Plate 48b). The wing house-fronts are defined by plain pilaster-strips around which are returned the first-floor platband, the crowning entablature, and the parapet coping. The ground-story face, rusticated with horizontal and vertical V-jointing, contains two windows and the door, this last being placed to the right side in those houses on the right of the centre, and to the left in the others. The windows have flat-arched heads centering on triple-keyblocks, and the door is surmounted by a star-pointed fanlight and recessed in an arch-headed opening. This is flanked by Doric pilasters with entablature-blocks supporting an open-bedmould triangular pediment. The pilaster shafts are panelled and each entablature frieze is adorned with an oval patera, generally formed of acanthus-leaves. The usual platband marks the first-floor level, and the upper part of each front, generally a plain face containing two tiers of evenly-spaced rectangular windows, is finished with an entablature, its modillioned cornice surmounted by a plain parapet. The house-fronts forming the centre and end pavilions have these additional ornaments: The three first-floor windows are underlined by a moulded sill and the middle light is framed by narrow pilaster-strips with consoles supporting a triangular pediment: The frieze of the entablature crowning the central house is enriched with fluting: Each house was originally finished with a triangular pediment, its tympanum containing a small recessed lunette.

PRINCE'S BUILDINGS

The site of Prince's Buildings forms part of an extensive tract of ground that the Merchants' Society granted to Samuel Powell on building lease, for a term of forty years beginning 1st May 1789. Powell had already built the Colonnade near the Hotwell House, of which he became lessee in 1790, and he also promoted the erection of St Vincent's Parade, situated on the lowest part of this ground. The plots for the houses in Prince's Buildings were sub-let to various people in June 1789, and in 1796 the property was conveyed by way of mortgage from Powell to William Paty, who was probably the architect of the houses.

The Prince-of-Wales's Crescent, as these buildings were at first named, was designed as a segmental range of fourteen three-storied houses, arranged in seven pairs which were linked by single-storied annexes. Now, however, the houses have been so greatly altered and added to that the original effect of this scheme is completely lost. The middle pair of houses is surmounted by a triangular pediment, its tympanum containing a small square panel enclosing a circular medallion carved with a representation of the Black Prince, above which is a bold relief carving of the Prince-of-Wales's feathers with a scroll bearing the motto 'Ich Dien'. Some of the houses have arch-headed doorways, flanked by Doric pilasters bearing entablature-blocks and a cornice, but Nos 8, 9 and 10 have fine Grecian porches that were added about 1830. In these the double-door is surmounted by a cobweb fanlight of oblong form, and framed between wide piers decorated with paired pilaster-strips. A channelled groove separates these from the simple entablature of frieze and cornice that is surmounted by a blocking-course, broken centrally by a tablet containing an oblong panel placed between quadrant fan ornaments (Plate 56d).

By far the most attractive architectural feature of this crescent is the return front to the south end house In this symmetrical composition the pedimented Doric doorcase and the arch-headed window over it adorn a narrow bay that is flanked by two semicircular bows, each having three rectangular windows, fitted with curved sashes on the ground and first floors, and one in the attic story above the simple main entablature. The windows are set without architraves in a plain ashlar face, and the attic story of the middle bay is decorated with a carved motif, consisting of a rampant beast framed in a rough oval formed of branches.

ST VINCENT'S PARADE

St Vincent's Parade is sited on the lower part of the ground granted by the Merchants' Society to Samuel Powell on 1st May 1789. This range, which was never completed, contains nine uniform houses that front on to a raised terrace walk, originally overlooking the fashionable tree-lined riverside promenade leading to the Hot-well House. The fronts of these houses, three stories high and three windows wide, are entirely faced with dressed freestone to a design almost identical with that used for the contemporaneous houses in The Mall.

WINDSOR TERRACE

The most fantastic of Clifton's Georgian buildings, Windsor Terrace owes much of its impressive effect to its magnificent situation on the edge of a rocky promontory high above the Avon, overlooking the Hotwells. The site formed part of Rownham Woods, one of the Clifton properties of John Power, and comprised some thirteen acres. About 1790 this land was conveyed to William Watts, a Redcliffe plumber who had amassed a small fortune from his invention of patent shot. By the terms of his lease Watts undertook to build a crescent of twenty houses, to cost not less than £20,000, and pay a ground rent of £100 per annum after the usual peppercorn period had elapsed. There is in existence a perspective drawing that shows the grandiose building scheme originally envisaged for this site. Windsor Terrace was to form a crescent of houses treated architecturally in a similar manner to Camden Crescent in Bath, with a giant order of columns and pilasters above a rusticated base, and pediment-crowned pavilions in the centre and at each end. Two similar ranges of houses, forming a broken crescent, were to be built on the higher ground behind Windsor Terrace. It seems highly probable that this was one of the three designs made for various Clifton sites by John Eveleigh of Bath.

On 7th August 1790 *Felix Farley* published an advertisement relating to Windsor Terrace, in the 'Notice to Masons and Quarrymen, willing to contract by the perch for building a Capital Wall, near the Hotwells, to deliver their proposals to William Watts, in College Green, by 14th August'. Watts spent most of his capital in completing the great retaining-wall and the vaults beneath the houses and terrace, and he was apparently obliged to sub-let the house-plots to other builders. An advertisement in *Felix Farley* for 12th November 1792, announced the sale, by order of Watts, of an 'unfinished house in New Windsor, in course of erection by Samuel Screen, builder, now bankrupt'. On 1st March 1794 a bankruptcy notice was issued against Watts, and the site of Windsor Terrace, with the shells of two houses, then reverted to the ground landlords. By a deed of 1807 the property was sold for £2,000 to Isaac Cooke, the attorney, and in 1808 Cooke and his mortgagees leased the unfinished houses of Windsor Terrace, described as 'now building', to John Drew, a builder, of Dial House, Clifton. Drew then finished the range by building eight more houses to a reduced design, and mortgaged them back to Cooke in order to raise funds for building The Paragon.

Only two of the houses, Nos 5 and 6, have fronts that were built in conformity with the original design for the terrace, and are entirely faced with dressed freestone (Plate 49b). These fronts, which are uniform, contain three lofty stories and are three windows wide. The ground-story is rusticated with horizontal and vertical V-jointing, each house having two tall windows, with arched heads rising from moulded imposts. A lower arch-headed opening, placed on the right, contains the door surmounted by a cobweb fanlight. An unskilled mason must have been responsible for cutting the arch voussoirs, for the V-joints radiate from points well below the arch centres, and they appear to be unrelated to the actual stone jointing which is correctly centred. Beneath each window is an apron, decorated with channelled cutting to form an oblong panel with incurved corners. The rusticated face is finished with a platband from whence rises an order of seven pilasters, with moulded bases, fluted shafts, and rich Corinthian capitals. These pilasters form bays framing the first- and second-floor windows, and support an entablature that has a modillioned cornice. A fluted string-course runs between the pilasters, about eighteen inches below the sills of the second-floor windows, and over the middle first-floor window of No. 5 is a carved decoration consisting of an oval patera flanked by husk festoons and pendants. The stonework over the corresponding window at No. 6 was boasted for a similar carving. A balustrade, with panelled dies centred over the pilasters, still surmounts the main entablature of No. 6.

The later houses were built on a much smaller scale, and Nos 5 and 6 thus became the disproportionately lofty central feature in an elevation that can only be described as a pathetic travesty of the original design. On either side of this centre are four houses, built to a frontage line that curves slightly forward. These form short wings and end-pavilions, each containing two houses, their fronts being indiscriminately dressed with giant Corinthian pilasters, some members of the entablature, and the

[227]

crowning balustrade intended for the first scheme. The absurdity of the result is most clearly seen in the four houses standing to the left of the middle pair, where three stories are introduced within the compass of the pilasters. The main architrave has been omitted, thus divorcing the entablature from the supporting pilasters, while the frieze and bed-mouldings of the cornice are cut into by the topmost tier of windows. Similar vagaries of treatment are exhibited in the four houses to the right, where the pilasters are unevenly spaced and the architrave is omitted for no apparent reason. Except for these stone adornments the fronts are faced with cement. The ground-story is treated to represent rusticated masonry, but the V-jointing is clumsily managed, especially around the arched heads to the door and window openings. The easternmost house No. 11, was also built by Drew, but has no architectural relationship to the rest of the range.

ROYAL YORK CRESCENT

The building of Royal York Crescent was the most spectacular of many such undertakings promoted about 1790 by James Lockier. From the character of the house-fronts it must appear that William Paty designed this crescent, although an entry in one of John Eveleigh's account-books sugests that he might have been employed in 1789 to survey and lay out the site, which formed part of the garden ground belonging to Clifton Manor House. Building was begun in the summer of 1791, and an immense sum was expended in erecting the deep substructure of vaults and basements required to raise the houses and terrace-walk to a constant level. By December Lockier was in financial difficulties which he sought to solve by promoting a tontine subscription to raise £70,000 in £100 shares, this sum being required to finish the buildings on which some £20,000 had already been spent. The trustees appointed to manage the scheme were John Cary, Joseph Harford, William Fry, William Gibbons, George Daubeny, and Richard Vaughan, but even these respected names failed to inspire public confidence in the proposal. Lockier's bankruptcy in May 1793 brought ruin to the builders engaged on the crescent, and in August the newspapers advertised forced sales of all loose materials on the site, belonging to the following:

John Coles	materials for 10 houses.
Michael Davis	materials for 9 houses.
Ezekial Evans	materials for 8 houses.
Richard Constant	materials for 7 houses.

The derelict buildings and adjoining land were offered for sale during May 1800, but no purchaser was forthcoming until July 1801, when it became known that the Government intended to buy the ground and the unfinished portion of the crescent, about three-quarters of the whole, and build barracks to accommodate a large body of troops. While this proposal was actively supported by Bristol's brewers, the local residents became thoroughly alarmed and strongly protested that the presence of such a building would ruin Clifton as a watering-place. So great was the pressure of opinion that the military authorities were induced to abandon their plans, although they had already purchased the property. In May 1809 the Barrack Department announced the sale of 15 unfinished houses, adjoining the 10 already completed at the west end, and in the following year a further sale was advertised of 'the remaining 21 unfinished houses, with a long range of void ground behind the same'. Much of the property passed into the hands of Isaac Cooke, the attorney, and the return of prosperity brought purchasers who were willing to finish the houses. A Bristol guide-book for 1815 described the crescent as 'nearing completion', but the last gaps in its continuity were not closed until about 1820. Throughout Clifton's heyday the Royal York Crescent was the favourite residence for people of wealth and fashion, but now its houses are mostly divided into flats and the blight of neglect has settled over the whole great ensemble.

Royal York Crescent consists of forty-six houses, forty being contained within the immense shallow concave segment, and three in each of the return fronts, which are built tangental to the arc. The short wing of five smaller houses at the east end is an addition of slightly later date. The crescent houses are very large, generally with a frontage width of 25 feet and an approximate depth of 50 feet. The interiors were well planned to meet the requirements of their time, but most of the houses have been considerably altered for conversion into flats. Generally, the ground-story contained a wide entrance-hall leading to the staircase and placed to one side of the front dining-room, about 16 feet wide and 27 feet deep, and a back parlour, about 14 feet wide and 19 feet deep. On the first-floor was the great drawing-room, 23 feet wide, 28 feet deep, and 13 feet high, generally furnished with double-doors opening to the back drawing-room, of the same size as the parlour below. On the second-floor were four principal bedrooms, with closets, and over them five garret-rooms in the double-mansard roof. The housekeeper's-room, servants'-hall, butler's-pantry, with a large kitchen and scullery, etc., were contained in the basement.

The fronts were originally uniform in appearance and built to a simple design in red brick, sparingly dressed with freestone. The brickwork has long since been stuccoed over and the whole face is now painted, each house generally differing in colour from its neighbours. The first house at either end of the segment has a wide front with four windows to each upper story, and the middle house in each return front is surmounted by a pilastered attic story, but the rest are three stories high and three windows wide. The middle pair of houses projects slightly forward from the general building line to form a central feature. The party-walls are defined by plain pilasters of stone, rising through the three stories to support projecting sections of the simple crowning entablature and plain parapet. Those houses lying east of the centre-line have their entrances placed to the left of the two ground-floor windows, while west of the centre this arrangement is reversed. The door, surmounted by a fanlight, is recessed in an arch-headed opening, framed by an unbroken moulded architrave. All the windows are without architraves and have flat-arched heads formed of five voussoirs, increasing in height and projection towards the key, which drops slightly below the general line of the head (Plate 50a, b). The upper wall face of the east end return-front is built of freestone, either a rebuilding or a departure from the original design.

Most of the houses have balconies and tent-shaped verandas at first-floor level, additions to the original design which give this crescent the finest array of early nineteenth-century ironwork to be found in or around Bristol. Nos. 1, 4, 22, 27–32, 41, and 43–5 have balcony railings of Gothic design, with tall and narrow arches ranged below a band of quatrefoils, while the veranda standards are filled with a pattern of interlacing segments. Nos. 5–7 and 11 have railings formed of elongated lozenges enriched with lead bosses at the intersections, and standards of similar design. The balconies at Nos. 8, 18, 19, 34–9 are railed with a diagonal trellis, having lead stars at the intersections. At Nos. 3, 16, 17, 21, 23–6, and 42 the balcony fronts have panels formed of interlacing segments, bordered by narrow margins of interlacing circles, while at Nos. 9 and 10 the railings are formed into panels, each containing diagonal bars that meet in small circles and are ornamented with scrolls. No. 33 has a Grecian railing, similar to those of Caledonia Place, while Nos. 2, 12, 20 and 40 have cast-iron balcony fronts and verandas of Victorian date, poor and rather florid in design.

The wide terrace-walk extending before the houses is raised well above the level of the roadway and supported on vaults, fronted with a simple arcaded wall that is broken at intervals by flights of steps. At the west end, where the roadway drops away, this wall becomes two stories high and three bays of the arcade were adorned with fluted Doric columns supporting entablatures. In decay this wall had achieved a truly Roman grandeur of effect, which harsh restoration has now effaced.

CORNWALLIS CRESCENT

The Lower, or Cornwallis Crescent was one of the most ambitious schemes undertaken during the heyday of speculative building in Bristol, being almost equal in size with the Royal York Crescent. Together, the two ranges represent a conscious attempt to reproduce at Clifton the splendours of the upper and lower crescents of Bath.

The site of Cornwallis Crescent belongs to the Merchants Society, who granted the ground on building lease in November 1791, for a term of 40 years, renewable at every 14 years. The lessee was Harry Elderton, a Bristol attorney, who promoted the scheme and had the ground laid out, then sub-letting the plots to various building tradesmen. Messrs Avard, Lewis and Mitchell the firm principally concerned in this venture, were made bankrupt in August 1793, and shortly afterwards their assignees held a sale of 'the loose materials on the premises called Lord Cornwallis's Crescent'. The unfinished houses were offered for sale on 19th August 1794, and their condition at that time can be adjudged from the following advertisement—'Nos. 1, 2 and 9, roofed in with timber; Nos. 3 to 6, built up to the withdrawing-room floor; No. 7, built up to the attic story; No. 8, built up to the garret floor'. The buildings remained in a derelict state for many years, eleven partly erected houses being offered for sale during 1809 (when some were taken by the Greenways) and nine more in July 1824. The Merchants' Society granted leases of several unfinished houses in April 1827, and the crescent was eventually completed except for the gap to the east of the centre, where a right-of-way had been established across the site. In common with so much of late eighteenth-century Clifton, Cornwallis Crescent has descended in the social scale and its fine houses, once occupied by wealthy families, are mostly converted into flats or tenements, with all the attendant signs of squalor.

This crescent was planned, probably by William Paty, as a shallow segmental range of forty houses, which, except for one at each end, were to be identical in their plan and dimensions, each measuring some 25 feet wide on the concave south front, and 40 feet deep, exclusive of the areas and the wide south terrace-walk. As the original design was not completed, however, there is a wide gap in the segment. The west block is the longest and contains twenty-three houses, while the east block has eleven, these being numbered 30 to 40. Each house is entered on the north front, the door opening into a small lobby beneath the first half-landing, thence into the stair-hall, with the secondary room placed to one side and the principal room beyond, occupying the full width of the south front. The accommodation is contained in three stories, a basement, and a garret story in the double-mansard roof.

The principal front is the concave one, facing south, which is wholly faced with dressed freestone (Plate 51a). Every house is three windows wide, and the fronts are defined by plain pilaster-strips that rise through the three stories to support forward breaks in the modillioned main cornice and surmounting parapet. The masonry of the ground-story is coursed with channel-jointing, the topmost joint returning to the flat-arched heads of the windows, which centre in triple-keyblocks. A platband marks the first-floor level and a continuous sill underlines the tall rectangular windows of this story. These, and the smaller windows of the top story, are set without architraves in a plain face. At each end of the crescent one front is broken slightly forward from the main building line, and these houses are flanked on the outer side by two-storied annexes with fronts containing two windows in each story. The two houses forming the intended centre of the crescent are also broken slightly forward. The wide terrace-walk before the houses is supported on vaults, the front wall displaying a rusticated arcade of wide segmental arches, one to each house, surmounted by a balustrade with solid dies placed above the piers. Most of the houses in the west block, and some of those in the east, are adorned at the first-floor level with balconies and tent-roofed verandas. These generally have iron railings of Gothic design, and simple trellis standards. The first-floor windows of the other houses open on to individual balconies.

The convex front, facing north, is built of red brick dressed with freestone, but the brickwork has been faced with stucco and the whole surface is now painted (Plate 51b). Here nothing marks the individual house-fronts, and there is no stringcourse other than the narrow main cornice, which is surmounted by a plain parapet. The houses numbered 1 to 20, west of the intended centre, have their doorways placed on the extreme right of the two ground-story windows. East of the centre this arrangement is reversed. Nos 34 and 39, at the east end, have projecting porches with semicircular fronts, built in stone to a design that appears to be a less successful variant of that used for the Paragon. Except for these, each house has a doorway surmounted by a false fanlight, recessed in an arch-headed opening and framed by Ionic plain-shafted pilasters that support an entablature having a modillioned cornice and a blocking-course. The ground-story windows, like the three to each upper story, are without architraves but have plain sills and flat arches formed of five voussoirs, increasing in height and forward projection towards the key.

SAVILLE PLACE, CLIFTON

Saville Place was begun in 1790, when building activity was at its height, the promotors intending to erect a large crescent of uniformly designed houses. Work was proceeding on eleven of these when the financial disasters of 1793 brought the undertaking to an abrupt close. Building was resumed early in the nineteenth century, when five of the houses, being sufficiently far advanced in construction, were finished in accordance with the original design, while the other six were built to a reduced scale with a different elevation.

The five large houses have uniform fronts, entirely faced with dressed freestone to a design almost identical with that used for so many houses of the time (Plate 46b). The manner in which the ground-story is raised above a semi-basement suggests the probability that it was intended to front this crescent with a raised terrace-walk. Narrow pilaster-strips define each front, rising from the basement plinth to support a break forward in the simple entablature and surmounting parapet. The ground-story face, rusticated with horizontal and vertical V-jointing, contains two flat-arched windows and an arch-headed doorway on the right. The plain upper face has two tiers of evenly spaced rectangular windows, without architraves. Each house has a veranda at first-floor level, the balcony having an iron railing of trellis pattern between narrow ornamental panels, while the tent roof is supported by trellis standards.

BELLE-VUE, CLIFTON

Belle-Vue, a terrace of nineteen uniform houses, is sited on the east slope of Clifton Hill, on ground leased from the Merchants' Society by Harry Elderton, for a term of forty years beginning 21st May 1792. These houses were among the latest begun during the height of building activity in Bristol, and all were abandoned in various states of incompletion when the financial crisis descended in 1793. For many years the range stood derelict, eight unfinished houses being offered for sale in July 1810, but shortly afterwards most of them found purchasers and the whole terrace was completed by about 1815. A house offered for sale in July 1812 was described as comprising 'spacious kitchens, servants' hall, suitable offices and cellars, two handsome parlours and an excellent drawing-room, fitted up in the best stile with elegant statuary and other marble chimneypieces, and richly corniced, the chambers are commodious, neat and lofty, with convenient dressing-rooms.' The houses are planned on similar lines to those of Cornwallis Crescent—the building of which was also promoted by Elderton—and the principal rooms are on the east front, where there is a wide terrace-walk before the ground-story of all the houses, with a large pleasure garden on the slope below. The ground opposite to the entrance front on the west was intended to be used for building coach-houses, etc. In view of the general condition of Clifton to-day, it seems scarcely necessary to record that the houses of Belle-Vue have descended to the status of tenements and appear to be falling into decay.

This range was built to conform with the north-to-south fall in the ground, so that each house steps down slightly below it northern neighbour, except for a level pair at each end. The east front is built of dressed freestone to a standard design that was commonly used at the time. Narrow pilaster-strips define each house-front, which contains three stories of three rectangular windows. All are without architraves and those of the ground-story are set in a face rusticated with horizontal and vertical V-jointing. A platband marks the first-floor level, and the plain upper face finishes with a simple cornice and plain parapet. The west elevation is built of rubble-stone and brick, faced with cement and sparingly dressed with freestone, This is used for the narrow pilaster-strips defining the party-walls, for the simple main cornice, and for the door surrounds that are the most decorative features of these fronts. The door, surmounted by a blind fanlight, is recessed in an arched opening between Doric pilasters with entablature-blocks supporting an open-bedmould triangular pediment. There is one window to the ground-story and each upper floor has two, set without architraves in a plain face.

THE PARAGON, CLIFTON

This crescent of houses, originally named Paragon Buildings, is sited on the higher part of the Rownham Woods ground that William Watts leased in 1790, to indulge in his ill-fated project of building Windsor Terrace. In 1807 the whole property was purchased by Isaac Cooke, the attorney who took over many of the Clifton houses left unfinished by the financial failures of 1793. On 1st April 1809 Cooke granted the higher ground on building lease to John Drew, the builder who had just finished Windsor Terrace on a reduced scale. Drew now covenanted to build a crescent of twenty-one houses—The Paragon—and pay a yearly rent of £325 for a term beginning 25th March 1812, by

which time the houses were to be completed. Ten houses had
been built, and the foundations laid for three more, when Drew
became bankrupt in December 1813, and a forced sale of his
properties was held on 12th March 1814, when the houses in
Windsor Terrace and Paragon Buildings were purchased by
Cooke. The unfinished houses in The Paragon were completed
by a builder named Stephen Hunter, who altered the original
design to the extent of adding an attic story in place of the roof
garrets common to the earlier houses. No. 15, the very large
house at the west end, is of later erection.

The houses form a quadrant range and the principal front is
the convex one facing south-east. This is entirely faced with
dressed freestone to the standard design adopted for so many of
Clifton's terrace-houses (Plate 52a). The party-walls are defined
by narrow pilaster-strips, rising through the three stories to
support forward breaks in the simple entablature and plain
parapet. Each front is built on the straight; there are three
evenly-spaced windows in the rusticated ground-story, and two
corresponding tiers of three in the plain upper face, which is
adorned at first-floor level with a tent-roofed veranda of simple
trellis-pattern ironwork. A wide terrace-walk, finished with a
stone balustrade, extends in front of the ground-story of the
houses, overlooking the sloping shrubbery.

The concave front is also composed of a series of straight
house-fronts, narrow in width because of the close radius of the
quadrant (Plate 52b). Except for the later houses that have attic
stories, each front is three stories high and two windows wide. Nos.
4 and 11–14 are stone-faced, but the rest are finished with cement
and sparingly dressed with stone. Most of the houses have well-
designed porches with bowed fronts (Plate 56c). The tall-
panelled double-door follows the curve and is recessed in a
rectangular opening, its moulded architrave being framed by a
plain marginal-surround. The upper angles of this surround are
overlaid by the stops of reeded consoles that rise to support the
corona of the cornice, and flank an oblong sunk panel placed
over the doorway. Below each console is carved a scallop-like
ornament, and a moulded margin adorns the sunk panel. The
flanking wall faces are coursed with channel-grooves, stopping
short of the door surrounds but continuing across the ground-story
of each house. Each tall first-floor window is framed with a

moulded architrave and finished with a plain frieze and cornice, these last members being linked by plain bands that project slightly from the wall face. Similar bands link the second-floor window architraves at sill level.

CLIFTON VALE, CALEDONIA PLACE and NEW MALL, CLIFTON

The houses of Clifton Vale were built about 1843, and those of Caledonia Place were begun a few years later, while the most westerly part of the New Mall, opposite the last, was described as being 'in process of building' in a work published during 1841. Therefore these fine terraces are not strictly Georgian in date, but they are entirely so in the spirit of their architecture, and the Grecian fronts designed by James Foster and William Okeley have a quality that demands their inclusion in any survey of Georgian building in Bristol.

The site of Clifton Vale has a steep fall from north to south, so that each of the fifteen houses steps down below its north neighbour. The fronts, facing west, are entirely uniform in design and faced with dressed freestone (Plate 53a). The ground-story face is regularly coursed with channel-grooves, and contains on the right of the centre a large window of rectangular form, with a narrow recessed margin and slender mullions that form the three lights, one wide between two narrow. On the extreme left is the doorway, having an eight-panelled door jointed to appear as a double-door, set beneath a fanlight in a rectangular opening. This is framed by a plain margin, wider at the base than at the head by reason of the tapered line to which the coursed face is broken back. The plain upper face, containing two tiers of two rectangular windows without architraves, is flanked by Doric plain-shafted pilasters that support a simple entablature surmounted by a plain parapet. Each house is adorned at the first-floor level with an elegant veranda. The balcony railing of tall and narrow round-ended panels extends between three ornamental standards that taper to a slightly decreased width at their heads. These support an architrave and a low-pitched pediment-head with an anthemion ornament rising from its apex.

Caledonia Place continues the line of the south block of The Mall, and is a most impressive terrace of thirty-one houses,

[237]

built on ground that slopes gently down from east to west so that the stepping down of each successive house-front is very slight (Plate 53b). The freestone fronts are entirely uniform and are generally similar in details to the Clifton Vale houses, although larger in scale. The ground-story, coursed with channel-grooves, contains two windows and a doorway on the left-hand side, this last being treated in a similar manner to those in Clifton Vale except that a slightly-projecting lintel is introduced to bridge the break in the coursed faces. Doric plain-shafted pilasters define the party-walls and flank the upper part of each front. This contains two tiers of three rectangular windows, set without architraves in a plain face, and has its individual main entablature, the deep frieze extending over the left-hand pilaster while the cornice overlays to a proportionate extent the lower cornice of the right-hand house. The attic story contains three windows and is flanked by short pilasters. The cornice-coping of each house is returned round the flanking pilasters, below or above that of the adjoining houses. The veranda at first-floor level calls for special notice. The Grecian balcony-railings, formed of trellis panels surmounted by openwork pediments and anthemion acroters, are placed in three arch-headed bays, with cobweb spandrels and openwork standards that support a scrolled band below the tent-roof. The stays to the standards are most ingeniously turned to ornamental account by being treated as arrows.

The shorter terrace, formerly called New Mall and now West Mall, consists of twenty-one houses that are similar in almost every detail to those opposite in Caledonia Place.

BIBLIOGRAPHY

Bristol's bibliography being very large, the following lists only those books, etc., that have any considerable reference to Bristol's buildings and building history.

General

BARRETT, William. *The History and Antiquities of the City of Bristol.* 1789.

BRAIKENRIDGE, George. *Collections for Bristol.*

EVANS, John. *A Chronological Outline of the History of Bristol.* 1824.

HARVEY, Alfred. *Bristol: A Historical and Topographical Account of the City.* 1926.

LATIMER, John. *Annals of Bristol in the 18th Century.* 1893. *Annals of Bristol in the 19th Century.* 1887.

NICHOLLS, J. F. and TAYLOR, John. *Bristol: Past and Present.* 3 volumes. 1881–2.

SEYER, Samuel. *Memoirs, Historical and Topographical, of Bristol and its Neighbourhood.* 2 volumes, 1821–3.

Architecture

BRIDGES, James and others. *Four designs for rebuilding Bristol Bridge, 1760; and other pamphlets relating to the same subject.*

DENING, C. F. W. *The Eighteenth-Century Architecture of Bristol.* 1923.

HARVEY, Alfred, and others. Various articles printed in the *Proceedings of the Clifton Antiquarian Society*, and in the *Transactions of the Bristol and Gloucestershire Archaeological Society.*

WOOD, John. *A Description of the Exchange of Bristol.* 1745. *An Essay towards a Description of Bath.* 1742 and 1749.

Original drawings by various architects, mostly early nineteenth. century. *Designs for Public Buildings in Bristol.*

Newspapers

Farley's Bristol News-Paper.

Felix Farley's Bristol Journal.

Sarah Farley's Bristol Journal.

BIBLIOGRAPHY

Bonner and Middleton's Bristol Journal.
The Bristol Mercury.
The Bristol Oracle.
CORPORATION OF BRISTOL. CITY ARCHIVES.
    Accounts and receipts for payments.
    Acts of Parliament.
    Apprentice Rolls.
    Bargain Books, relating to Corporate Property leases.
    Burgesses Rolls.
    Chamberlain's Audit Books.
    Committee Minutes (Exchange, etc.).
    Common Council Proceedings and Minutes.
    Plan Books, relating to Corporate Property.
    Property deeds, indentures of lease, etc.

INDEX

Adam, Robert, archt., 42
Albemarle Row, 24, 31, 198–201, 202, 207; *Pls. 41, 55c, d*
Alfred Street, 25
All Saints' Street, 39
Allen, James, archt., 30, 77, 84, 85
Allen, John, joiner, 30
Allen, Ralph, 96, 98
Anne, Queen, visits Bristol, 143
Arcades, Upper and Lower, 29, 34
Armstrong, William, archt., 205
Arno's Court, 24, 32, 40, 45, 181–9; *Pls. 35a, b, 55b, 61a, b*
    Bath-house, 185–6; *Pls. 36a, 63a*
    Castle, 32, 181, 187–9; *Pls. 37a, b*
    Gateway, 186–7; *Pl. 36b*
Arthur, Nathaniel, smith, 31, 57, 166
Ashley Down, 27
Assembly Rooms, Clifton (see Clifton Hotel and Assembly Rooms)
Assembly Room, Prince Street, 23, 38, 108–14
Assembly Room Lane, 109, 110
Auriol, John L., 130, 131
Avard, Lewis & Mitchell, builders, 231

Badminton Church, 74
Baily, E. H., sculptor, 138
Baker, William, 154
Baldwin Street, 68
Bank of England, Broad Street, 33
Baptists' College, Stokes Croft, 35
Barber-Surgeons' Company, 91
Barber-Surgeons' Hall, 45, 46, 91–2
Barnes, William, 109
Barrett, William 'History of Bristol' references, 67, 105, 128
Barrow, J., mayor, 136

BATH, Somerset, 25
    Avon Street, 92
    Beauford Square, 45, 92
    Camden Crescent, 26, 226
    Guildhall, 41
    Kingsmead, 45
    Lansdown Crescent, 26
    Queen Square, 147
    Rosewell House, 46, 92, 171
    St. James's Square, 26
Bayly, Richard, 171, 172
Bayly, Robert, 223
Becher, Cranfield, 109
Becher, John, 154, 161
Belle Vue, Clifton, 27, 234
Berkeley Crescent, 41, 214, 216; *Pl. 46a*
Berkeley Place, 30
Berkeley Square, 25, 26, 27, 28, 41, 214–17, 222; *Pls. 45a, b*
Biggs, William, mason, 98
Bird, Edward, painter, 81
Bishop's House, Clifton, 23; *Pl. 64a*
Bishop's Park, 210
Blackburne, archt., 81, 82
Blaise Castle, Henbury, 43
Blomfield, Sir R., quoted, 102
Boyce, Thomas, 202, 204
Boyce's Buildings, Clifton, 202–4
Braikenridge Collection, reference, 52
Brandon Hill, 25
Brewer, J. N., quoted, 166
Bridge Street, 25, 41
Bridges, James, archt., 24, 30, 31, 32, 41, 49, 66, 67, 114, 116–22, 181, 188, 191, 192
Brigden, Thomas, clerk-of-works, 136

Q

[241]

Bristol Bridge, 24, 31, 41, 46, 48, 49, 65, 66, 114–23, 191; *Pl. 18a*
  Trustees' ledger, references, 66, 122
Bristol Cathedral, 49
Bristol Directories, references, 39, 174
Bristol Guide books, references
  Mathews, 78, 129
  New Bristol Guide, 30
  Shiercliff's, 55, 114
Bristol Journal, references, 42, 43
Bristol Oracle, references, 38, 160
Broad Street, 33, 73, 90, 135, 137, 138
Brooks, William, joiner, 56
Brunel House (Royal Western) Hotel 29
Brunswick Square, 24, 36, 48, 77, 174, 204–9; *Pls. 43a, b*
Bubb, J. G., sculptor, 135
Budge, Christopher and Mary, 198, 199
Bullock's Park, 211, 214

Caledonia Place, 29, 34, 231, 237–8; *Pl. 53b*
Campbell, Colen, archt., 167, 168
Carolina Row (Court), King Square, 174, 175
Carracci, Annibale, painter, 60
Cathay, Redcliffe, 30
Chamberlain's Audit-books, references, 39, 48, 90, 93, 146
Champion, Nehemiah, 62
Chandos correspondence, reference, 45
Chapel Row, Dowry, 47, 158, 159; *Pl. 27a*
Charlotte Street, 27, 41, 44, 214
Christ Church, 25, 40, 41, 72–6; quarter-jack figures, 39, 74; altar-piece, 75–6; *Pls. 8b, 11a, b*
Circular Stables, Stokes Croft, 49
Clare Street, 25, 41
Clark, Thomas, sculptor, 138
Clifton Club (formerly Assembly Rooms), 131
Clifton Court, 38
Clifton Hill House, 23, 24, 34, 40, 47, 171–81; *Pls. 34a, b, 58b, 60b, 62b, 64c*
Clifton Hotel and Assembly Rooms, 35, 109, 130–4; *Pl. 19b*

Clifton Manor House, 228
Clifton Parish Church, 29, 34, 88
Clifton Vale, 29, 34, 88, 237, 238
Cockerell, C. R., archt., 29, 32, 88
Coles, John, builder, 229
College Green, 39, 48, 210, 211
College Street, 25, 41, 210–11
Colonnade, Hotwells, 213–14, 224; *Pl. 44b*
Combe, Henry, mayor, 98, 162
Comfort, Robert, mason, 121, 201, 202
Commercial Rooms, 28, 32, 134–5; *Pls. 20a, b*
Congregational Chapel, Brunswick Square, 205
Constant, Richard, builder, 229
Cooke, Isaac, attorney, 36, 226, 227, 229, 235, 236
Coopers' Hall, 23, 38, 91, 105–6, 124, 172; *Pl. 17b*
Corn Street, 90, 99, 108, 134, 136, 137, 138
Cornwallis Crescent, 27, 28, 35, 43, 231–3, 234; *Pls. 53a, b*
Corporation of Bristol, 71, 98, 135, 136
  Bargain-books, references, 109, 141–3, 190
  Minute-books, references, 90, 95, 96, 106, 108, 140, 141, 152, 153
  Plan-books, references, 32, 38, 172
Corsham Court, 45, 186
Cossins, John, 23, 32, 38, 54, 55, 59, 164
Cossins, Martha, 59, 164
Council House, 29, 44, 135–9; *Pls. 21a, b*
Council House, old, 23, 90–1
County Gaol, 29, 44
Court, W. & G., joiners, 76
Crispin, J., joiner, 136
Crook, Nathaniel, 198
Cumberland Street, 205, 207, 209
Curtis, John, 109
Customs House, 44
Customs House, old, 144, 146

Dance, George, the elder, archt., 96, 97

Dalton, John, brickmaker, 175
Daniel, William, builder, 84, 121
Daubeny, George, 125, 228
Davis, Gilbert, house-carpenter, 125
Davis, Michael, builder, 229
Davis & Husband, builders, 214, 220
Day, John, 143, 171
Day, Nathaniel, 143, 148, 211
Deanery Road, 210
Denmark Avenue, 154
Dighton family, 174, 175
Dighton Street, King Square, 174, 175
Dixon, Cornelius, decorator, 133
Donne's Plan of Bristol, 212; *Pl. 3*
Doolan, Colonel, 35
Dove House, Dowry Square, 159
Dowbiggin, Lancelot, archt., 178
Dowry Chapel, 24, 48, 61, 88, 158
Dowry Parade, 158, 201–2; *Pl. 42a*
Dowry Square, 22, 47, 156, 157–61, 174, 201, 205, 207; *Pls. 27b, 33a, 54d*
Drawbridge, 37
Drew, John, builder, 28, 227, 228, 235, 236
Duke Street (Court), King Square, 174, 175, 176
Dyer, Charles, archt., 29
Dyer, George, 134
Dymond, George, archt., 139

Edgar, Alexander, 124
Edkins, Michael, painter, 125, 127, 196
Edkins, William, painter, 136
Edney, William, smith, 33, 70
Elderton, Harry, attorney, 231, 234,
Elton, Sir Abraham, mayor, 99, 143, 147, 205
Elton, Jacob, 170
Eugene Street, 30
Evans, architect, 74
Evans, Ezekial, builder, 229
Eveleigh, John, archt., 26, 223, 226, 228
Exchange (Corn Exchange), 23, 24, 34, 37, 40, 48, 49, 95–105, 106, 108, 134; *Pls. 15, 16, 17a.* Building Committee, 95–9.

Exchange Avenue, 91, 92
Exchange Coffee-house, 100
Exchange Tavern, 100

Farley, Felix (*Felix Farley's Bristol Journal*), references, 38, 40, 41, 43, 48, 49, 66, 67, 70, 105, 114, 115, 116, 119, 120, 121, 124, 126, 130, 174, 187, 190, 191, 202, 204, 208, 209, 210, 211, 214, 223, 226
Farley, Sarah (*Sarah Farley's Bristol Journal*), references, 25, 26, 210, 220
Fear, James, house-carpenter, 198
Fisher, Paul, 177, 180
Foote, William, mason, 125
Fort, The, see Royal Fort
Foster, James, archt., 29, 34, 136, 237
Foster, Thomas, archt., 34
Foster & Okeley, archts., 29, 34, 237
Foster & Son, archts., 34
Fowles, Francis, joiner, 142
Frampton Court, 46, 167
Franklin, smith, 125
Freemasons' Hall, see Philosophical and Literary Institute
French Protestant Chapel, 154
Friends' Meeting House, The Friars, 24, 48, 61, 62–5; Building book, references, 62–4; *Pl. 7b*
Full Moon Inn, 48, 204

Garrick, David, actor, 125
Gay, Robert, mason, 121, 142
Gaunts Lane, 154
George III statue, Portland Square, 223
Georgian House Museum, 217–20
Gibbon, John, mason, 106
Gibbs, Elizabeth, 156
Gibbs, James, archt., 42
Glascodine, Joseph, archt-carptr., 34, 81, 82
Glascodine, Samuel, archt-carptr., 34, 37, 98, 106, 108, 178
Gloucester Street, 207, 209
Goldney, Thomas, 62, 63
Grapes Tavern, 91

Great George Street, 25, 27, 41, 43, 44, 212, 217–20; *Pls. 47a, b, 64d*

Greenway, Benjamin & Daniel, carvers, 98

Greenway, Francis H., archt., 35, 36, 131

Greenway, Messrs., archts. & builders, 28, 35, 36, 131, 232

Griffin, John, plasterer, 98

Grinden, Joseph, tiler and plasterer, 136

Greville, Giles, apothecary, 173

'Guide to all the Watering-Places' reference, 131

Guinea Street, Nos. 5, 6 and 7, 47; Nos. 10, 11 and 12, 156–7; *Pl.* 26

Hague, Daniel, archt.-mason, 26, 30, 36, 41, 77, 81, 84, 220

Halfpenny, John, draughtsman, 38

Halfpenny, William, archt.-carptr., 23, 37, 38, 40, 54, 55, 56, 60, 95, 96, 99, 105, 110, 111, 144, 147, 163, 164, 172; 'Perspective made Easy' references, 37, 38, 96, 110, 144

Harding, Robert, plasterer, 45

Harford, Mark, 62

Harford family, 174

Harris & Byfield, organ-builders, 52

Henwood, Luke, archt., 38

Heylyn, John, 109

High Street, 41, 65, 106

Hill, Thomas, joiner, 56

Hilliard monument, St. Mark's Church, 41

Hobbs, John, merchant, 23, 45, 46, 143, 162, 163

Hollidge, James, 143

Hollidge, John, 146

Holy Trinity Church, 29, 33, 88–9; *Pl. 13c*

Holy Trinity Church, Leeds, 37

Hope Square, 199

Hospital of Queen Elizabeth, 152

Hot-well, 108, 158, 200, 202, 213, 226

Hot-well House, 29, 37, 44, 223, 224, 225

Hotwell Road, 88

Hunter, Stephen, builder, 236

Infirmary, 25, 36, 38, 41

Jacob's Wells, 38

Jacob's Wells Theatre, 124

Jamaica Street, 175

Jefferies, alderman, 96, 97

Jelf, John, 162

Jones, Henry, poet, quoted, 42

Jones, Joseph, house-carpenter, 90

Jones, Robert, builder, 214

Jones, William, mason, 121, 124

Kay, Joseph, archt., 131

Kilby, Thomas, mason, 39

King, Thomas, statuary, 41, 42

King Street, 66, 93, 105, 106, 123, 124, 125, 127, 128, 129, 140

King's Parade, 27

King Square, 24, 47, 48, 173–7, 205; *Pl. 33b*

King Square Avenue, 175

King's Weston House, 23, 106

Kingsdown Parade, 25, 28

Labelye, Charles, engineer, 119, 122

Lady Huntingdon's Chapel, 109

Langley, Batty, archt., 37, 42, 67, 119, 185

Lawford's Gate, 48, 186

Lawrence, William, house-carpenter, 175

Lewin's Mead, 82

Lewis, David, clerk-of-works, 99

Library, Central, 94

Library, City, King Street, 39, 93–4; *Pl. 14a*

Lightoler, Thomas, archt., 45, 110, 195

Limekiln Lane, 35, 41, 210

Little King Street, 142

Lockier, James, building-promoter, 26, 27, 214, 220, 228

Lockier, MacAulay & Co., builders, 27

Lodge Street, 41

LONDON
    College of Physicians, 137
    Lincoln's Inn Fields, 141

LONDON (continued)
Royal Exchange, 77, 78
St. Martin's in-the-Fields Church, 74
St. Stephen's Wallbrook Church, 66
Theatre Royal, Drury Lane, 124
Westminster Bridge, 118, 122
London Magazine reference, 49
Long Rooms, Dowry, 109
Lord Mayor's Chapel, see St. Mark's Church
Loscombe, Joseph, 205

Malcolm, James, antiquary, quoted, 27, 78, 220
Mall, The, Clifton, 27, 130, 131, 133, 223-4, 226; Pl. 48b
Mall, The New, 29, 34, 237, 238
Mangotsfield Parish Church, 30
Manley, Isaac, mason, 205
Manley, Thomas, mason, 36, 121, 205, 209
Markets, High Street, 49, 106-8
Marsh Street, 161
Marsh, The (Queen Square), 140, 141, 143, 161
Mathews' Guide, see Bristol Guide-books
Matthews, Richard, gardener, 159, 160
Merchants' Hall, 41, 127-30; Pl. 18b
Merchants' Society, 70. 98, 127, 146, 202, 213, 224, 225, 231, 232, 234
Merchant-Taylors' Hall, 94-5
Milk Street, 150
Millard, Daniel, mason, 108
Millerd, James, Plan of Bristol, 21, 127, 140, 161; Pl. 1
Modern Builder's Assistant, references, 110, 195
Montague Tavern, 174

Narrow Quay (Wood Key), 110, 140, 161
Nash, John, archt., 43, 135
Neale, Alexander, 154
New Street, 48
Newgate, 186

Okeley, William, archt., 34, 237
Oldfield, Thomas, building-promoter, 47, 158, 159
Orchard Street, 22, 34, 47, 144, 152-6, 158; Pls. 25a, b, 54c
Oxford Street, 25

Padmore, engineer, 66
Paragon, 28, 227, 235-7; Pls. 52a, b, 56c
Park Street, 25, 40, 41, 48, 211-13
Parsons, Robert, mason, 98
Paty, or Patty
James Patty, carver, 39
James Paty (1), carver-mason, 39, 74, 93, 168
James Paty (2), carver-archt., 40, 71, 122, 124, 211
John Paty, son of James Paty, carver, 40
John Paty, son of Thos. Paty, archt., 24, 41, 42, 43
Thomas Paty, carver-archt., 24, 25, 31, 32, 40, 43, 55, 57, 59, 60, 61, 63, 66, 69, 71, 72, 81, 98, 101, 108, 122, 128, 161, 178, 181, 191, 192, 193, 195, 198, 199, 202, 204, 205, 210, 211, 212, 214, 217
William Paty, carver-archt., 24, 26, 29, 34, 41, 42, 43, 76, 210, 224, 228, 232
Paty and Sons, archts., etc., 72, 108, 210, 212, 214, 217
Paul Street, 25
Payne, Henry, glazier, 136
Peloquin, Stephen, 143
Philips, Joseph, mason, 136
Phillips, John, surveyor, 118, 121
Philosophical and Literary Institute, 29
Pithay, 108
Pope, R. S., archt., 29, 139
Pope, Thomas, builder, 220
Portland Square, 26, 27, 36, 76, 77, 78, 220-3; Pls. 48a, 49a, 56b
Post Office, Old, Corn Street, 35, 108; Pl. 17a
Powell, Samuel, 213, 224, 225
Power, John, 158, 226

Price, John, house-carpenter, 21, 47, 143, 154, 170

Prigg, Peter, house-carpenter, 174

Prince Street, 21, 23, 38, 46, 109, 110, 144, 161–3, 171–3; No. 40, 23, 38, 171–3; No. 66, 68 and 70, 23, 46, 162–3; *Pls. 28, 32*

Prince's Buildings, 224–5; *Pl. 56d*

Probert, Benjamin, house-carpenter, 174, 201

Prospect House, Clifton Green, 204; *Pl. 42b*

Queen Charlotte Street, 45, 46, 142, 146; No. 59, 45, 46, 170–1; *Pl. 29b*

Queen Square, 21, 22, 23, 31, 37, 108, 136, 140–9, 150, 156, 161, 170; No. 29, 148–9; Nos. 36–38, 147–8; *Pls. 22a, b. 23a, b, 55a.* Temple for Fireworks Display, 32

Queen's Parade, 216

Rawlings, Thomas, house-carpenter, 214

Reade, Rev. John, 141, 142, 146

Red Lodge, 25

Redcliffe Parade, 209–10; *Pl. 44a*

Redland Chapel (St. Katherine's Church), 23, 31, 38, 40, 46, 54–61, 166; *Pls. 4, 5a, b, 6a, b*

Redland Court, 23, 31, 32, 33, 40, 46, 54, 55, 59, 96, 164–70; *Pls. 30a, b, 31a, b, 57a, 58a, 60a, 62a, 64b*

Redland Green, 54

Redland High School for Girls (Redland Court), 164

Redland Hill House, 32

Redwood, Robert, 93

Reeve, William, 181, 182, 187, 188

Regency Theatre (Assembly Room, Prince Street), 110

Repton, Humphrey, landscape-gardener, 27, 191

Reynolds, Thomas, mason, 93

Richmond Place, 27

Rock House, Hotwell Road, 213

Rocque, John, Plan of Bristol, 150, 174; *Pl. 2*

Rogers, Woodes, 143

Rosewell, John, 92

Rosewell, Thomas, 92

Rownham Woods, Clifton, 226, 235

Royal Fort, 24, 32, 40, 45, 70, 182, 185, 190–8; *Pls. 38a, b, 39, 40a, b, 56a, 57b, 59a, b, 60c, d, 63b*

Royal Western Hotel, 29

Royal York Crescent, 26, 27, 28, 43, 228–31; *Pl. 50a, b*

Ruddock, Andrew, 154

Ruddock, Noblett, 161, 163

Rumley, Henry, archt., 147

Rysbrack, Michael, sculptor, 59, 129, 146

St. Augustine's Back, 109, 123, 153

St. Augustine's Church, 40, 41

St. Clement's Chapel, 127

St. Ewen's Church, 136

St. George's Church, Brandon Hill, 29, 44

St. George's Parish Poor-House, 43

St. James's Barton, 45, 105; No. 12, 46, 163–4; *Pl. 29a*

St. James's Church, 76

St. James's Market, 41

St. James's Square, 22, 149–52; *Pls. 24a, b, 54a, b*

St. Mark's Church (Lord Mayor's Chapel), 34, 41

St. Mary's on-the-Quay Church, 29

St. Mary Redcliffe, 30, 33, 38, 84; organ-case, 46, 52–4

St. Michael's Church, 25, 41, 46, 49, 70–2; *Pl. 9b, 12a*

St. Michael's Hill, 31

St. Michael's Hill House, 46

St. Nicholas' Church, 24, 31, 33, 41, 45, 65–70; altar-piece, 70; iron-work, 70; *Pls. 8a, 9a, 10*

St. Nicholas' Gate, 65

St. Nicholas' Street, 68

St. Paul's Church, 25, 30, 36, 76–81, 220, 221; *Pls. 8c, 12b*

St. Thomas's Church, 30, 84–8; altar-piece, 87; organ-gallery, 87–8; *Pl. 13b*

St. Thomas's Street, 30, 85

St. Vincent's Parade, 223, 224, 225–6
St. Werburgh's Church, 24, 31, 187, 188
Saunders, Capt. Edmund, 52, 156
Saville Place, 27, 233–4; *Pl. 46b*
Scheemaker, Peter, sculptor, 146
Screen, Samuel, builder, 226
Seward, Henry H., archt., 29, 44, 136
Shakespeare, surveyor, 122
Shambles, 48
Shewring, Daniel, 114
Shiercliff's Guide, see Bristol Guide-books
Sidnell, Michael, carver, 40
Sion Hill, Clifton, 130
Sion Row, Clifton, 25
Simpson & Tidway, masons, 52
Small, Rev. J. Atwell, 77
Smirke, Sir Robert, archt., 29, 44, 136, 137
Smirke, Sydney, archt., 44
Smith, Morgan, 109
Smith, Wm., of Warwick, surveyor, 48
Spring Hill, King Square, 175
Stibbs, John, house-carpenter, 47
Stock, William, carpenter, 84, 136
Stocking, William, plasterer, 24, 32, 44, 69, 181, 192, 210
Stokes Croft, 49, 123
Stone Bridge, 48
Stoney Hill, 30
Strahan, John, archt., 23, 37, 45, 52, 54, 70, 92, 96, 162, 163, 164, 171, 191
Stratford, Ferdinando, engineer, 31, 46, 49, 116, 117, 118, 119, 122
Sumsion, Thomas, mason, 90
Swayne, Walter, smith, 76
Swymmer, William, 153, 154
Symons, Thomas, 124

Taylors' Court, Broad Street, 94
Teast, Sydenham, 209
Temple Church, 33
Tenteman, J., builder, 82
Tetbury Church, Old, 48
Theatre Royal, 40, 67, 110, 123–7; *Pl. 19a*

Thomas, Joseph, plasterer, 44, 47, 110, 156, 178
Tijou, Jean, smith, 33, 103, 128
Tolzey, 95
Townsend, George, mason, 90
Tully, George, archt-carptr., 22, 24, 30, 38, 47, 61, 62, 63, 97, 158, 159, 174, 205, 211
Tully, William, archt-carptr., 47, 48, 63, 114, 121
Tyley, H., statuary, 89
Tyndall, Colonel T., 27, 191
Tyndall, Thomas, 32, 190
Tyndall's Park, 26; Scheme for building a Crescent, Square, Circus, etc., 26–7

Underwood, Charles, archt., 29
Underwood & Co., smiths, 136
Union Street, 25, 41
Unitarian Chapel, Lewin's Mead, 25, 81–4; *Pl. 13a*
Upper Berkeley Place, 41
Utting, Thomas, joiner, 56

Vanbrugh, Sir John, archt., 23, 106, 167
Vanderbanck, John, painter, 60
Vaughan, John, 124
Vaughan, Sir Richard, 166, 228
Vaughan, T. G., 26, 190
Victoria Rooms, Clifton, 29

Walker, George, mason, 93
Wallis, John, archt-builder, 31, 46, 48, 49, 115, 116, 117, 118, 121, 122, 190
Wallis's Wall, Durdham Down, 49
Walpole, Horace, references, 67, 181
Watts, Robert, 124
Watts, William, 226, 235
Webb, John, 198, 199
Wells Assize-Hall and Market, 41
Wesley, John, 61
Wesley's New Room, Broadmead, 24, 48, 61–2; *Pl. 7a*
West, mason, 84
West Mall, Clifton, see New Mall
Whippie, Thomas, 88
Whiting, Charles, plumber, 136
Wilder Street, 49, 205

INDEX

Wilkins, Peter, house-carpenter, 21, 143, 154

William III equestrian statue, Queen Square, 146

Williams, Richard, house-carpenter, 55

Wilstar, John Jacob de, surveyor, 38, 96

Windsor Terrace, 26, 28, 226–8, 235, 236; *Pl. 49b*

Wine Street, 73

Wood, John, the elder, 23, 37, 49, 66, 95, 96, 97, 98, 99, 100, 101, 102, 103, 104, 105, 106, 108, 191; Description of Bath, quoted, 45, 46, 54, 167; Description of

Wood, John, the elder (*continued*) Bristol Exchange, quoted, or referred to, 97–105

Wood, John, the younger, 49, 116, 117, 118, 119, 121, 122

Workman, Edmund, house-carpenter, 48, 205

Worrall, Samuel, 27, 204, 210

Worsley, John, 154

Wyatt, James, archt., 26

Yate, Robert, 161

York Hotel, Clifton, 109

York Place, 27

York Street, 207

PLANS

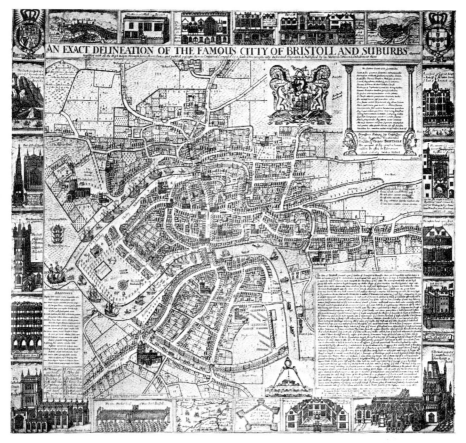

1. A Plan of Bristol by Jacobus Millerd, published in 1673

2. A Plan of Bristol by John Rocque, published in 1745

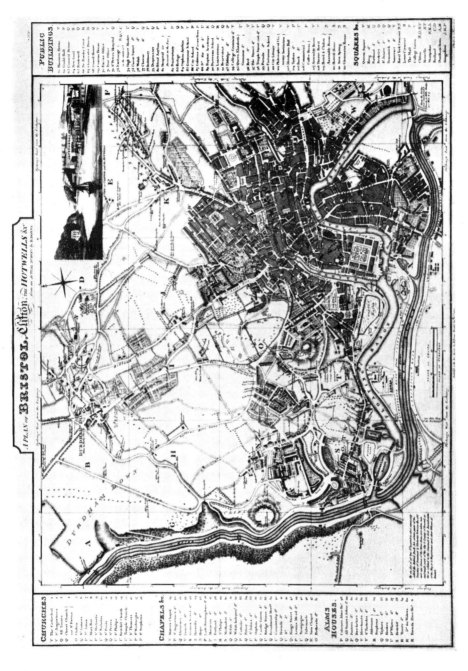

3. A Plan of Bristol by Benjamin Donne, published in 1826

4. Redland Chapel, The exterior from the south-west

5a. Redland Chapel. The interior, looking east

5b. Redland Chapel. The interior, looking west

6a. Redland Chapel. Detail of the altar-piece

6b. Redland Chapel. Detail of the dado-capping

7a. Wesley's New Room. The interior

7b. The Friends' Meeting House. The Friars. The interior

8a. St. Nicholas' Church. The steeple

8b. Christ Church. The steeple

8c. St. Paul's Church. The steeple

9b. St. Michael's Church.
The exterior from the south-west

9a. St. Nicholas' Church.
The exterior from the north-west

10. St. Nicholas' Church. The interior, looking east

11a. Christ Church. The interior, looking east

11b. Christ Church. The interior, looking south-west

12a. St. Michael's Church. The interior, looking east

12b. St. Paul's Church. The interior, looking east

13a. The Unitarian Chapel. Lewin's Mead. The principal front

13b. St. Thomas's Church.
The east front

13c. Holy Trinity Church, Hotwells.
The south front, central feature

14a. The old City Library. The exterior. (Drawing by E. Cashin, 1823)

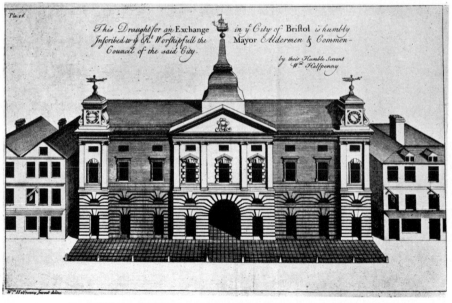

14b. William Halfpenny's first 'Draught for an Exchange'

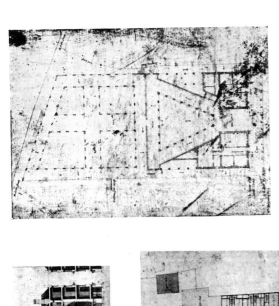
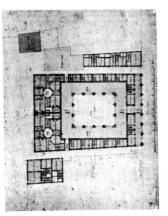
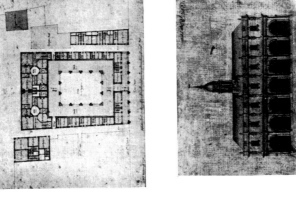
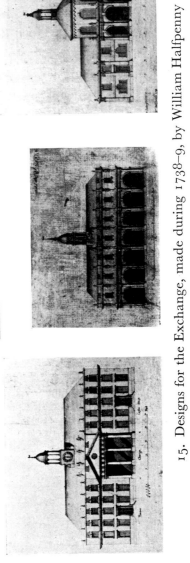
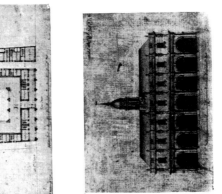
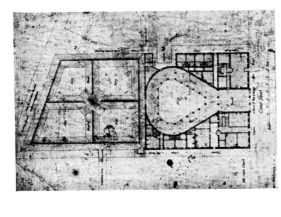

15. Designs for the Exchange, made during 1738–9, by William Halfpenny

16. The Exchange. The principal front in Corn Street

17b. Coopers' Hall. The exterior

17a. The old Post Office and part of the Exchange

18a. Bristol Bridge. (Drawing by H. O'Neill, 1823)

18b. Merchants' Hall. The exterior. (Drawing by H. O'Neill, 1823)

19a. The Theatre Royal. A general view of the auditorium from the stage

19b. The Clifton Hotel and Assembly Rooms. The front facing The Mall

20a. The Commercial Rooms. The front in Corn Street

20b. The Commercial Rooms. The lantern-light of the great room

21a. The Council House. The exterior

21b. The Council House. The former Council-chamber

22a. Queen Square. The north-east angle,
looking into Queen Charlotte Street. (Drawing by S. Jackson, 1824)

22b. Queen Square. A general view of the south-east angle.
(Drawing by T. Rowbotham, 1827)

23b. Queen Square. The south row. Front of No. 29

23a. Queen Square. The south row. Front of No. 38

24a. St. James's Square. Houses on the west side

24b. St. James's Square. Houses in the south-east angle

25a. Orchard Street. The south block on the east side

25b. Orchard Street. The north block on the west side

26. Nos. 10–12 Guinea Street

27a. Chapel Row, Dowry Square

27b. Dowry Square. Houses on the north and east sides

28. Nos. 66, 68 and 70 Prince Street

29b. No. 59 Queen Charlotte Street

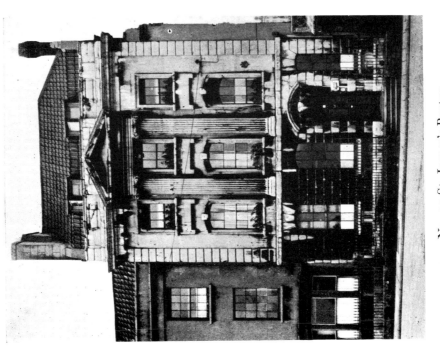

29a. No. 12 St. James's Barton

30a. Redland Court. The south front

30b. Redland Court. The south front. Detail of pedimented centre

31a. Redland Court. The south front.
(Engraved drawing by J. and H. S. Storer, 1825)

31b. Redland Court. The north front

32. Prince Street. The west side, with No. 40 and the Assembly Room
(Drawing by E. Cashin, 1825)

33a. Dowry Square. Houses on the west side

33b. King Square. The south-west side

34a. Clifton Hill House. The design for the elevation,
from Ware's 'Complete Body of Architecture'

34b. Clifton Hill House. The garden front, facing east

35a. Arno's Court. A general view of the exterior

35b. Arno's Court. The entrance front

36a. Arno's Court. The Bath-house. The exterior

36b. Arno's Court. The Gateway

37a. Arno's Court. The Castle. A general view of the exterior from the south
(Drawing by T. Rowbotham, 1827)

37b. Arno's Court. The Castle. The courtyard, looking west

38a. The Royal Fort. The architect's model

38b. The Royal Fort. The architect's model with the upper stories removed

39. The Royal Fort. The west front

40a. The Royal Fort. The south front

40b. The Royal Fort. The north front

41. Albemarle Row

42a. Dowry Parade

42b. Prospect House, Clifton Green

43a. Brunswick Square. The south side

43b. Brunswick Square. The east side

44a. Redcliffe Parade

44b. The Colonnade and Rock House, Hotwells

45a. Berkeley Square. The west side

45b. Berkeley Square. The north side

46b. Saville Place

46a. Berkeley Crescent

47b. Great George Street. The front of No. 7
(The Georgian House)

47a. Great George Street. The front of No. 3

48a. Portland Square. The west side

48b. The Mall, Clifton. The south side

49b. Windsor Terrace. Nos. 5 and 6

49a. Portland Square. The central feature of the south side

50a. Royal York Crescent. A general view from the west end
(Engraving by Willis, c. 1850)

50b. Royal York Crescent. A general view from the east end

51a. Cornwallis Crescent. The concave front, facing the garden

51b. Cornwallis Crescent. The convex front, facing the roadway

52a. The Paragon. The convex front, facing the garden

52b. The Paragon. The concave front, facing the roadway

53a. Clifton Vale

53b. Caledonia Place

54a. No. 10 St. James's Square.
Entrance doorway

54b. No. 16 St. James's Square.
Entrance doorway

54c. No. 28 Orchard Street.
Entrance doorway

54d. No. 7 Dowry Square.
Entrance doorway

55a. No. 16 Queen Square.
Entrance doorway (now removed)

55b. Arno's Court: The mansion.
Entrance doorway

55c. No. 2 Albemarle Row.
Entrance doorway

55d. No. 7 Albemarle Row.
Entrance doorway

56a. The Royal Fort.
The entrance doorway

56b. Portland Square.
A typical doorway

56c. The Paragon.
A typical porch

56d. Prince's Buildings.
The porch of No. 9

57a. Redland Court. The entrance hall

57b. The Royal Fort. The entrance hall

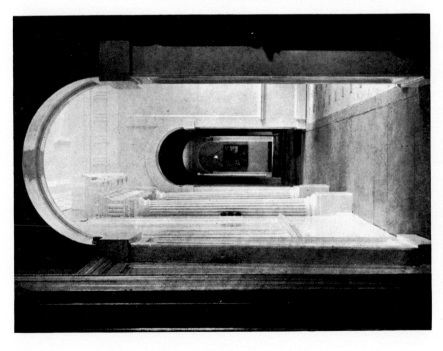

58a. Redland Court. The main corridor

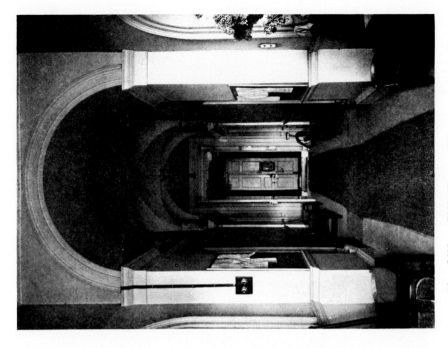

58b. Clifton Hill House. The entrance hall

59b. The Royal Fort. The staircase hall

59a. The Royal Fort. The main corridor

6oa. Redland Court. Ceiling of the
main staircase well

6ob. Clifton Hill House. Ceiling of
the staircase hall

6oc. The Royal Fort. The staircase
hall, wall decoration

6od. The Royal Fort. Ceiling of the
staircase hall

61a. Arno's Court. The dining-room ceiling

61b. Arno's Court. Ceiling of the staircase hall

62a. Redland Court. The south-east reception-room

62b. Clifton Hill House. The north-east reception-room

63a. Arno's Court. Interior of the Bath-house

63b. The Royal Fort. The large drawing-room

64b. Redland Court. The main staircase

64d. No. 7 Great George Street. Detail of the staircase balustrade

64a. Bishop's House, Clifton Green. The hall and staircase

64c. Clifton Hill House. The staircase